Social Security Advisory Committee

RESEARCH PAPER **8**

Helping Disabled People to Work: A Cross-National Study of Social Security and Employment Provisions

A Report for the Social Security Advisory Committee

Patricia Thornton
Roy Sainsbury
Helen Barnes

Social Policy Research Unit
University of York

London: The Stationery Office

ISBN 0 11 762555 8

Printed in the United Kingdom for The Stationery Office
J22684 C14 9/97 5673

CONTENTS

CHAPTER 3
FINLAND

CHAPTER 5
GERMANY

CHAPTER 6
NETHERLANDS

CHAPTER 7
SWEDEN   90

CHAPTER 8
UNITED KINGDOM   104

LIST OF TABLES

ACKNOWLEDGEMENTS

In a desk-based review of policy in seven countries, retrieval of comprehensive and accurate information, as well as insight and understanding, can be achieved only through the active and close involvement of national experts. In this study we were particularly fortunate in our team of national informants drawn from leading research institutes and departments in six countries - Tony Eardley, Social Policy Research Centre, University of New South Wales, Australia; Anna Metteri, Department of Social Policy and Social Work, University of Tampere, Finland; Dominique Velche, Centre National d'Etude et de Recherche sue les Handicaps et les Inaptations, Paris, France; Markus Körbel and Werner Friedrich, WSF Wirtschafts- und Socialforschung, Germany; Edwin de Vos, NIA-TNO, Amsterdam, the Netherlands; and Eskil Wadensjö, Swedish Institute for Social Research, Stockholm University, Sweden. We are grateful to them not only for their written contributions, but also for their willingness to expand and elaborate on request within a short time-frame. We also acknowledge the help of research and policy colleagues in the Department of Social Security. Thanks go to Sally Pulleyn, Teresa Frank and Lorna Foster for their secretarial and editing work. The information contained in this report was obtained over the period November 1996 to April 1997, with some late additions, and is, as far as possible, the latest available. The policy context is undergoing rapid change in a number of countries, including the UK, and unavoidably some information may already have been overtaken by events.

Patricia Thornton
Roy Sainsbury
Helen Barnes

Social Policy Research Unit
University of York

July 1997.

PREFACE

The research on which this report is based was undertaken on behalf of the Social Security Advisory Committee (SSAC) with support from the Department of Social Security (DSS). The evidence presented and the views expressed in the report are the responsibility of the authors, and do not necessarily reflect the position of either SSAC or DSS.

HELPING DISABLED PEOPLE TO WORK:

A CROSS-NATIONAL STUDY OF SOCIAL SECURITY AND EMPLOYMENT PROVISIONS

The Study

CHAPTER ONE

INTRODUCTION

In October 1996, the Social Policy Research Unit was commissioned by the Social Security Advisory Committee, through the Department of Social Security, to carry out an international comparison of approaches to supplementing the income from work and supporting the employment of disabled people with partial capacity for work. The UK had introduced a new form of partial capacity provision into the social security system in 1992; previously, the only opportunities to work and claim incapacity benefit were very restricted. The chosen approach, an in-work social security benefit to supplement to low earnings (Disability Working Allowance), had not met policy expectations. The study was commissioned by the Social Security Advisory Committee to compare the UK experience with alternative approaches to 'partial capacity provision' in Australia, Finland, France, Germany, the Netherlands and Sweden.

BACKGROUND

There is widespread international interest in promoting employment among disabled people, for both social and economic reasons - to enhance equity and reduce social exclusion, to increase independence and self-reliance, to reduce social security expenditures, and to increase tax and national insurance revenues, and to increase labour market efficiency.

The characteristics of disabled people wanting work are changing. New groups are entering the labour force because of increased life expectancy, deinstitutionalisation and the shift away from segregated employment and services. Many people with learning difficulties now expect to participate in, and enjoy the rewards from the mainstream labour market. The exclusion from the mainstream of people with mental illness is increasingly recognised. Work is now an aspiration for some people with deteriorating conditions. At the same time, chances to remain in employment are put at risk by the onset of disability or deterioration in health, and an increasing proportion of employees find their working opportunities are limited because of their health condition.

Consequently, there is a growing group in the labour force able to do some work, but unable to work full or normal hours or to achieve full productivity, whose employment prospects are limited and whose earning capacity is reduced.

Recognition of the employment and income needs of disabled people with partial capacity for work has challenged employment and social security policy traditions which assumed that disability is incompatible with work and which, in many countries, led to 'all or nothing' systems where an individual was deemed either completely fit for or totally incapable of work. In the last few decades, several industrialised countries have introduced systems to support both the integration into employment and the earnings potential of disabled people with partial working capacity. In certain countries, it is now taken for granted that partial disability is compatible with work; in others, the notion remains under-developed.

Changes in the world of work, such as the rise of part-time employment, flexible working hours and the casualisation of work, may increase opportunities for people with partial working capacity to engage in the labour market. On the other hand, such changes lead to low wages which, alone, are inadequate, reduce income security and pose particular challenges to systems for income support.

WHAT CAUSES PARTIAL-CAPACITY?

Some disabled people's capacity for work can differ from that of people who are not disabled for a range of reasons which can be classified into two main types; those connected with a person's impairment or illness, and those connected to the disabling effects of many working environments.

People with certain physical or mental impairments or illnesses can be limited in their working capacity in a number of ways. Fatigue, pain or stress, for example, may limit the number of hours they are able to work in the day or week or restrict the times of day when they can work. Fluctuating conditions, or the need for rest periods or treatment during the day, may make it difficult to keep regular working hours.

Limited working capacity can also result from the characteristics of particular working environments, such as inappropriate physical surroundings, unsuitable machinery and equipment, barriers to communication in the workplace and inflexible organisation of work. Barriers in getting to work, such as inaccessible transport or unco-ordinated personal care services, may also affect some disabled people's capacity for work.

As a result of one, or a combination, of all the above reasons, a person may have a 'partial capacity for work'. The degree of an individual's capacity for work depends on how far the environment, working conditions and the organisation of work can be adapted to minimise the effects of impairment or illness. Measures to prevent disabling work environments include legal requirements to make adjustments for disabled employees, grants towards the costs of adaptations and personal support services at the workplace, as well as action taken voluntarily by employers to suit an employee's circumstances. Not all impairments and illnesses can be accommodated, however, and pain, fatigue, stress, limited mobility and other consequences of mental or physical impairment or illness may affect ability both to engage in full or regular employment and to meet the demands of the job.

The study reports on different policy approaches to accommodating partial capacity for work. Particular attention is given to opportunities for part-time working and to social and environmental measures which aim to maximise capacity for work.

PARTIAL-CAPACITY, DISCRIMINATION AND ECONOMIC DISADVANTAGE

Partial capacity for work can limit capacity to earn. People with partial capacity for work may be restricted to part-time employment, typically less well paid than full-time work. If productivity is reduced, they may be remunerated for output rather than for hours worked. Earnings may fluctuate if regular hours cannot be sustained. Structural disadvantages, such as lower levels of education, fewer skills, and under-employment, mean that the income which disabled people can command is lower than that of those who are not disabled. Moreover, for some disabled people there are extra costs associated with working.

For some disabled people the problems of accessing employment which suits their particular needs and is commensurate with their skills, in a competitive labour market, may be compounded by discrimination on the part of employers and prejudiced attitudes about the productive abilities of disabled people.

The combination of limited availability for work, restrictions on productivity, low levels of remuneration, extra costs and barriers to suitable employment means that for many disabled people earnings may be insufficient to guarantee a sustainable adequate income.

Opportunities for employment will be limited in the absence of state provision to supplement their earnings.

APPROACHES TO SUPPLEMENTING EARNINGS

There are several ways of supplementing the in-work earnings of disabled people with partial capacity to work or to earn. They fall into two broad types; payments and allowances paid directly to the disabled employee, and wage supplements and subsidies paid to the employer.

There are four main arrangements for directly enhancing disabled people's income from work:

- income maintenance benefits paid through contributory and non-contributory social protection schemes
- fiscal measures, such as allowances against personal income tax
- one-off payments, usually on taking up work, paid by special rehabilitation funds or through the benefit system
- benefits, allowances and assistance in kind to meet extra costs of working, available from a range of special funds and benefit systems, at national, regional and local levels.

In addition to direct payments by the state to the disabled worker, the wage costs of disabled people may be supported by schemes to supplement or subsidise wages. We can identify two main types:

- supplements to the wage-packet of a disabled worker with reduced productivity where the employer is allowed to pay lower wages
- subsidies to compensate the employer for losses resulting from reduced productivity where there is a requirement to pay a minimum wage or a normal salary.

The first type, the wage supplement, is necessary in order for the disabled worker to receive an adequate wage. Wage supplements for many years have formed part of income security policies for workers in sheltered employment. As workers with reduced productivity are diverted from sheltered settings to open employment, this mechanism is becoming increasingly important, both as a permanent wage supplement and as a temporary rehabilitative measure. The second type of measure, wage subsidies, acts more as an incentive to employers to hire and retain disabled employees who must receive a normal wage. Wage subsidies also play a significant role in active labour market policies in many countries, where the aim is to divert public funds to create additional jobs for groups with lower activity or employment rates.

The two main approaches to supplementing earnings of disabled people in the study countries are social security benefits (partial capacity benefit) and wage supplements and subsidies. Both approaches are used, to a varying extent, in all countries in the study.

In the UK, the former approach is more prominent. Providing a benefit to the employee reflects the UK policy emphasis on encouraging the incentive to work. Some other countries lay more emphasis on incentives to employers to take on and retain disabled workers, in many cases reflecting their general labour market policy approach. Outside the UK, the notion of financial incentives to work is less usual. Although the UK is by no means alone among the study countries in its concern to reduce the growth of disability benefits, policy responses elsewhere in Europe have focused more on prevention, rehabilitation and increasing employer responsibilities than on changing individual behaviour.

Taking the UK situation as its starting point, the enquiry began with an examination of partial capacity in the social security system but extended its brief to look at the alternative, and often complementary, approach of promoting employment opportunities and enhancing income through financial incentives to employers.

The main focus of the study was on *regular* supplements to the earnings of people with partial capacity to work and to earn. However, *one-off* payments, such as bonuses on taking up work or grants for special purposes, which may have an incentive effect or help with the extra costs of work, were also surveyed and are reported here.

Support for transition to work emerged as an issue during the design stages of the study. Some partial capacity provision, such as the Disability Working Allowance in the UK, does not bridge the gap between unemployment or non-employment and paid work. Accordingly, the study examined the experience of other countries in providing *short-term* financial support for rehabilitation, transition to employment and trial work periods.

PARTIAL-CAPACITY PROVISION IN CONTEXT

Provision to supplement income is one element in the gamut of income support, labour market and employment policies and practical services to promote employment of disabled people with partial capacity for work. The role of partial capacity provision in any national system must be interpreted within the context of labour market developments and policy responses, disability employment policy and how it has evolved and the social security system as it affects disabled people.

SELECTION OF STUDY COUNTRIES

The selection of countries for inclusion in the study was guided by the suggestions of the SSAC, by comparative studies of national policy approaches to promoting employment of disabled people (Lunt and Thornton, 1993; Thornton and Lunt, 1997), by comparative studies of disability benefits (Lonsdale, 1993; Einerhand *et al.*, 1995) and by the pragmatic consideration of access to nationally based information and research expertise. No attempt was made to select countries theoretically, by distinguishing, for example, between 'ameliorative' and 'corrective' policy approaches (Haveman *et al.*, 1984). The study countries broadly divide historically into those two analytical categories, but recent developments in disability employment policies limit their contemporary relevance (Lonsdale, 1993).

The brief was to compare partial capacity provision in the UK with that in other countries but, to our knowledge, no other country provides an in-work benefit quite like the Disability Working Allowance. The UK also stands out for the high priority it accords to individual rather than employer incentives. As we will show, the countries selected demonstrate a mix of approaches to supplementing the income of people with partial capacity for work, through labour market policies, employment policies for disabled people and social security provision.

STUDY METHODS

The study was entirely 'desk-based' and did not allow for information-gathering visits to the study countries. It drew on documentary evidence such as statistical sources, legislative texts, policy documents, governmental reviews, evaluation reports and academic studies.

The tasks of gathering and interpreting national material were divided between the research team in SPRU and six national informants based in non-governmental research organisations in Australia, Finland, France, Germany, the Netherlands and Sweden. The research team gathered contextual information about the labour market and disabled people, policies for employment of disabled people and social security provisions in the study countries. Main sources were recently completed and on-going cross-national studies in related fields of enquiry and information already gathered from government officials and policy researchers in the study countries.

Detailed information about approaches to supplementing income was collected by national informants. They completed a standardised questionnaire and collated official documents, research reports and 'grey literature'. The research team then compiled draft country reports which were passed to national informants for comment and verification.

There was unavoidable variation in the breadth and depth of material available to the study, depending in large part on the current policy priority attached to partial capacity provision. The UK and Australia stand out from the other study countries in having introduced within the past six years a new system which allows disabled people to combine work and benefit. The Dutch system of general disability benefits, and those in the UK and in Australia, have also seen major reforms in the same period. Not surprisingly, therefore, the amount of evaluative material from those countries was much higher than from France and Germany where change to the well-established disability benefits systems has been minor and incremental. The amount and type of statistical data on benefit receipt was also uneven. Particularly surprising was the lack of hard information on numbers of partial capacity benefit recipients in employment in four of the seven countries.

STRUCTURE OF THE REPORT

The following seven chapters comprise comprehensive reports of policy and provision in the seven study countries. Each chapter first describes the national context as it affects disabled people; labour market characteristics and policy developments, employment and social security policies, provision for disabled people in the social security system, and concepts of partial capacity. Direct provisions to supplement earnings are then described, covering in sequence partial capacity benefits, other disability benefits which can be combined with work, provision for extra costs of working and benefits for rehabilitation or transition to work. Wage supplements and subsidies paid to employers are then described.

Chapter Nine presents summaries of the seven countries. The final chapter of the report draws some comparisons between the UK and other national approaches to partial capacity provision, comments on the relative significance of the benefit-based approach in the national systems reviewed and identifies some features of possible value to the UK.

REFERENCES

Einerhand, M., Knol, G. and Prins, R. (1995) *Sickness and Invalidity Arrangements: Facts and figures from six European countries*, The Hague: VUGA.

Haveman, R., Halberstadt, V. and Burkhauser, R. (1984) *Public Policy Towards Disabled Workers*, Ithica: Cornell University Press.

Lonsdale, S. (1993) *Invalidity Benefit: An international comparison*, Department of Social Security Analytical Services Division, Social Security Branch, London: Department of Social Security.

Lunt, N. and Thornton, P. (1993) *Employment Policies for Disabled People: A review of legislation and services in fifteen countries*, Research Series No.16, London: Employment Department.

Thornton, P. and Lunt, N. (1997) *Employment Policies for Disabled People in Eighteen Countries: A review*, York: Social Policy Research Unit.

CHAPTER 2

AUSTRALIA[1]

OVERVIEW

The social security system in Australia has no social insurance features. Benefits, including those for disabled people, are means-tested according to income and assets. The general principle is that benefits are paid at a flat-rate and withdrawn when income or assets exceed defined maximum levels; thus benefit receipt can be combined with work.

The current policy approach to disabled people (in and out of work) reflects the principles behind the Disability Services Act of 1986 that disabled people have the same fundamental rights as other people and that services should be oriented towards realising those rights. That Act most notably attempted to shift the funding emphasis away from segregated sheltered employment towards competitive employment and supported employment.

The Disability Reform Package (DRP), introduced in 1991, derived from the philosophy of the government of the time, expressed in its 'active society' framework, which argued that people had more chance of achieving independence and self-determination if they had better access to the labour market. The DRP reforms to the system of income and employment support for disabled people were radical, given a long history of reliance on an 'all or nothing' invalid pension and of exclusion of disability pensioners from Commonwealth employment services programmes. The system was reoriented towards pensioners who might benefit from rehabilitation services, labour market programmes and other elements in a Workforce Transition Package, as identified by cross-departmental Disability Panels. The new arrangements are designed to allow work - typically part-time - backed by an income support payment, with easy transitions off and back to the benefit as the need arises.

In addition to direct support for disabled people through the benefit system, there are government schemes providing wage subsidies for up to 26 weeks and bonuses to employers who take on unemployed people. Some are open to disabled and non-disabled people alike, while others are specifically for disabled people.

THE LABOUR MARKET AND DISABLED PEOPLE

Labour market characteristics and trends

Unemployment in Australia rose from 6.2 per cent in 1989-90 to 9.5 per cent in 1994, and in early 1997 stood at about 8.7 per cent. The structure of the labour market is changing, with a growth in part-time and casual employment. Service sector employment has increased, while the manufacturing sector has continued its longer-term decline (Office of Disability, 1995).

Labour market policy

A series of major policy changes is affecting the entire labour force. In March 1996 the national administration changed from a Labour Government to a Liberal-National Coalition. The 1996 Budget proposed cuts in mainstream labour market programmes of 28 per cent. One result is that access to mainstream labour market provision will be increasingly competitive.

---

[1] Tony Eardley, Social Policy Research Centre, University of New South Wales, was national informant for Australia.

Minimum wages in Australia are determined by industry and job under the national award system. The industrial relations system is currently undergoing reform, which attempts to remove much the protection currently available under awards, and increasingly wages and conditions are determined under local 'enterprise agreements'. From 1997, employers will also be able to introduce individual contracts (Australian Workplace Agreements). However, even in the latter case the agreement has to be ratified by a new Employment Advocate and the wage package is supposed, on balance, not to be inferior to the previous award. Nevertheless, although most lower paid workers are still covered by awards, there is not one national 'minimum wage'.

Disabled people in the labour market

There is no coherent system for collecting information on the number of disabled Australians but the Australian Bureau of Statistics (ABS) and Australian Institute of Health and Welfare put this at about 18 per cent of the total population (Australian Law Reform Commission, 1996). The ABS (1993) survey estimated that 3,176,000 (18.0 per cent) of the Australian population had a disability, and 14.2 per cent were handicapped.[2]

Rather under half of the number of people with a handicap or disability aged between 15 and 64 years of age were in the labour force in 1993. This compared to three-quarters of non-disabled people. Employment rates were similar for *disabled* men (82 per cent) and women (82.6 per cent) (Briggs, 1994). ABS statistics (cited in Briggs, 1994) show that participation rates are slightly higher for those with a disability than for the general population without disability but rates for those with a *handicap* are considerably lower.

The rise in unemployment has made it difficult for disabled people to obtain and maintain employment, particularly those without work experience (Office of Disability, 1995). Employment rates for those with handicaps dropped between 1987 and 1993 (Briggs, 1994). Baume and Kay (1995) quote ABS figures that suggest that a further 123,000 people could benefit from the Disability Services Programme (see below), 38,800 of whom are unemployed, 57,700 are permanently unable to work, and 26,700 are not in the labour force.

EMPLOYMENT AND SOCIAL SECURITY POLICIES FOR DISABLED PEOPLE

In the last decade there have been extensive changes in policies to promote economic integration of disabled people.

Employment policies

Commonwealth disability discrimination legislation was enacted in 1992, as part of the then government's social justice agenda for disabled people, complementing similar state legislation. The Disability Discrimination Act (DDA) differs from the UK legislation; it applies to all employers and a Disability Discrimination Commissioner has powers to investigate alleged and potential transgressions. Some states and government departments require the preparation and implementation of equal opportunity plans for groups which include physically disabled people.

---

[2] Consistent with the International Classification of Impairments, Disabilities and Handicaps, the Australian Bureau of Statistics defines disability as a range of impairments or restrictions likely to last more than six months, and a handicap as a disability limiting the capacity to perform tasks associated with daily living, such as self-care, mobility and verbal communication.

Reviews in the 1970s and 1980s of the basic approach to provision of income support and services to disabled people led to the Disability Services Act (DSA) of 1986. Its aim was to encourage innovation in the development and delivery of employment services.

One feature of the 1986 Act was to shift funding emphasis from segregated employment services, particularly sheltered workshops, to forms of open employment which bring disabled employees the same relative levels of pay and conditions as those available to other workers. Two main employment models were identified under the Act: Competitive Employment Training and Placement (CETP) schemes, which provide training and support for disabled people to earn a full award wage; and Supported Employment (SE) services for people needing a higher level of training and ongoing support to earn full award or productivity-based wages.

SE services are funded to provide a variety of employment models, including small business opportunities, mobile work crews and 'enclaves' (small production units within a regular business or industrial setting). Older-style sheltered workshops only receive funding if they can demonstrate adequate plans for transition into de-institutionalised services. The difficulties involved in the transformation of this sector are discussed in a paper by Chapman (1994).

In October 1993, just over 2,300 CETP clients and 65 per cent of the 1,000 clients of SE schemes were in open employment (Disability Task Force, 1995).

Definitions of disability

The Disability Discrimination Act takes a broad view of disability, considering it to be physical, intellectual, psychiatric, sensory, neurological or learning disabilities. The Act also includes discrimination against a person because they have some disease-causing organism (such as the AIDS virus) present in the body.

The Disability Services Act does not include a definition of disability but specifies its target groups as those persons with a disability that:

● is attributable to an intellectual, psychiatric, sensory or physical impairment or a combination of such impairments
● is permanent or likely to be permanent, and
● results in a substantially reduced capacity for communication, learning or mobility, and the need for ongoing support services.

Social security policies

All benefits are funded from general revenue, mainly taxation. There are no social insurance arrangements.

The current Australian approach emphasises the role of income support within an 'active society'. If permanent full-time employment is not achievable, then combining part-time or casual earnings with income support is considered preferable to extended periods of total reliance on income support payments (Briggs, 1994).

Income support for disabled people was first introduced in 1908. Sickness benefit was introduced in 1944 for those with temporary incapacity from employment. The premise underlying invalid pension was that disabled people would be unable to (re)gain employment. To obtain a pension they had to be classified as permanently incapacitated for work. Prior to reforms in

1991, pensioners were not eligible for Commonwealth employment services programmes to access employment or training.

The number of people receiving those two benefits grew considerably in the 1970s and 1980s. Details of the growth are provided by Lonsdale (1993). Sickness benefit (SB) escalated from 9,000 to 73,000 beneficiaries. A 1983 study found that more than half of its recipients had transferred from unemployment benefit, special benefit, or had never been employed. Duration on SB also increased, particularly among men aged over 45, half of whom in 1987 had stayed on the benefit for over two years. The number of recipients of invalid benefit (IB) increased by 150 per cent over the two decades, to stand at 334,000 in 1991, largely due to the big increase in male beneficiaries. According to a source cited by Lonsdale, during the 1980s the number of people transferring to IP from unemployment benefit increased and about two-fifths of SB recipients transferred to IP. These trends were a strong impetus to the restructuring of the income support programme.

The current social security provisions for disabled people were shaped mainly by a government policy review of services for disabled people which began in the mid-1980s under Labour administrations. Under the Social Security Review in the late 1980s, a paper was published, called *Towards Enabling Policies: Income Support for People with Disabilities* (Cass *et al.*, 1988), which reinforced the principles behind the DSA. As a consequence of the paper, an inter-departmental Disability Task Force was established to develop options for reform.

The outcome of the Task Force's work was the Disability Reform Package, introduced in November 1991, aimed at creating a more active system of support which encouraged disabled people to maximise their employment potential through rehabilitation, training and labour market programmes. It stressed the need to ease transition to employment for those who could work part-time (International Social Security Association, 1996). The package was also designed to improve co-ordination between the relevant Departments.[3]

The Disability Reform Package replaced Sickness Benefit with Sickness Allowance, with eligibility largely limited to a period of 12 months. It replaced Invalid Pension with Disability Support Pension, based on a minimum impairment of 20 per cent and an ongoing inability to work full time at full award levels. Previously, eligibility for IP had been assessed in terms of medical condition, interacting with socio-economic factors. Under the new arrangements, people considered likely to benefit from rehabilitation, training or special assistance have their workforce participation reassessed and may be placed in an 'active' category of Disability Support Pension recipients. A new Workforce Transition Package aimed to help disabled people to re-enter the labour market.

The basic structure of benefits has not been altered by the new Liberal-National coalition government which took office in 1996 but there have been changes which indicate a possible alteration in policy approach that could bring more changes in later years. Current policies on income support for disabled people also have to be seen in the context of broader policy development in this field, including the strategic review of the Disability Services Programme (Baume and Kay, 1995) and the review of the Commonwealth State Disability Agreement (Yeatman, 1996), the current round of which expires in 1997. The Disability Reform Package itself was reviewed in 1995 (Disability Task Force, 1995).

---

[3] Although this process sounds progressive and rational, the original proposals were not without their critics at the time and the eventual shape of the package only emerged after intensive lobbying by interest groups.

Institutional responsibilities

The Department of Employment, Education, Training and Youth Affairs (DEETYA) is responsible for mainstream labour market programmes.

The Department of Health and Family Services (DHFS) has primary responsibility for funding specialist services under the Disability Services Act. It administers the Disability Services Programme (DSP) and, through it, funds employment services for disabled people who require ongoing support to get and retain employment.

Under the Commonwealth/State Disability Agreement of 1991, the Commonwealth Government administers employment services for disabled people and the State Governments take responsibility for accommodation and other support services.

The States are responsible for medical rehabilitation and the Commonwealth Rehabilitation Service uses a network of regional rehabilitation units for vocational and social rehabilitation and training.

Advice on all social security payments lies with the Department of Social Security (DSS). Service-related disability pensions are administered by the Department of Veterans' Affairs (DVA).

However, benefits and services for disabled people have, at least in principle, been integrated at Commonwealth level through the Disability Reform Package (since 1991), which brings together the DSS, DEETYA and DHFS.

Assessment of entitlements

Eligibility for benefits is assessed in the first instance by assessment officers in regional DSS offices. Specialist Disability Support Officers (DSOs) deal with complex decisions and provide advice to general staff. They also identify Disability Support Pension recipients who might benefit from training, rehabilitation or job search assistance and convene Disability Panels, made up of representatives of the Departments involved in the Disability Reform Package, including Disability Job Seeker Advisers from DEETYA. These Panels work with the DSOs to establish suitable goals with and for the recipient and to help them access programmes run by DEETYA and the Commonwealth Rehabilitation Service (CRS), or other special employment services funded by DHFS. Participation in assessment by the Panel and any subsequent referrals are voluntary.

Recent developments

The Commonwealth Employment Service (CES) (a division of DEETYA) is being largely abolished, with its remaining functions moving into a new 'one-stop shop' service delivery agency based on the DSS administration and payments network and also involving sections of DHFS services. The Disability Support Officers will operate from the new agency, along with the DEETYA Disability Job Seeker Advisers. A recent document on community consultation about the employment service reforms canvasses the possibility that in the new unified agency the coordinating panels may not be necessary (DEETYA, 1996a).

Two main types of government scheme designed to supplement the wages of disabled employees can be distinguished. In this section we concentrate on social security benefits paid directly to disabled people. In a later section, we look at subsidies paid to employers to encourage them to take on disabled workers or to create jobs.

The main benefits allowing a combination of substantial disability and work are:

- *Disability Support Pension*: paid to people with a disability who have limited capacity for working and which allows them to keep some earnings from employment
- *Disability Wage Supplement*: a top-up benefit for people in the Supported Wage System, which compensates employers for employing disabled people
- *Mobility Allowance*: paid where a disabled person cannot use public transport to get to work or a place of education.

Of these benefits, Disability Support Pension far exceeds the other two in its relevance and importance for disabled people who wish to work.

Disability Support Pension

Disability Support Pension (DSP) was introduced in 1991, replacing the former benefit, Invalid Pension.

Eligibility criteria

To qualify for DSP, a person must have a physical, intellectual or psychiatric impairment of at least 20 per cent (based on a set of impairment tables). People who are permanently blind qualify automatically for DSP.

A person must also have a continuing inability to work in order to qualify for DSP. 'Continuing inability to work' is defined as being prevented by the impairment, within the next two years, from doing any work and undertaking education, vocational or on-the-job-training likely to reskill the person for work. 'Any work' in this context means work for at least 30 hours per week at 'award' wages.[4] Thus DSP recipients are able to work part-time.

DSP is available only to people aged 16 or over and under the age for receipt of the Age Pension (from July 1997, 65 for men, 61 for women). No period of residence is required if the inability to work or blindness occurs while the recipient is an Australian resident. Otherwise (apart from temporary absence) residence rules are as for the Age Pension (basically ten years of continuous residence, but with some exceptions).

Receipt of DSP is subject to a means test, covering both income and assets. DSP recipients can earn the following amounts before their benefit is affected:

Single person	$98.00 per fortnight
Couple (combined)	$172.00 per fortnight
For each dependent child	add $24.00 per fortnight

---

[4] The minimum industry- and job-based rates laid down, at present, by the Industrial Relations Commission.

For every dollar that earnings or other income exceed these amounts, the full rate of payment for a single person is reduced by 50c, or by 25c for each member of a couple. If a recipient's partner does not receive a pension, the pensioner receives the couple rate, reduced by 25c for every dollar of income above the disregarded income for a couple. Thus, for single people payment would stop if their gross fortnightly income was $801.60 or more, while for a couple the limit would be $1,338.40 per fortnight.

DSP is both an in-work and out-of work benefit, so moving into and out of work within the parameters of benefit eligibility does not affect entitlement to the benefit or any of the 'passport' entitlements, described below, except through the income test.

People not qualifying for DSP because they are assessed as having an insufficient impairment, or one that does not substantially reduce their capacity to work, would be able to claim an unemployment benefit - Job Seekers Allowance or Newstart Allowance - which also allows the recipient to keep some earnings from employment. These benefits have an activity test.

Assessment

DSP claimants have to provide a report on their impairment and capacity to work from their own doctor, using a standard form. Unless this indicates 'manifestly' that they have a qualifying impairment, they would normally also be required to be examined by a Commonwealth Medical Officer. The determination is in two stages. The first is based on the impairment level, according to the Impairment Tables. The second stage involves assessing the claimant's current and potential ability to work, or be retrained, within the next two years. Work Ability Tables are being developed and trialed but are not currently in use.

Guidance sets out a detailed set of steps for assessment officers in making determinations, but the Impairment Tables in particular are controversial and decisions are frequently appealed. From January 1997, the Impairment Tables have been revised to remove from eligibility 'those customers whose impairments have a relatively small impact on their overall ability to work'.

From January 1997, all those DSP recipients who were previously receiving Invalid Pension, or who are blind, have had to undergo a medical review. This is intended to make sure that people are 'receiving the most appropriate form of income support' (Ministerial press release, 9/12/96).[5]

Recipients of Disability Support Pension
Table A.1 shows the trends in the numbers of people receiving Disability Support Pension (and its predecessor Invalid Pension) since 1986, by sex, and recipients and other related pensioners as a proportion of the population.

---

[5] Budget forward estimates of expenditure on DSP suggest that it is assumed that substantial numbers might be taken off benefit (and presumably moved on to an activity tested unemployment allowance).

14

Table A.1
Invalid/Disability Support Pension recipients, by sex, June 1986-1996 (000s)

At 30 June or for year ending 30 June	*1987*	*1988*	*1989*	*1990*	*1991*	*1992*	*1993*	*1994*	*1995*	*1996*
Men	213.3	219.2	227.3	233.3	244.7	273.7	291.5	309.1	324.7	340.3
Women	75.8	77.8	80.5	83.5	89.5	104.9	115.1	127.1	139.8	159.0
Total	289.1	297.0	307.8	316.8	334.2	378.6	406.6	436.2	464.4	499.2
% of recipients with only part payment	12.4	12.6	12.7	13.9	14.2	14.3	-	-	14.1	15.6
Recipients as % of population aged 16-64 (men) or 16-59 (women)	2.74	2.76	2.79	2.82	2.94	3.30	-	-	-	-
Pensioners (including Wife and Carer) as % of total population	2.28	2.30	2.33	2.35	2.40	2.72	-	-	-	-

Sources: DSS, 1993; 1996

The table shows that the proportion of recipients who are women has been increasing slowly, but they are still less than a third of the total.

In June 1996, a large majority (nearly 70 per cent) of DSP recipients were aged between 30 and 59, but the men tend to be older than the women (DSS, 1996).

Information supplied by the DSS for 1994 shows that, for those awarded DSP after November 1991 (i.e. not those transferred from Invalid Pension or other payments), the main medical conditions registered were musculo-skeletal (42 per cent of awards), psychological/psychiatric (19 per cent), circulatory (nine per cent) and respiratory (six per cent).

DSP recipients in employment

Table A.1 above shows, where the information is available, the rising percentage of recipients who have reduced rate payments partly, but not only, because they have assessable earnings.

The introduction of the Disability Reform Package as a whole does appear to have some impact on both the proportion of DSP recipients with earnings from work and the level of these earnings. In June 1991, before the DRP was introduced, 3.8 per cent of Invalid Pensioners had some earnings, most below the 'free area' level (equivalent to the earnings disregard in the UK). Once the DRP was in place, with a raised earnings review trigger, this percentage increased to six per cent overall and remained at this level through to 1994 (over a period when the labour market was contracting). Table A.1 suggests that the figure may have risen slightly since then.

However, the real increase took place among the former Invalid Pension recipients. The percentage of them in work rose from 3.8 in 1991 to 7.6 by June 1994, while for new DSP recipients it was only 2.9 per cent in 1994. There seem to be several reasons for this. First, former IP recipients had to volunteer for DRP assistance rather than being directed towards it and thus may have been more motivated. The DRP evaluation recommended that this group should be involved more systematically in the DRP. Secondly, tighter criteria for DSP means that new recipients tend to have higher levels of disability than former IP recipients and thus may experience greater problems getting work.

The report on the Disability Reform Package by the Disability Task Force (1995) includes a breakdown of employment characteristics of those recipients who were working, based on sample surveys carried out twice at 12 month intervals (reproduced as Table A.2 below). It includes both people receiving payments before the reform package (pre-DRP) and those awarded it later (post-DRP). Almost all the post-DRP respondents who were working were still receiving benefit, compared with 83 per cent of the pre-DRP respondents.

Table A.2 demonstrates the very high proportion of post-DRP recipients working part-time and the prevalence of casual employment. It should be noted that almost half of the working post-DRP recipients were in voluntary work.

Table A.2
Employment characteristics of pre-DRP and post-DRP pensioners who were working

Granted Disability Support/ Invalid Pension	Pre-DRP1 %	Pre-DRP2 %	Post-DRP1 %	Post-DRP2 %
Average hours:				
Part-time	67.5	74.3	87.6	85.2
Full-time	32.5	25.7	9.9	10
Job status:				
Permanent employment	41.8	44.6	33	26.6
Temporary employment	17.8	16	17.6	11.6
Casual employment	39.1	38.4	49.1	61.8
Type of work:				
Wage and salary earner	50.4	32.3	49.8	38.9
Own or family business	_3.2_	8.8	_7.7_	9.3
Sheltered employment	16.3	11.3	_6.8_	6.7
Voluntary work	22.4	40.2	32.6	44.8
Other	7.2	7.4	_3.2_	_0.3_
Occupation:				
Same as before grant	18.8	16.2	8.1	9.2
No occupation before grant	24.4	23.5	28.6	18.2
Income per week:				
Less than $100	53.7	67.9	81.7	76.7
$100 to $499	18.2	14.1	15.3	15.2
$500 or more	28	16.7	3	8.1
Weighted population	824	1,203	1,093	1,209
Sample total	38	196	72	86

Note: Figures underlined and in italics have an estimated relative standard error in excess of 20 per cent and should be used with caution

Source: Disability Task Force, 1995

The latest information about income levels of people receiving DSP is from June 1996 (DSS, 1996). This shows that of the 99 per cent of people qualifying under the income test, 42 per cent had no assessable income, 43 per cent had income up to $47 per week, and 14 per cent had income above this level (based on individual assessable income of both single people and members of couples). There is, however, thought to be some underestimation of income of DSP recipients, partly because adjustments to entitlements are usually made annually and people do not always report earnings until then, and partly because of unreported earnings below the 'free area'. It is not possible to tell how many recipients have income from paid work, as opposed to interest on savings, other pensions, property and so on, but the small percentage with income above the free area suggests that the amount of work undertaken is still small.

Claims and awards

Data on claims[6] for the period up to 1994, taken from the DRP evaluation, indicate that between 1991 and 1993 there was an increase in the number of claims for DSP. However, since the introduction of the reform package the grant rate (success rate) fell from 72 per cent in the last year of Invalid Pension to 70 per cent in 1992 and 64 per cent at June 1994. This was regarded by DSS as a desirable outcome of tighter eligibility requirements under DSP, but was offset by the increasing number of claims (rising from 101,900 in 1991-92 to 114,100 in 1993-94).

The growth in the number of claims seems largely to be explained by changes in eligibility, including the incorporation of Rehabilitation Allowance and Sheltered Employment Allowance into DSP, demographic factors such as the ageing of the population and greater numbers of single women, and reduced access to some other forms of income support, including Widow B pensions[7] and some DVA pensions (Perry, 1994).

The single largest reason for the reduction in the grant rate up to June 1994 was the new 20 per cent impairment criterion (40 per cent of rejected claims). A further 16 per cent failed the work capacity test in spite of a having a 20 per cent impairment. Only five per cent were rejected on grounds of excess income.

Disability Wage Supplement

Disability Wage Supplement (DWS), introduced in 1994, provides supplementary assistance to people participating in the Supported Wage System, administered by the Department of Health and Family Services (DHFS).

The Supported Wage System provides the legal framework for the payment of an agreed wage to a disabled person at a pro-rata level of the normal award rate, based on a nationally consistent assessment of the person's skills and productive capacities. Previous schemes had allowed payment at below award wages. The Supported Wage System was introduced on the basis of studies which concluded that some disabled people needed a productivity-based wage system. Initial assessment, on-the-job support and workplace modifications to help maximise performance are also available through DHFS.

During 1995/6, 681 people with disabilities were approved as supported wage system participants, representing 79 per cent of the target number (DHFS, 1996). Early data from the scheme (*Work in Progress*, 1996) show that participants are predominantly male, aged under 35 and with some type of intellectual disability; average assessed productivity is around 60 per cent, the average hours worked are 23, and weekly earnings $140.

To be eligible for the Disability Wage Supplement disabled people must qualify under the rules outlined above for Disability Support Pension. Once an award of DWS is made, recipients do not have to demonstrate a continuing inability to work in order to continue to qualify. DWS can also be received for up to 12 months after a recipient achieves the full award rate, subject to the income test.

---

[6] Information on claims, as opposed to awards, is not routinely published by the Department of Social Security and is not easily obtainable.

[7] A pension for widows without dependent children and aged 50 and over (available up to retirement age) being phased out over 15 years from 1987.

Applications to join the Supported Wage System are assessed by the Supported Wage Management Unit within the DHFS. Separate application must be made for DSP/DWS at DSS regional offices, where they are dealt with as described above. There are rules covering movement back on to DSP from DWS, which allow for easy transition without further assessment within a specified period.

Recipients of Disability Wage Supplement

There is little official data about Disability Wage Supplement. However, what data does exist shows that take-up of the benefit has been extremely limited.

In December 1996, the total number of recipients of DWS was 284, of whom 181 were men and 103 women. Single people account for 95 per cent of awards. (One possible explanation for this is that disabled people in dual earner households are likely to be excluded from eligibility for DWS on the grounds of their joint income.) Most recipients (98 per cent) did not own their own homes. The age structure of recipients was skewed towards the younger age bands (eight per cent were between 16 and 20 years, 81 per cent between 20 and 39 and eight per cent between 40 and 59).

A recently concluded sample survey of DSP recipients may provide more information on people who receive DWS, but at the time of writing no findings have been published.

Mobility Allowance

Mobility Allowance provides help for people in employment, vocational training or voluntary work, who are unable to use public transport without substantial assistance because of a physical, psychiatric or intellectual disability.

To qualify, a person must:

● be aged at least 16 years
● spend at least eight hours per week in paid employment (including sheltered employment), or self-employment, voluntary work, and/or vocational training
● undertake job search as part of an activity plan agreed with a Disability Panel or a Competitive Employment Training Placement programme, or receive an unemployment allowance
● not have received a sales tax exemption on a motor vehicle within the last two years as a result of the disability, and
● not be provided with a car by the Department of Veterans' Affairs.

A claimant must be an Australian resident and be in Australia when claiming and receiving the allowance. Legislation was put forward to deny this payment to new migrants until they have been resident for 104 weeks, but at time of writing this has not been passed by the Senate.

Trends in awards of Mobility Allowance

The number of Mobility Allowance recipients was fairly stable from the mid-1980s up to 1993, rising from around 11,400 in 1986 to 13,900 in 1992. From 1993 it increased substantially, reaching almost 25,000 in mid-1996 (DSS, 1996). This increase mainly resulted from DRP-related reforms, which eased eligibility to include people undertaking eight hours or more of voluntary work, and DSP/Sickness Allowance recipients with job search included in their DSS activity plan.

In 1994 the majority (61 per cent) were undertaking employment rather than some other eligible labour market activity.

The sex breakdown of recipients has consistently been about 56 per cent men and 44 per cent women. The most common types of disability registered in 1994 were intellectual and learning disabilities (57 per cent), congenital abnormalities (22 per cent), nervous system disorders (nine per cent), musculo-skeletal and connective tissues (four per cent) and psychiatric disorders (three per cent) (Disability Task Force, 1995).

Concessions and lump-sum payments

Recipients of DSP and DWS (and other recipients of pensions) are automatically issued with a Pensioner Concession Card (PCC). This gives access for the recipient and their dependants to Commonwealth health benefits including cheaper prescriptions, free basic dental treatment and free hearing aids. The card also gives access to some State concessions, which vary by State, but include such things as rate reductions, cheaper public transport and energy, and motor registration reductions. PCC holders can also get help with cost of having a telephone through Telephone Allowance; this is paid quarterly at $15.40 per quarter.

Mobility Allowance recipients not eligible for a PCC automatically receive a Health Care Card, which gives access to a similar range of concessions.

Recipients of all of these payments also receive Pharmaceutical Allowance, which is paid in with the pension at a rate of $5.40 per fortnight (single or couple) or half this amount if only one partner in a couple is eligible.

Until they were abolished in March 1997, both unemployed and disabled people had access to Employment Entry Payments. For DSP recipients the payment was $300 and was available if they took work for more than 30 hours per week or if earnings exceeded the qualifying threshold.

DSP recipients still have access to Education Payments, worth $200 annually for DSP recipients who start or continue studying and who are eligible for the Austudy (student grant) pensioner education supplement. From March 1997 Education Payments were abolished for unemployment beneficiaries but not pension recipients.

Under the Disability Reform Package, DEETYA introduced schemes to support training for disabled job seekers including Disability Supplement for People with Disabilities which assists access to formal training by providing equipment, transport and so on worth up to $5,000 per annum.

Benefits for Vocational Rehabilitation

There are no longer any specific benefits for rehabilitation in Australia. Prior to 1991 disabled people could claim Rehabilitation Allowance but this was merged with the new Disability Support Pension as part of the Disability Reform Package. All recipients of DSP can retain their benefit while participating in any rehabilitation work or training.

The Commonwealth Rehabilitation Service (CRS) (part of the Commonwealth Department of Human Services and Health) provides vocational and social rehabilitation services without charge to recipients of DSP, Sickness Allowance, unemployment benefits and veterans' pensions, as well as to clients referred from compensation and insurance programmes (Zeitzer, 1995). Around one in five are referred by a DRP panel.

As part of the rehabilitation programme, CRS clients may be placed in a work environment for up to three months under the Work Training Scheme, a joint agreement with the Australian Council of Trade Unions. The CRS provides any specialised clothing or tools needed and usually pays the participant a training allowance, which is in addition to their benefit (Zeitzer, 1995).

WAGE SUBSIDIES

Schemes for supplementing wages to employees (and thus allowing employers to pay relatively low wages) have been discussed above. This section concentrates on schemes providing direct subsidies to employers. All are administered by DEETYA and funded through general revenue. There are both generalist and specialist programmes. Subject to the normal eligibility rules and the means test, workers in subsidised employment can continue to receive their in-work disability benefits.

General wage subsidy schemes

Jobstart has been the main generalist programme available to long-term unemployed or other disadvantaged people in recent years. It was introduced in 1991, and expanded and reorganised in 1994 (as part of the Working Nation initiative). It provides by far the largest number of subsidised placements.

Disabled people receiving DSP and referred by a Disability Panel with an endorsed Activity Plan are immediately eligible for Jobstart, while others with disabilities and registered with the Commonwealth Employment Service are eligible after four weeks.

Subsidies for Jobstart are temporary, paid for a minimum of 13 weeks and up to 26 weeks, plus a lump-sum establishment fee of $1,000 for people unemployed for over 18 months. The employer is expected to keep the employee on for at least three months after the subsidy period. The rates of subsidy vary depending on the length of time the person has been unemployed, but for adult full-time positions they ranged in 1995-96 from $150 to $325 per week. Employers must pay award (or enterprise agreement) wages and conditions, but subsidies are payable pro-rata for part-time work of at least 80 hours per month (or less for DSP recipients depending on the nature and severity of a disability).

National Training Wage is designed to place long-term unemployed people, especially school leavers, in work that includes approved training. From 1994 the programme brought together a variety of training awards. The subsidies are similar to those of Jobstart and can also include completion bonuses to employers.

Wage subsidy schemes for disabled people

Wage subsidy schemes specially for disabled people are *Disabled Apprentice Wage Subsidy*, which provides apprenticeship opportunities with subsidies and completion bonuses to employers as in the trainee scheme, and *Work Experience Programme for People with Disabilities* (WEPD).

Under the WEPD scheme, wages are fully reimbursed up to $3,600 (1995-96 figures) per client referred by a Disability Panel for around 12 weeks for full-time positions or about 20 weeks for part-time positions of at least 20 hours per week. Employers can also be reimbursed up to $2,000 per client for necessary additional costs, such as buying special equipment and making necessary adaptations.

A grant scheme, *Workplace Modification Allowance*, provides up to $5,000 to private sector employers who employ disabled participants in a DEETYA programme, to cover the cost of essential equipment, or of modifying the workplace to enable disabled people to undertake employment. Eligibility comes with access to the other relevant programmes, but depends on the particular needs of the employee and the workplace.

The 1995-96 allocation for wage subsidy schemes was $397 million for around 167,000 places, of which around 1,600 were for DSP recipients within Jobstart.

It should be noted that the wage subsidy schemes are, after a transitional period, to be 'cashed out' into the new employment placement enterprise 'single funding stream', under the 1996/97 Budget plans. Although the Government has talked about ensuring disabled people receive appropriate assistance, it is not clear yet how this will work in practice and was raised as a concern by a number of organisations in the consultation report (DEETYA, 1996a).

Policy rationales

The broad policy objective behind wage subsidy schemes is to give employers incentives to take on people whom they otherwise would not, in the hope of demonstrating that they can be valuable workers, and therefore worth retaining. The Government policy document, *Working Nation*, (Commonwealth of Australia, 1994) states that 'the experience of the last few years indicates that many employers will hire long term unemployed people once they have the opportunity to consider them, if the incentives provided by the Government are right' (p.119). In relation to people with disabilities, subsidies are generally paid at a higher level, in order to overcome the special reluctance employers may have to take them on, and come with additional grants or allowances to help with special costs of adaptation, equipment etc. The restructuring of Jobstart under *Working Nation* was intended to increase incentives by extending periods and levels of subsidy.

It is difficult in official policy statements to distinguish between the aims of providing incentives to disabled people and to employers. Generally the incentive issue is phrased in terms of the employers, while programme objectives also include reductions in public expenditure, but all these tend to be expressed within a rhetorical framework of offering assistance and encouragement to disabled people to maximise their potential, social justice and equity, and so on.

Characteristics of disabled workers subject to wage subsidies

The evaluation of the DRP shows that between 1992 and mid-1994, 14,400 DRP clients commenced some form of labour market programme, out of a cumulative total of 19,300 clients registered. The total number of people with disabilities starting a programme (including those not eligible for the DRP) was 203,000, representing about 13 per cent of the total of 1.53 million commencements.

In 1992, 23 per cent of all disabled clients undertaking a programme entered subsidised employment under Jobstart, increasing to 30 per cent in 1993 and 33 per cent in the first half of 1994. Among just the DRP clients (mainly people receiving DSP), the percentages for Jobstart use were a little lower but similar, while over 20 per cent were also consistently using the other subsidy scheme, WEPD.

Qualitative research findings indicated that WEPD was the most highly regarded of the DEETYA programmes for disabled people and appeared to lead to particularly satisfactory outcomes when used to lead on to a Jobstart placement. Thus the two schemes were linked more formally in 1994.

We have not been able to ascertain any 'take-up' measures for the wage subsidy schemes from the employer side. However, the DRP evaluation indicates that virtually all the employment schemes have been oversubscribed and the complaints were about waiting lists and lack of opportunities for people assessed as needing assistance by Panels. The general view is that there has been considerable unmet demand for places.

Effectiveness of subsidising employers

Earlier experience of wage subsidy schemes for disabled people suggested that they were not particularly effective, possibly because output rather than price variables were more influential in determining employment (Mangan, 1990). It is difficult to disentangle the results for disabled people from the (fairly limited) data available on the impact of Jobstart and the other more recent schemes, but it does appear that overall, the wage subsidy schemes have been the most effective of all the *Working Nation* programmes, especially for the unit costs. Twelve month post-programme monitoring data from DEETYA show that in 1995, a year after completing a Jobstart placement, 59 per cent of participants were in unsubsidised employment - roughly the same percentage as after three months (DEETYA, 1996b). This percentage was only bettered by the self-employment support scheme and the Australian Traineeship Scheme, and was considerably higher than for most of the other schemes. Figures for WEPD are not presented separately in this analysis.

The Australian Economic Planning and Advisory Commission (EPAC) estimated that the average cost per person in Jobstart was $1,900 - the second lowest after Skillshare - and the cost per unsubsidised employment outcome was $3,500, easily the lowest of all the schemes (EPAC, 1996). However, wage subsidy schemes are known to involve deadweight, substitution, and replacement effects which can account for up to 95 per cent of all jobs created. For Jobstart it has been estimated that only 11-25 per cent of jobs are genuinely additional, but the substitution may nevertheless have given some particularly disadvantaged people an employment opportunity.

The DRP evaluation provides some estimates of the outcomes achieved by DRP clients as opposed to other participants between 1993 and 1994. This suggests that in the first half of 1994 69 per cent of DRP Jobstart participants achieved a 'positive outcome' (defined as unsubsidised employment, a traineeship or other unsubsidised education or training about three months after completing a programme), compared with 63 per cent of other participants. WEPD participants have no comparison group, but achieved a 58 per cent positive outcome rate in 1993, falling to 49 per cent in the first half of 1994 (Disability Task Force, 1995).

It is difficult to get a clear picture of which particular groups of disabled people have been benefiting from wage subsidy schemes. The interactions between different schemes and forms of support for disabled people entering work also make it hard to isolate the impact of particular schemes. The most that can be said at this stage is that wage subsidies do appear to have some positive effect on disabled people employment chances, at a relatively low cost compared with some other kinds of labour market programme.

The main constraint on the effectiveness of wage subsidy schemes appears to be the amount of resources the Government is prepared to put into them, as there is unmet demand for places. Surveys of employers for the DRP evaluation suggested that while employers tended to show the usual reservations about employing disabled people, there appeared to have been some improvement in attitudes since the introduction of the package. However, there is little evidence as to how much further take-up of wage subsidy schemes by employers might go.

COMMENTARY

In Australia, evaluation of the specific policy of enabling people with partial incapacity to combine benefits and work has to be seen within the wider context of the whole raft of reforms introduced since the late 1980s, but especially the Disability Reform Package.

The Disability Task Force's evaluation of the DRP judged it to be a success overall, though with shortcomings in some areas. The promised programme places under the DRP were created and filled - in fact the demand for places was considerably greater than the provision. Participation in one of the various programmes run either by DEETYA or CRS, or funded through DHFS, seemed to improve people's employment chances relative to non-participation (though there were no random experimental trials which would have established whether success was due to the characteristics of those selected). The establishment of the Disability Panels also seems to have improved inter-departmental co-ordination and has resulted in disabled people having access especially to DEETYA programmes, for which they were not previously eligible. The wage subsidy schemes appear to have been the most effective.

Certainly, the package has had the effect of increasing the numbers of DSP recipients with some earnings, and in increasing the level of these earnings. The DSS argues that the benefits (including Sickness Allowance) are now better targeted in terms of people's levels of impairment and work capacity, though appeals evidence shows that this remains a contested area. The policies have not translated into fewer DSP recipients, partly because of demographic and other factors increasing claim levels, and partly because of a downturn in demand for labour. Also DSP arrangements are not really designed to get people completely off benefit *per se*, but rather to allow work, backed up by a social security payment, and reasonably smooth transitions off or back on to benefit as the need demands.

Thus the work transition package has been important. Some community groups have regarded this as one of the most successful elements of the DRP. It is difficult to assess the direct impact of these measures, but there are some data which give an indication. For example, the number of recipients with benefit suspended (rather than cancelled) due to return to work rose from 265 in June 1992 to 1,834 in June 1994. A small survey for DSS showed that of 437 people who had their benefit suspended by September 1994, 32 per cent returned to DSP by June 1993 (Hetherington and Van Meurs, 1994). Most of these had worked in casual or temporary jobs and returned to benefit after completing their contract, but most of those in permanent jobs went back on to benefit for medical reasons.

The DRP evaluation estimated that in spite of the higher than expected growth in the numbers of DSP recipients, the package overall achieved some savings in its first few years, mainly through reductions in Sickness Allowance payments, but also through changes in DSP eligibility criteria and part-rate payments resulting from higher earnings levels. Expenditure would probably have increased considerably faster if the DRP had not been introduced. These savings were also projected to increase in future years.

Shortcomings identified in the DRP related mainly to especially disadvantaged groups, to medical assessment for DSP, and to the performance of the Panels. Aboriginal and Torres Strait Islander people, people from non-English speaking backgrounds, people with psychiatric and

severe disabilities requiring high levels of support, and older people, were the groups identi
fied as not having had access to adequate services.

Medical assessment for DSP, and especially the role and performance of the Commonwealth
Medical Officers attracted considerable criticism from community groups. CMOs were said to
lack understanding and expertise in disability. As a result, special training was introduced for
CMOs on disability assessment and cultural diversity. Although the Panel system has been
generally regarded as successful and effective in improving co-ordination and access across
services and departmental areas, some Panels were criticised as bureaucratic and inflexible. The
relatively poor services provided to the special groups listed above also suggested that Panels
needed to be more sensitive to their needs, and would benefit from better linkage into State
and local governments and private and community sector organisations locally.

Overall, Australian policies to break down the rigid barriers between disability and paid work
may be said to have had modest, but not insignificant, success. It appears that the Disability
Wage Supplement, however, is barely used at all. It remains to be seen what impact the new
Government's policies to reduce public expenditure will have on disabled people. In the
context of continuing high unemployment, the cuts to labour market programmes seem likely
to reduce opportunities for transitions to work, even if some special programmes receive extra
places.

REFERENCES

Australian Bureau of Statistics (1993) *Survey of Disability, Ageing and Carers*, Canberra: ABS.

Australian Law Reform Commission (1996) *Report 79*, (electronic version) Uniserve Law:
Electronic Publishing Group.

Baume, P. and Kay, K. (1995) *Working Solution: report of the Strategic Review of the
Commonwealth Disability Services Program*, Canberra: Australian Government Publishing
Service.

Briggs, L. (1994) 'Meeting the challenge: Australian labour market trends and the income
support system', in proceedings of the international research meeting Social Security: *A time
for redefinition?*, Geneva: International Social Security Association.

Cass, B., Gibson, F. and Tito, F. (1988) *Towards Enabling Policies: Income Support for People
with Disabilities*, Social Security Review Issues Paper No.5, Canberra: Department of Social
Security.

Chapman, J. (1994) *Out of the Bunker: The case of Sheltered Workshops in Transition*, Working
Paper No.20, Centre for Australian Community Organisations and Management, Sydney:
University of Technology.

Commonwealth of Australia (1994) *Working Nation*: Policies and programmes, Canberra:
AGPS.

Department of Employment, Education, Training and Youth Affairs (1996a) *Reforming
Employment Assistance: Report on Public Consultations*, Canberra: DEETYA.

Department of Employment, Education, Training and Youth Affairs (1996b) 12 *Month Post
Program Monitoring Survey*, EMB Report 3/96, Canberra: DEETYA.

Department of Health and Family Services (1996) *Annual Report 1995-96*, Canberra: Australian Government Publishing Service.

Department of Social Security (1993) *Ten Year Statistical Summary, 1982-1992*, Canberra: DSS.

Department of Social Security (1996) *DSS Customers: a Statistical Overview*, Canberra: DSS.

Disability Task Force (1995) *Evaluation of the Disability Reform Package: Main Report*, Canberra: Australian Government Publishing Service.

Economic Planning and Advisory Commission (1996) *Future Labour Market Issues for Australia*, Commission Paper No. 12, Canberra: Australian Government Publishing Service.

Hetherington, E. and Van Meurs, L. (1994) *Clients Reactivating their Disability Support Pension Post-employment*, Canberra: Department of Social Security.

International Social Security Association (1996) 'Employment and reintegration measures for disabled or unemployed workers', *International Social Security Review*, 49, 2, 111-126.

Lonsdale, S. (1993) *Invalidity Benefit: An international comparison*, Department of Social Security Analytical Services Division, Social Research Branch, London: Department of Social Security.

Mangan, J. (1990) 'Integrating disabled persons into the Australian workforce: are wage subsidies effective?', *International Social Security Review*, 2, 203-212.

Office of Disability (1995) *Review of the Disability Task Force*, Commonwealth Department of Human Services and Health, Canberra: DSS.

Perry, J. (1994) 'Trends in Disability Support Pension Population 1987-1993', Department of Social Security (unpublished).

Yeatman, A. (1996) *Getting Real: The Final Report of the Review of the Commonwealth/State Disability Agreement*, Canberra: Australian Government Publishing Service.

Zeitzer, I. (1995) 'Quality, effectiveness and efficiency of rehabilitation measures', International Social Security Association Study Group on Rehabilitation (SG/Rn/18/2).

CHAPTER 3

FINLAND[1]

OVERVIEW

The inclusion of disabled people within Finnish society and securing equal opportunities are widely accepted policy goals. These goals are pursued via rights legislation, and through service provision that best supports these objectives. Principles of integration and normalization help to shape the direction of disability policy in different social policy areas.

Finland has always had an approach to labour market policy which is based on active policies (including advice, training, placement and rehabilitation) rather than a more passive reliance on labour market forces as a means of promoting and ensuring employment. In line with this dominant approach, the employment needs of people with limited capacity for work have been recognised (since 1973) in social security legislation, with the provision of a partial employment disability pension.

The most important influence on the labour market in general, and on the employment of disabled people in particular, has been the severe economic recession experienced by Finland in the early 1990s. High levels of unemployment affected disabled people disproportionately, although the position has improved in the last two years or so. However, it is difficult to isolate the proportional effects of a general upturn in economic activity and of specific labour market policies based on social security, rehabilitation or wage subsidies to employers. Furthermore, many of the measures to combat unemployment are still in their early years and there is little evidence yet about their impact (Labour Market Institute for Economic Research/ECOTEC, 1997).

THE LABOUR MARKET

Labour market characteristics and trends

As a result of economic recession, Finland, like other Western European economies, is experiencing major changes in the structure of production, labour utilization, and types of available work. In the three years from 1990, economic output declined by 12 per cent, the worst drop recorded in any OECD country in recent decades. The supply of traditional jobs decreased while temporary, fixed-contract and short-term opportunities increased. Economic restructuring has led to a reduction in the overall level of demand for labour, which has affected marginalised groups disproportionately. The general unemployment rate rose from 3.4 per cent in 1990, peaking at 18.4 per cent in 1994, and stood at 16.3 per cent in 1996.

Out of a population of 5.1 million in 1995, the working age population of Finland was 3.3 million. Two-thirds of employment was in the service sector, and a third in industry and manufacturing (European Commission, 1996a). Finland has a history of high levels of workers in full-time employment compared with most other European countries. Only 12 per cent of workers were in part-time jobs in 1995 which, although a relatively low figure, is higher than in the previous decade when part-time rates varied only between six and eight per cent (European Commission, 1996). However, in 1996, the majority of new jobs (60 per cent) were either temporary (with a fixed termination date) or part time.

[1] Anna Metteri, Department of Social Policy and Social Work, University of Tampere, was national informant for Finland.

27

The labour market participation rate, although falling since the early 1980s, at 75 per cent is still high, particularly when compared with other OECD countries (Eardley *et al.*, 1996), despite a strong trend towards early retirement in the 1980s. Finland has always had a high level of labour market participation in comparison with most other countries. By 1990, women comprised 47.5 per cent of the total workforce, and around two-thirds of workers in the public sector. Unlike many other countries, women are mostly in full-time employment (Glendinning and McLaughlin, 1993). There appears to be a continuing preference for full-time working; almost half of those working part-time reporting doing so because of difficulties obtaining full-time work (Statistics Finland, 1995).

Table Fin.l: Key labour market indicators in Finland, 1995

	Men	*Women*	*Total*
Employment rate (% age 15-64)	63.5	59.9	61.7
Self-employed (as % employed)	18.7	9.6	14.3
Part-time (% total employed)	8.1	15.7	11.8
Activity rate (% age 15-64)	77.3	71.8	74.6
Unemployment rate (% labour force)	17.6	16.7	17.2
Long-term unemployment (% unemployed)	47.3	31.6	37.2

Source: European Commission (1996a), *Employment in Europe 1996*

Labour market policy

Finland has a history and tradition of active labour market policies, aimed at getting people into work and sustaining people in existing employment, rather than a passive reliance on social security benefits to maintain people out of work. Even before the economic recession of the early 1990s, new policies, under the 1987 Employment Act, were being put into place to help young people and the long-term unemployed in particular.

Economic recession has contributed to the eight-fold rise in social security expenditure on unemployment in the last decade. Unemployment expenditure is now more than double the cost of active labour market operations but has given a new impetus to economic and employment policy. The Government's principal aim in recent years has been to regenerate the Finnish economy, reduce inflation and cut unemployment (Labour Market Institute for Economic Research/ECOTEC, 1997). One specific target is to halve unemployment by 1999 (MISEP, 1996). A number of active programmes are now in place, under a general policy initiative called *the Employment Programme 1996-1999*, which build on existing programmes, and which are intended to promote employment and stimulate the labour market. The *Programme* includes, among its 52 different measures, policies to ease the burden of taxation on employees, reforms of employment legislation to remove some of the barriers to hiring workers, new vocational training programmes, promotion of self-employment, and investing in the construction and environmental protection sectors.

Government schemes to promote part-time work, for example through subsidies to employees who transfer from full-time to part-time work, have had very limited impact (Marullo, 1995).

Disabled people in the labour market

The position of disabled people in the labour market in Finland must be seen in the context of economic recession. The general demand for labour affects the relative position of disabled people, and economic recession particularly impacts on disabled jobseekers (Haapasalo *et al.*, 1994; Mannila *et al.*, 1992). In 1994 eight per cent of the working population were in receipt of a disability pension or early disability pension.

Between 1987 and 1990, there were 40,000 to 43,000 disabled jobseekers[2] registered in the Finnish Employment Services; between seven and eight per cent of all jobseekers. Since that time, the proportion of disabled jobseekers to all jobseekers has fallen due to the sharp rise in unemployment, despite the numbers of disabled jobseekers having risen to 58,000 in 1994. At the end of 1994, while the overall unemployment was around 18 per cent, it was estimated to be almost twice as high among disabled people (Ministry of Labour, 1995). The long-term unemployment of disabled people and their exclusion from the labour market have increased (Ministry of Labour, 1995). About 40 per cent of the unemployed disabled people seen by the employment service in the first half of 1995 had been unemployed for over a year (European Commission, 1996b).

EMPLOYMENT POLICIES FOR DISABLED PEOPLE

Disabled people are recognised as a disadvantaged group in the labour market, along with, for example, young people and the long-term unemployed. The range of active labour market measures are as open to disabled people as they are to all unemployed people, and integration into mainstream employment programmes is the preferred policy approach.

Of particular relevance to disabled people are the vocational rehabilitation services, which include information services and, more actively, vocational guidance, and employment assistance. Employment assistance entails the employment office and the unemployed person working together to produce an individual plan which may include training, rehabilitation, apprenticeship or other workplace training, or measures to enable the person to start their own enterprise (MISEP, 1996). Employment assistance may also be integrated with job creation subsidies paid to employers. Subsidised employment has grown in importance as a method of placing disabled jobseekers in work.

The Finnish employment services use an extensive definition of disability, in accordance with ILO Convention 159[3]: a person whose prospects of securing, retaining and advancing in employment are substantially reduced as a result of a duly recognised physical or mental impairment. In Finland, the existence of an impairment must be validated by a medical certificate.

Wide reform of the rehabilitation legislation since the late 1980s aimed to reduce transfer to disability pensions or other long-term benefits, guaranteed rights to vocational training and retraining for disabled people with significantly reduced working capacity, and attempted to improve co-operation between agencies to ensure that rehabilitation is begun at an early stage. Employers are responsible for measures to maintain working capacity.

There is no compulsory employment legislation (such as a quota system). Nor is there comprehensive disability discrimination legislation but recent changes to the Constitution Act and penal code included rights not to be placed in a different position because of disability and sanctions for infringement, and labour legislation outlaws some aspects of employer discrimination on grounds of state of health.

---

[2] Not all those registered as disabled jobseekers are unemployed as some register while still working and others while on training and rehabilitation schemes.

[3] International Labour Organisation (ILO) Convention Concerning Vocational Rehabilitation and Employment of Disabled Persons No. 159, 1983.

Responsible bodies

The Ministry of Labour has the overall responsibility for making labour market policy and for designing practical programmes. The *Employment Programme 1996-1999*, however, is coordinated in conjunction with the Ministries of Education, Finance, and Trade and Industry. A high level steering group of the representatives from the Ministries, the Prime Minister's Office and employers and trade union representatives oversees the *Programme*.

Responsibility for delivering services is shared principally between the Ministry of Labour, the Social Insurance Institution, Employment Pensions Institutes and the municipalities (local government).

- Employment offices at local level, guided by objectives set by Labour District Offices, provide vocational guidance and rehabilitation, job placement services, labour market training and information on vocational services. In 90 offices there are specially trained officers to help disabled people.
- The Social Insurance Institution has the main responsibility for carrying out social security policy, including arrangements for training and rehabilitation.
- The municipalities have a responsibility to provide counselling on rehabilitation and arrange sheltered employment (which had over 3,000 disabled workers in 1993).

SOCIAL SECURITY POLICY FOR DISABLED PEOPLE

The Ministry of Social Affairs and Health is responsible for policy, legislation and overall implementation of the social services and social insurance schemes in Finland. In recent years, social security policy in relation to disabled people has been a concern of the Government and a national working group, headed by the Ministry of Social Affairs and Health, reported in Spring 1997. Prime concerns identified were the barrier to labour market activity presented by the disability benefits system and the need to target resources more effectively to support disabled people in finding and staying in work. The working group's recommendations for existing provisions and innovative proposals are reported in the section which describes the main benefits that disabled people can claim and combine with work.

Social security benefit provision

Finnish social security pensions fall into three categories. A national pension scheme covers all permanent residents. Secondly, an earnings-related insurance-based employment pension scheme covers all employees, self-employed persons and farmers. Most pension recipients draw from both schemes simultaneously. Thirdly, there are special plans for people injured at work, in road traffic accidents, or through military service.

National pensions, which are operated by the Social Insurance Institution, take the form of old age pension (including an early old age pension payable to someone aged between 60 and 64), unemployment pension (payable under certain conditions to those aged between 60 and 65 out of work for a lengthy period) survivors' and veterans' pensions and disability pensions.

The ordinary disability pension in the national scheme is payable to those aged between 16 and 64 who have been found unfit for work. An *individual early retirement disability pension* is payable to someone aged between 58 and 64 with permanently reduced working capacity who either stops working altogether or cuts down on work to a significant degree.

Employment pensions in the private sector are the responsibility of the six Employment Pension Institutes and 150 smaller pension funds. Employment pensions for public sector employees are covered by a further two main schemes. Employment pensions include old age pension and unemployment pensions, a part-time pension for employees aged 58 to 64 who switch to part-time work, and disability pensions.

Disability pensions under the employment pension scheme include a *partial employment disability pension*, unlike in the national scheme where there is only a full pension. The partial employment disability pension is half the amount of the full employment disability pension. The employment disability pension can be claimed by insured people with an employment history whose work capacity is reduced because of illness, injury or disability and whose incapacity for work is estimated to last for at least one year. In the private sector account is also taken of ability to earn an income from such available work the claimant is considered capable of doing (taking into consideration age, education, previous work experience and so on). In the public sector, incapacity for one's own position or job is a sufficient criterion.

Under the employment pension scheme there is also an individual early retirement pension for those with a long work history aged between 58 and 64 whose work capacity has been permanently reduced to the extent that they cannot be expected to continue in the same place of work in their present job or occupation. Assessment of work capacity considers health status, ageing factors affecting work performance, the physical or mental strain of the job and the working conditions.

In both schemes, disability pension can follow a maximum of 300 days receipt of sickness allowance, which is payable under the Health Insurance Act to all employed and self-employed people (and to students and housewives) who are incapacitated from work. However, since January 1996, recipients of sickness allowance no longer move to fixed disability pensions but are entitled to time-limited *rehabilitation support* from the Employment Pensions Institutes.

Separate from pensions are disability benefits, paid by the Social Insurance Institution 'to compensate for the handicap and financial strain imposed by the disability' (Social Insurance Institution, 1996). The main cash benefit is *disability allowance*, one of the eligibility criteria for which is that the claimant's ability to carry out normal physical or mental functions has been affected by some impairment due to illness, injury or disability.

Discretionary benefits for increased costs due to disability are administered by the municipalities (*local authority disability benefits*).

COMBINING DISABILITY BENEFITS AND WORK

Here we consider in detail four of the disability-specific pensions and benefits that can be combined with work in Finland:

- partial employment disability pension
- individual early retirement pension
- disability allowance
- local authority disability benefits.

Partial employment disability pension

Employment disability pensions are payable to insured people who are unable to maintain themselves through their normal or comparable work. When the system was introduced in

1956, it was an 'all-or-nothing' system which contained no provisions for those with a reduced, partial working capacity. This situation was rectified from 1973 onwards with the introduction of the partial employment disability pensions which had the explicit aim of keeping people in some form of work for as long as possible, reflecting the general policy objective of promoting employment but also as a means of reducing expenditure on employment pensions.

Administration of employment disability pensions for the private sector is the responsibility of the six Employment Pensions Institutes and 150 smaller employment pension funds. The information and figures presented here refer to the six main partial employment disability pensions in the private sector. The two main schemes for the public sector are not included in detail. (Around three-quarters of the labour force are in the private sector and the remaining quarter in the public sector.) The Central Pension Security Institute has a central co-ordination and monitoring role, including the collation of national statistics.

To establish entitlement to partial employment disability pension a person must be able to fulfil a number of criteria, including:

- they must have been a registered employee with a satisfactory record of social insurance contributions, and their employer must have paid the appropriate contributions to the pension fund
- due to illness, permanent disability or injuries, they must be unable to carry out their usual work. The claimant can move to part-time work or change job or become unemployed searching for new work
- they must have worked for at least 12 months prior to the disability that reduced their working capacity
- they must claim within 12 months of the onset of the relevant disability (though this period can be extended for a number of reasons including when the claimant takes up educational benefits or has time off for child care), and
- they must have been a Finnish resident for five years.

The partial pension, which corresponds to half of the full employment pension, is awarded if the ability to work is reduced by between 40 per cent and 59 per cent. (The claimant is eligible for a full pension if their reduced capacity is assessed at 60 per cent or more.)

New regulations were introduced in 1996 which changed the period used for the calculations for partial pension awards. The changes will be phased in over a ten year period, but by the year 2006 awards will be based on the wages of the claimant over the previous ten years. The effect of this will be that the level of awards will decrease.

The various partial employment disability pension schemes are funded by contributions from employees, private employers and the state and the municalities (in their role as employers).

Assessment

Claimants do not necessarily apply separately for a partial benefit but are assessed on their capacity and then awarded the appropriate level of pension. Decisions are based on an assessment of the claimant's capacity to carry out their regular work or any other kind of work which, considering their age, occupation, education, and place of residence, would be suitable for them.

Final assessments of the capacity to work are made by doctors working within the insurance institutions, who have a strong controlling and guiding role in relation to doctors making assessments on the basic level. There is some evidence that the doctors within the insurance institutes are basing their decisions more on purely medical factors than in the past when reports of, for example, social workers or psychologists, on a claimant's social circumstances were given more weight.

Awards and recipients

In 1995, in the six main private sector schemes, there were 8,192 partial employment disability pensions in payment (52 per cent to men, 48 per cent to women), of which 1,556 were new awards in that year (44 per cent to men, 56 per cent to women). Nearly seven out of ten new and current awards were made to people over 50 years old. In the same year, a total of 40,600 employment disability pensions were awarded (including new and renewal claims). In the public sector scheme run by the Local Government Pensions Institute at the end of 1995 there were 1,618 partial employment disability pensions in payment.

In the six main private sector schemes in 1993 the four most common disabling conditions of partial employment disability pension recipients (accounting for over three-quarters of all recipients) were diseases of the musculo-skeletal system and connective tissue (44 per cent of all cases), diseases of the circulatory system (12 per cent), mental disorders (12 per cent), and injuries and poisoning (nine per cent).

There are no data published by the Employment Pension Institutions on the numbers of recipients of partial employment disability pension in work. The number is thought to be low, in view of the limited opportunities in the labour market and for part-time work in particular.

Table Fin.2 shows the range of values of the pension (paid monthly) in the six main private sector schemes in 1995.

Table Fin.2
Value of the private sector partial employment disability pension (in FIM per month), 1995

Value of pension (FIM)	Number	Percentage
0-999	3,532	43
1000-1999	2,181	27
2000-2999	1,463	18
3000 and over	1,016	12
Total	8,192	100

Source: Central Pension Security Institute (1996) *Statistical Yearbook of the Employment Pensions Schemes, Part I*

The table shows that seven in ten partial employment disability pension awards were below 2,000 FIM per month compared with an average wage of around 6,800 FIM[4].

[4] Average income figure is for 1994.

Individual early retirement pension[5]

Early retirement pension is strictly an out-of-work benefit for people aged 58 or over who cease work for health reasons. However, in practice some people combine receipt of the pension with employment.

The benefit was introduced in 1986 to improve the incomes of people who after long working careers were forced to retire on health grounds but who were not sufficiently disabled to qualify for a disability pension. The qualifying age was initially 55 but was raised to 58 in 1994.

Eligibility is based on a long employment record (in the region of 20 years in most cases) and, in the employment pension scheme, on a satisfactory record of contributions. The amount of *full* pension depends on the number of years the claimant has worked and on their level of wages.

Claimants are allowed to earn up to a statutory ceiling and still receive the full pension. If earnings are above the ceiling, but still lower than 60 per cent of the normal wage for the individual, then a *half* pension is payable.

An interesting feature of the benefit is that a decision in *principle* can be obtained by a person while they are still in work. The decision is valid for a period of nine months, allowing the worker time to make related decisions about their retirement. Table Fin.3 shows the number of preliminary decisions on individual early retirement pensions between 1989 and 1995 and the percentage of claims disallowed in the national pension scheme.

Table Fin.3
Preliminary decisions and disallowances on national individual early retirement pensions, 1989-1995

Year	Number of preliminary decisions[a]	Percentage of claims that were disallowed
1989	15,199	31
1990	14,836	37
1991	13,121	39
1992	13,301	41
1993	13,368	43
1994	14,157	47
1995	9,270[b]	45

a. Claimants may obtain a 'preliminary decision' which remains valid for a period of nine months.
b In 1994 the qualifying age for individual early retirement pension was increased from 55 to 58 years.

Sources: Statistical Yearbooks of the Social Insurance Institution.

The table shows the relatively stable application rate between 1989 and 1994 when the increase in the qualifying age led to a sharp decrease in claims. However, during the same

[5] 'Individual early retirement pension' is the translation from the Finnish adopted by the Social Insurance Institute in its English publications, although an alternative, and possibly more accurate translation is 'individual early disability pension'.

period the disallowance rate increased from 31 per cent in 1989 to a peak of 47 per cent in 1994.

As mentioned above, early retirement pensions were not initially intended to act as an in-work benefit. In line with the current general policy emphasis on reducing early retirement, the intention is to restrict the number of claimants and recipients (the increase in the qualifying age is an example), and to encourage greater interest and commitment to the rehabilitation of older workers among employers, employees and health care professionals.

Disability allowance

Disability allowance is the main benefit for helping meet the costs of disability. It can be combined with work, but the benefit has other objectives of normalisation; that is, the aim is to help persons with disabilities manage their lives, in work, in education, and in day-to-day activities. The benefit is aimed at disabled people of working age who do not receive one of the range of national pensions, excluding those who are in publicly funded institutional care. The main aim of the benefit is to provide compensation for disability due to the need for assistance and the need to meet special expenses caused by the illness or injury. Claimants do not have to be in work in order to receive the benefit.

Disability allowance is awarded to claimants who fulfil the relevant eligibility criteria, which include:

- the relevant disability must last for at least one year
- functional capacity must be impaired
- the claimant must be aged between 16-64
- the claimant must not be receiving any out-of-work benefits, disability pension, or any corresponding benefits based on the occupational, accident of traffic insurance or war disability insurance
- the claimant must reside in Finland
- there must be extra financial costs due to disability.

There are three payment categories which are assessed according to the degree of disability, or the need of continuous help, or the extra costs based on the disability. In the highest payment category, the special disability allowance is paid to a severely disabled person or to a disabled person, who needs the daily help of another person or who has particularly high expenses because of the illness or injury. A blind person, a person not able to move and a person deaf from infancy is always categorised severely disabled.

The benefit is not means-tested. It is funded from central government.

Disability allowance decisions are made by officials of the Social Insurance Institution based in a network of local offices (though some decisions are made in the national central office).[6]

Decisions are based on information provided on an application form plus a medical statement (making doctors the effective gate-keepers to receipt of the benefit).

Between 1990 and 1995 the number of new claims to disability allowance in each year has varied between 2,500 and 3,000. The success rate of claims has been around two-thirds, with

---

[6] In Finland there is some concern about differences between local offices in the criteria used for decision making and in the decision made. This has led to discussions between medical professionals and administrators.

the higher age groups being more successful than younger claimants. In the same period the number of awards in payment has risen from 10,200 to 11,300.

Table Fin.4 presents a breakdown of awards in 1995 by sex and by level of award.

Table Fin.4
Analysis of disability allowance awards, 1995

Level of award	Men	Women	Total
Smaller allowance	1,299	2,197	3,496
Larger allowance	1,060	1,102	2,162
Special allowance	1,084	996	2,080
(Benefit awarded under earlier legislation)	1,922	1,645	3,567
Total	5,365	5,940	11,305

Source: Statistical Yearbook of the Social Insurance Institution, 1995

There are no official statistics on the proportion of disability allowance recipients who are in employment, but unofficial estimates suggest that as many as 80 per cent could be in some form of paid work.

The costs of disability allowance are of concern to government and the level of benefit is being held at 1995 levels until 1998. The national working group headed by the Ministry of Social Affairs included in its remit the future of disability allowance.

Local authority disability benefits

People who are defined as 'severely disabled' (using a set of statutory criteria established in 1987 under the *Decree on Services for the Disabled*) can claim a disability benefit from their local authority (Municipality) to contribute to some of the costs associated with their particular disability, such as transport, interpretation services, or a personal assistant. Municipalities also have discretion to award additional amounts for the costs of special foods or clothing.

Local authority disability benefits are funded jointly from municipal taxation and from the state. They are not means-tested. Eligibility is based on medical reports and on an assessment by the local authority social services department.

Local authority disability benefits are not primarily intended as means of supporting disabled people in work but they can be combined with work and with other benefits. For example, it is permissible to receive both a partial employment disability pension and a local authority benefit.

There is some evidence that local authority disability benefits are not easy to obtain and that there are wide disparities between awards in different municipalities. The need to reduce expenditure has led municipalities to introduce tighter policies for the award of benefits.

Policy recommendations

A national working group headed by the Ministry of Social Affairs and Health published its conclusions and recommendations on the future of social security policy and provision for disabled people in Spring 1997.

A main conclusion was that the disability pension is not the most desirable means of ensuring that disabled people have an adequate amount to live on, because it acts as a barrier to people being active in the labour market, and because it is expensive. The working group devoted some effort to finding new ways of targeting resources more effectively to support disabled people finding and staying in work. One possibility considered was the inclusion of partial employment disability pension within the national pension system which would extend the opportunity for combining work and benefit to those who have no previous work history and who are therefore ineligible for a partial disability pension. However, no conclusion was reached on this issue because employment pensions were outside the terms of reference of the working group.

One of the main suggestions of the working group was the introduction of a new type of benefit, an incentive support (*kannustintuki*) to people with disabilities to combine work and social benefits. Another suggestion was to extend the duration of a disability pension to two years, while the disabled person is entering or re-entering the labour market. This would make work trials less of a risk than at present, giving people a longer opportunity of returning to the pension, if they did not succeed in the labour market.

A further recommendation of the working group, though not directly related to benefits, was the development of local authority disability services into a statutory obligation on the municipalities, including the expansion of the system of personal assistants, transportation services and interpretation services.

Benefits for Vocational Rehabilitation

Encouraging earlier return-to-work and facilitating work retention are current policy priorities in Finland. People whose work and earnings capacity is significantly impaired by illness or injury are entitled to the vocational training necessary to maintain their working capacity, to financial assistance or interest-free credit to help with self-employment, and the basic education needed to enter vocational training.

A wide reform of rehabilitation legislation was carried out in Finland, to improve the population's capacity for work and activity, including three important new acts which came into force at the beginning of October 1991. Rehabilitation activities of the Social Insurance Institution are governed by these three acts:

- Act on Co-operation in respect of Rehabilitation Issues
- Act on Rehabilitation to be provided by Social Insurance Institution
- Rehabilitation Allowance Act.

The changes have been aimed at reducing the need for workers to transfer to disability pensions or other long-term social benefits, clarifying responsibilities and increasing co-operation. The changes sought to reduce the regional differences in the availability of rehabilitation services and brought some new groups into its scope. Attempts to ensure that rehabilitation is begun at an early stage, particularly around the workplace, were consolidated. The responsibility for undertaking measures to maintain working capacity, and for obtaining practical results lies with employers. The changes also provided for the standardisation of subsistence benefits paid for the period of rehabilitation, and clarified division of responsibilities (Ministry of Labour, 1995).

Rehabilitation allowance is paid for services arranged by the Social Insurance Institution. The allowance is paid only if the objective is for the client to remain in, either, or re-enter employment. The Social Insurance Institution arranges medical rehabilitation for those persons with severe disabilities who are not in institutional care and occupational rehabilitation for persons whose capacity for work is essentially reduced. In 1994, over 9,000 disabled people participated in the vocational training and pre-training arranged by the Social Insurance Institution.

Incentives are built into the social security system to encourage people to undertake rehabilitation programmes. A disability pension can be retained by a claimant while undergoing rehabilitation and, according to which organisation arranges the rehabilitation, the amount of an award will be enhanced. After completing 30 days of rehabilitation arranged by the Social Insurance Institution, participants will receive an increase in their benefit of ten per cent. Employment pension institutes pay rehabilitation allowance to disabled or partially incapacitated employees who come from the labour market and who are returning to the labour market which is set at 33 per cent above the level of the amount of disability pension they would have received. For people already in receipt of a pension, a *rehabilitation increase*, equivalent to an increase of 33 per cent of the award, is paid.

Table Fin.5 shows the number of these allowances distributed to disabled people between 1988 and 1995 by the Social Insurance Institution.

Table Fin.5
Number of rehabilitation allowances, 1988-1995

Year	Number
1988	8,097
1989	8,781
1990	9,598
1991	9,974
1992	9,825
1993	9,082
1994	8,010
1995	5,736

Source: Ministry of Labour (1995)

Financing is provided through employer and employee contributions and from the state budget. The Social Insurance Institution manages the funds, and can provide or reimburse costs of other rehabilitation services with special earmarked funds.

WAGE SUBSIDIES

Under the Employment Act of 1987 a government employment office will attempt to match unemployed persons in the open labour market, or arranges training to widen opportunities. Failing both of these, job opportunities may be improved by providing temporary employment subsidized by employment funds. Special attention has been paid to improving the labour market competition of those with the weakest standing in the labour market: young people, those experiencing long-term unemployment, and disabled people.

Employers taking on an unemployed person can claim a government subsidy for between six and ten months for non-disabled workers and for a maximum of two years for disabled people. Individuals have a work contract with employers and receive a wage. Since 1995, tightened rules mean that the duration of the contract for a previously unemployed person must exceed the subsidy period. For work in central government, the employment subsidy covers the entire wage. The exact amount of the subsidy varies from person to person and is between FIM2,500 and 4,500 per month.

'Traineeships' are a more recently introduced subsidy for on-the-job training. Trainees have no work contract; the employer enters into a contract with the employment service. The measure is directed primarily at young people. There are also subsidies to support self-employment.

At January 1996, a total of 57,000 people were employed on wage subsidies, including traineeships, apprenticeship training and self-employment. Table Fin.6 shows the distribution.

Table Fin.6:   Numbers on wage subsidies by type of employment, January 1996

Type	Number
State employer	6,967
Employment service	1,735
Municipal wage subsidies	25,650
Municipal apprenticeship training	1,107
Private employers	6,068
Self-employment	2,394
Traineeships	1,526
Part-time work	6,033
Private sector apprenticeships training	5,552
Total	57,032

Source: Statistics of the Ministry of Labour, 1996

The table shows that most subsidised employment is in the public sector. The share of the private sector is small but increasing, having more than doubled between 1991 and 1994.

Recently the sustainability of subsidised employment in its present form has been threatened by reductions in the permanent workforce in the public sector, due to budgetary deficits (Mannila, 1995) and policy debate has focused on ways of increasing provision by private sector employers. The problem is found to lie with the design of the scheme which discourages or prevents employers from substituting subsidised labour for a permanent workforce. Employers, for example, must issue workers with contracts and subsidies can last only a maximum of ten months (for non-disabled workers). Consideration is therefore being given to reforming these aspects of the wage subsidy scheme. In addition, the Ministry of Labour is consulting on a proposal to extend the scheme beyond private and public sectors, where subsidies are mainly focussed, to include non-profit organisations.

Subsidised employment for disabled people

Wage subsidised employment is considered the most important individual means available to the employment authorities both to promote the employability of disabled job-seekers and to give those disabled people unsuccessful in the competitive labour market a chance to work; it is thus considered both a step towards the competitive labour market and an end in itself (Mannila, 1995). According to Ministry of Labour (1995) statistics, in 1994 out of 58,000 disabled jobseekers seen by the employment offices almost as many were channelled to subsidised employment (13,000) as to open employment (13,600).

The absolute number of disabled people in subsidised employment has remained fairly constant since 1991 but the number as a proportion of all disabled job-seekers has decreased; overall, a higher proportion of disabled than of all jobseekers has been channelled into subsidised employment (Mannila, 1995).

The wage subsidy is intended to compensate the employer both for the employee's reduced productivity stemming from disability and for the extra costs of workplace modifications or training.

A major study of wage subsidies (reported in Mannila, 1995), found that disabled persons in subsidised work had positive images of work, while their employers had positive images of the subsidised workers. From the employees' point of view, the disadvantages were, above all, job insecurity and low pay, although the wage is usually somewhat higher than unemployment benefit and considered a socially legitimate income (Mannila, 1995).

In addressing whether subsidies affected transfer to open employment, Mannila's research found that in 1990, one-third, and in 1992, one-quarter of all disabled employees engaged in subsidized employment in 1988 had found jobs in the competitive labour market. These statistics are comparable both to the experiences of disabled people who had undergone training, and also nondisabled people who had previously been in subsidized jobs. Mannila also found that those disabled people in private sector jobs were more likely to find employment in the competitive sector than those working in comparable public sector jobs.

Grants for aids and adaptations

Other financial support is available to employers, including grants for adapting the working conditions of disabled people. This funding can also be provided for job assistance. The Social Insurance Institution provides grants for technical aids and adaptations to the workplace and for training. It includes costs of alterations to machinery and working environment, and can be used to cover extra costs arising from help a fellow worker gives to a disabled person at work.

The Ministry of Labour and its local labour administration provide grants for workplace adaptations and equipment, and compensation to employers for up to two years if the disabled employee needs the help of another employee. In 1993 various supportive measures for job placement were paid in 3,800 cases.

COMMENTARY

The approach in Finland to disabled people and the labour market differs from many countries, including the UK, in a number of respects. First, for nearly 25 years there has been recognition within the social security system of the potential for disabled people to have a reduced capacity for working. Secondly, Finland has had a tradition of implementing active labour market policies that aim to get people into work and help them sustain employment, in comparison with more passive policy approaches which provide income replacement benefits and rely more on individual disabled people to (re)establish themselves in the workforce.

Thirdly, there are incentives built into social security for people to undertake rehabilitation into the workforce, based on increases to existing benefits, rather than on the introduction of a new benefit. Hence, there is no risk in participating in rehabilitation programmes, in terms of losing entitlement to existing benefits.

Although the social security system has features which can facilitate entry into the labour market by disabled people, those who have no employment history are particularly disadvantaged since they are not eligible for a partial employment disability pension (which is insurance based) and therefore are unable to combine part-time work and benefits.

Subsidised employment is increasingly the likely destination for unemployed disabled people helped into work by employment services, both as a route to competitive employment and as an end in itself. However, wage subsidised employment has been a predominantly public sector measure and enhancing take-up by private sector employers may involve further avoidance of normal employment contracts between employers and wage-subsidised workers.

Despite policies to help disadvantaged groups get work and official commitments to maintain people in work, the harsh effects of the 1990s economic recession have made it more difficult for people with a partial capacity to work to find employment. For many people, partial capacity means not being able to work full-time, but the dominant form of work in Finland has traditionally been full-time working (including for women). There have for many years been relatively few part-time opportunities for partially incapacitated people, although one effect of recession has been a recent increase in the proportion of the workforce in part-time jobs. As a result the partial employment disability pension has not been popular. Similarly, it is not common to combine an individual early retirement pension with work.

There is no doubt, though, that one of the principal driving forces behind much recent social welfare reform in Finland, including social security, has been to reduce government expenditure. Government policy has been geared towards getting people into some form of activity (work, training, or rehabilitation) and away from benefits. The tradition in Finland of retiring from the workforce relatively early is being challenged, and policies (such as changing the basis on which early retirement pensions are awarded) are designed to make retirement less attractive.

Nevertheless, Government departments, the Social Insurance Institution and the employment pensions institutes have made efforts to change the dominant full-time model of working and to encourage more flexible working practices. The changes in legislation, encouragement of early rehabilitation, work sharing, and other measures in workplaces are together beginning to change the attitudes and thinking of many employers, although there is evidence that people who have a reduced capacity for work, or who have had a reduced capacity in the past (even if they are fully able to work subsequently) still find it harder than other people to find work.

The future of social security benefits for disabled people in Finland is uncertain, although the report of the Ministry of Social Affairs working group is likely to be influential.

REFERENCES

Central Pension Security Institute (1996) *Statistical Yearbook of the Employment Pensions Schemes, Part I*, Helsinki: Central Pension Security Institute.

Eardley, T., Bradshaw, J., Ditch, J., Gough, 1. and Whiteford, P. (1996) *Social Assistance OECD Countries: Country Reports*, DSS Research Report No. 47, London: HMSO.

European Commission (1996a) *Employment in Europe 1996*, Luxembourg: Office for Official Publications of the European Communities.

European Commission (1996b) *The 1995 Multiannual Programmes for Employment of the EU Member States*, V/436/96, Brussels: DGV.

Labour Market Institute for Economic Research/ECOTEC (1997) *Labour Market Studies: Finland*, Luxembourg: Office for Official Publications of the European Communities.

Glendinning, C. and McLaughlin, E. (1993) *Paying for Care: Lessons from Europe*, Social Security Advisory Committee, Research Paper 5, London: HMSO.

Haapasalo, S., Levo, H. and Ravaja, N. (1994) *Employment after vocational education: Educational and working careers of students graduated from vocational institutions of the Association for the Disabled*, Research Reports 43, Helsinki: Rehabilitation Foundation.

Mannila, S. (1995) 'Subsidized employment for Finnish disabled jobseekers?', in Bengtsson, S. *(ed) Employment of persons with Disabilities: Colloquium in connection with a research project*, Copenhagen: Social Forsknings Instituttet.

Mannila, S., Tynkkynen, A. and Eronen, M. (1992) *Disabled Jobseekers and the Services of the Employment Authorities*, Research Reports 33/1992, Helsinki: Rehabilitation Foundation.

Marullo, S. (ed) (1995) *Comparison of regulations on Part-time and Temporary Employment in Europe: A briefing paper*, Research Series No. 52, London: Employment Department.

Ministry of Labour (1995) *Operational Programme for the Community Initiative Employment in Finland 1995-1999*.

MISEP (1996) *Basic Information Report Finland Institutions, procedures and measures*, Employment Observatory, Brussels: European Commission.

Social Insurance Institution (1996) *Overview of Benefit Programmes*, Reprint from the Statistical Yearbook of the Social Insurance Institution, Finland, Helsinki: Social Insurance Institution.

Statistics Finland (1995) *Supplementary Labour Force Survey, Autumn 1993*, Helsinki: Statistics Finland.

CHAPTER FOUR

FRANCE[1]

OVERVIEW

In France, the prime policy concern is long-term unemployment and disabled people are a target group for a number of active labour policy measures. For the past ten years economic integration of disabled people has been viewed as the responsibility of the economic actors, rather than, as previously, a social responsibility founded on principles of compensation. There is now an extensive programme of grants and subsidies to employers for recruitment and retention of disabled workers.

Expenditure on disability benefits is not a policy concern. Nor is benefit dependency an issue. The level of the invalidity pension is low and numbers have remained static at around 430,000 for over a decade. The pension is a continuation of sickness benefit, administered within the health care system. It is suggested that the inadequacy of the pension by itself may serve as an incentive to seek paid work. It is only in the last ten years that invalidity pensioners have become eligible for employment support services and the number in employment is low.

The notion of individual incentives to enter or return to work is novel in France. Traditionally, incentives have been directed at employers, as wage subsidies or relief of national insurance contributions. The only direct financial incentive to disabled workers, other than help with extra costs of work, is a lump-sum integration bonus; a similar bonus is also paid to the employer.

Financial incentives are administered by different bodies, depending on the category and employment circumstances of the recipient. A new Fund was established to redistribute the voluntary levies paid by employers as a way of fulfilling their employment obligation under the new law of 1987 in favour of the employment of disabled people. That Fund appears more flexible and imaginative in use of resources than State institutions.

The employment needs of people with partial capacity for work are beginning to be recognised with some growth in part-time appointments and increasingly available help in the workplace. However, the financial help specifically directed at sustaining the income of people with reduced working capacity is little used in open employment.

THE LABOUR MARKET AND DISABLED PEOPLE

Labour market characteristics and trends

The population of working age is 37 million. The rate of labour market participation has remained constant in the last decade at around 68 per cent, with the participation rate for women showing a slight increase. The previously low level of part-time work has risen steadily from around 11 per cent in 1985 to close on the EU average of 16 per cent in 1995 (European Commission, 1996a).

In the first half of the 1990s there has been a significant fall in the demand for labour. (Between 1991 and the end of 1993, almost one in 20 non-agricultural jobs disappeared.) The unemployment rate fell in 1996 for the first time in the 1990s (to 11.5 per cent) but the share

---

[1] Dominique Velche, Centre National d'Etude de la Recherche sur les Handicaps et les Inaptations (CTNERHI) was national informant for France.

of long-term unemployment rose to 40 per cent in that year. Young people, women and disabled people have been particularly hit by long-term unemployment.

Table F.1
Key labour market indicators in France, 1995

	Men	*Women*	*Total*
Employment rate (% age 15-64)	68.5	52.9	60.6
Self-employed (as % employed)	15.3	6.9	11.6
Part-time (% total employed)	5.1	28.9	15.6
Activity rate (% age 15-64)	75.6	61.2	68.3
Unemployment rate (% labour force)	9.5	13.8	11.5
Long-term unemployment (% unemployed)	39.2	41.1	40.2

Source: European Commission (1996a) *Employment in Europe 1996*

Labour market policy

Labour market strategies are directed at reducing unemployment. Key elements are training initiatives to bridge the skill-gap, measures to increase flexible working, notably part-time employment, and reduction of the indirect costs of labour (European Commission, 1996b).

Since the early 1980s there have been several policy measures to promote part-time working, mainly to reduce unemployment and to encourage more flexible use of working time and work organisation by employers, but also to allow individuals more choice in their use of time (Glendinning and McLaughlin, 1993). Legislation in 1982 which allowed civil servants rights to opt for part-time work was followed in 1991 by laws which gave the right to employees in all sectors. Part-time workers now enjoy the same employment rights as full-time workers.

Part-time working has not grown as much as was hoped and recently financial incentives have been introduced, including an experiment to encourage employers to decrease the hours of work and simultaneously increase the number of staff (European Commission, 1996b).

Financial incentives to employers to recruit and retain disadvantaged groups are central to active labour market policies in France. A relaunched programme of wage subsidies and reductions of employers' social security contributions is targeted at the recruitment of those who have been unemployed or received social assistance for two years. These *Contrats Initiative Emploi* (CIE) aimed to place a total of 350,000 in employment in 1996.

The employment service (ANPE) plays a central part in strategies to bring down unemployment, as in France over 90 per cent of the unemployed use the public employment service as the main means of job search (European Commission, 1996a). In 1992, ANPE launched a special placement initiative for the long-term unemployed.

Disabled people and the labour market

An estimated 1.2 to 1.5 million disabled people are capable of working. Over 100,000 are in sheltered work and between 500,000 and 700,000 in open employment. Of the 200,000 to 400,000 disabled people who are fit for work but unemployed, 70,000 are registered with ANPE (European Commission, 1995).

Disabled people have been hit by the falling demand for labour and high unemployment. The increase in the number of disabled people among the unemployed has been greater than that for job seekers as a whole. The average period of unemployment is very long (587 days) and is closely related to severity of disability. Half of the disabled but only one third of all job seekers have a low level of qualification. Unemployed disabled people are older than average. (European Commission, 1995).

Disabled people are a priority group for labour market measures, including agreements on gradual early retirement and recruitment incentives.

Disabled people in employment

Recent information about employed disabled people is available only for those in private sector establishments with over 20 staff subject to the law of 1987 in favour of disabled people (see below). Detailed information is presented in a report on the application of the law of 1987 in 1994 and 1995 (Ministry of Labour and Social Affairs, 1996). In 1994, 248,000 disabled people were employed. Half worked in the industrial sector and two-fifths in the service sector. Over 70 per cent were aged over 40 and three-quarters of the total were men.

It is not possible to summarise the types or extent of disability because of the different ways of categorising disabled employees in the French system. In 1994, 46 per cent were people who had suffered work-related injury or disease and 30 per cent of the total were classified as moderately or severely disabled.

Over half of the new recruits counted under the quota scheme work part-time, although overall 86 per cent of the beneficiaries work full-time. It is suggested that the rise reflects the number of more severely disabled people taken on, as well as the general trend towards part-time work (Ministry of Labour and Social Affairs, 1996).

EMPLOYMENT POLICIES FOR DISABLED PEOPLE

There are three main elements in policy to promote open employment of disabled people:

- a legal obligation on employers of over 20 staff to contribute to raising the representation of disabled people in the workforce to meet an overall target of six per cent

- an extensive programme of financial aid to employers, and latterly to disabled workers, boosted in recent years by the funds gathered as levies

- specialist agencies at département level which assess the social and employment needs of disabled people and arrange placements.

Overview of disability employment policies

Measures to favour the employment of certain groups of disabled people stem from just after World War I with legislation giving war-disabled people a right to retraining and to employment under a quota scheme. Rights were extended in 1930 and 1945 to people disabled by occupational accident and disease. The first financial incentives to employers appeared in 1949. An act of 1957 consolidated the quota system, covering both public and private sectors, and some reserved employment. It also provided for sheltered employment. It introduced a committee, at département level, which classified disabled workers.

A comprehensive act of 1975 authorised the *Commission Technique d'Orientation et de Reclassement Professionel* (COTOREP) to recognise disability, grant allowances and provide vocational guidance. Other new provisions included a right to a minimum wage in open and in sheltered employment. The 1975 act views integration of disabled people as a national obligation. It covers education, social security, access to buildings and employment matters.

More recent policy changes include a law in 1991 to improve access to public establishments and workplaces and in 1990 an amendment to the penal code to outlaw discrimination on grounds of state of health or disability.

The law of 1987 in favour of the employment of disabled workers marked a shift in policy based on obligations to victims of disability and stressed the responsibility of the economic actors for the integration of disabled workers. The law introduced four new features. It imposed an obligation on public and private sector employers of at least 20 eligible staff to employ people defined as disabled by the law in order to meet an overall target of six per cent. Secondly, beneficiaries[2] were extended to include people entitled to an invalidity pension under compulsory social security schemes. The third novel feature was a mechanism to encourage employers' and employees' organisations to formulate joint plans and agreements (*accords*) for the integration of disabled workers into the workforce; such action, if approved by the state, counts as meeting the employment obligation.

Finally, the law of 1987 established a Fund to dispense voluntary contributions from employers. The policy intention is to allow those employers unable for economic reasons to promote the employment of disabled workers to discharge their obligations financially. The Fund then redistributes the money to enterprises, of all sizes, for the recruitment and retention of disabled workers. Funds also may be used for research, promoting attitudinal change, training, removal of architectural barriers and for support for the disabled person at the workplace. A range of organisations and disabled people themselves may apply. The Fund has become an important means of promoting recruitment and retention of disabled workers and AGEFIPH, (*Fonds pour l'insertion professionelle des personnes handicapées*), the quasi-governmental body which administers it, has since taken over the administration of some grants and subsidies previously administered by the State.

Incentives to employers are the main financial instruments for promoting employment of disabled people in France. Disabled people are one of the priority groups in the system of 'employment incentive contacts' which relieve employers of the obligation to pay their national insurance contributions and provide monthly grants. Disabled people are also a priority group in arrangements for subsidised temporary work of benefit to the community.

A number of bodies are involved in policy and service delivery. The Employment Delegation, within the Ministry of Labour and Social Affairs advises on policy and manages the employment agency (ANPE) which has specialist services for the placement of disabled people. At département level COTOREP directs workers it recognises as disabled towards guidance, training and placement in open and sheltered employment. Working in collaboration with ANPE and COTOREP are around one hundred specialist 'preparation and follow-up teams' (EPSR: *Equipes de Préparation et de Suite du Reclassement*) for the guidance of disabled people seeking (re)employment.

---

2 The main beneficiaries (private and semi-public sectors) are: workers recognised as disabled by COTOREP; those with an occupational injury or disease leading to incapacity of at least ten per cent; invalidity pensioners; and war disabled pensioners.

Most recent policy emphasis has been placed on service delivery at département level. It is at this level that the various bodies concerned with employment of disabled people connect. COTOREP has been reformed and the EPSR strengthened. Plans to co-ordinate local initiatives have been in place since 1992 and a pilot programme has shown encouraging results in terms of the number of disabled people placed in employment. An agreement between AGEFIPH and the EPRS, signed in 1994, has facilitated placement.

A number of established national disabled persons' associations play a significant role, through placement agreements with ANPE and by providing support services. Training is provided through the apprenticeship system, mainstream training centres, or a range of public and private centres for vocational rehabilitation.

In addition, there is an expanding sheltered employment sector. Sheltered workshops are intended for people whose work capacity is at least one-third of normal. In 1995 there were 14,000 employees. They are commercial production units. The *centres d'aide par le travail* (CAT) cater for people whose working capacity is less than one-third and whose condition does not permit a normal working life. Around three-quarters of the 80,000 users of CAT have learning disabilities and a further fifth have other mental disorders. The CAT are heavily subsidised. Although they work like companies, they are social service institutions and the users are not legally workers.

SOCIAL SECURITY POLICIES FOR DISABLED PEOPLE

In France, income maintenance for people whose capacity for work is limited through disability is provided through compensation for occupational injury and disease and for war disability, insurance-based invalidity pensions and social assistance allowances. Essentially, all these schemes are based on compensatory principles.

Public expenditure on disability benefits is not a prominent policy concern. The level of the invalidity pension is relatively low and the number of beneficiaries has remained constant for over a decade. However, there have been plans to control the escalating costs of the health care Fund, which also covers sickness and disability benefits, through social reforms. The Fund has suffered from a deficit in insurance contributions, because of unemployment, alongside an increasing demand for health care.

Disability benefits and allowances

Legislation dating from 1898 covers victims of work accidents. It provides for compensation for the disability suffered, compensation for the occupational implications of the accident (based on an occupational scale), and damages linked to the degree of occupational risk. The award of a permanent pension varies in proportion to the degree of disability.

Compensation for physical injury caused by war, to both civilians and members of the armed forces, has been covered since 1919 by several enactments. The right to a pension and the degree of disability are assessed on the basis of a scale, codified in 1951.

Disability insurance (dating from 1930 and 1945) provides earnings-related invalidity pensions to persons insured under the social insurance system who have been unfit for work for more than three years. A person who suffers a two-third reduction in working or earning capacity is deemed to be disabled. The degree of disability is not based on a quantitative scale, but on the insured person's residual working capacity, general state, age, physical and mental faculties, and suitability for occupational training.

The Disability Act of 1975 introduced means-tested benefits for those not covered under other legislation, replacing various allowances paid as social assistance or by the family allowance offices:

● A minimum social allowance payable to adult disabled people (AAH) is subject to a certified minimum disability level of 80 per cent, or inability to obtain employment as a result of disability

● A Compensation Allowance both provides a seriously disabled person with assistance from another person and compensates for specific extra costs incurred in connection with work. Payment is dependent on an 80 per cent incapacity for work.

Responsible bodies

The French system of social security and social assistance benefits can be divided broadly into three institutional 'structures': the *Régime Général* comprising insurance Funds (*caisses*) for old age, health and family support; a second structure covering unemployment insurance; and a third covering state-funded social assistance for elderly and disabled people as well as for others not covered elsewhere (Bolderson and Mabbett, 1997). The Fund for health care, sickness and invalidity benefits (CNAM) is the largest in the *Régime Général*. It encompasses health insurance and is mainly involved in financing provision of health services.

Different bodies are involved in delivering invalidity pensions, AAH and the compensation allowance although there is some overlap at département level (see Bolderson and Mabbett, 1997). It should be noted that COTOREP is not involved in the process of delivering the invalidity pension.

Definitions of partial capacity

There is no distinct concept of partial capacity in the French system. Rather, there are degrees of incapacity. Different definitions are used for different benefits. For occupational disability benefits, disability is assessed on a scale from one to 100 per cent. The main test for sickness benefit and invalidity pension is inability to earn two-thirds of the previous wage. For means-tested social assistance benefits, the person must be assessed by COTOREP as 80 per cent disabled.

Assessment by COTOREP is the gateway to many social services and concessions as well as to training and opportunities in sheltered and open employment. Committees have two sections with different assessment procedures. The second section, which assess eligibility for the means-tested benefits referred to above, applies a general incapacity rate (such as 80 per cent) based on a functional limitation scale (*barème*), according to assessments by a doctor and psychologist. Although the scale is now based on a test of functional limitations, the claimant is still asked to declare the diagnosis (Bolderson and Mabbett, 1997).

The first section of the Committee attributes the status of 'disabled worker'. Disabled workers recognised by COTOREP are the main beneficiaries of the law of 1987 in favour of disabled workers. COTOREP classifies disabled workers into three groups (A, B and C) according to the severity of disability.

In France the concept of supplementing low incomes is unusual as workers are guaranteed a minimum wage. Normally, workers are hired at a wage level which is equal to the 'convention' level; a nationally negotiated level for every employee in a given economic sector and fixed in a collective agreement. Disabled workers are a special case, as employers may reduce their wages in line with their productivity. Accordingly, the State provides a supplement (*garantie de ressources*), paid to the employer, to bring the wage packet up to the minimum wage level.

There are no significant arrangements specifically for combining disability benefits with income from work. The insurance-based partial invalidity pension is awarded to disabled people transferring from sickness benefit after three years who are judged capable of some work. The system does not explicitly promote their return to work, however. Rather, the very low level of the pension means that they are forced to find paid work in order to achieve an adequate income.

The only other possible arrangement is to combine a very low wage, due to part-time or discontinuous work, with part of the AAH but an evaluation found very few instances (Roussel and Velche, 1995).

Recently, a system of lump-sum integration bonuses has been introduced, directed at both the disabled person seeking employment and the employer. This integration bonus appears to be the only significant direct financial incentive to disabled people.

As in other countries, there are various grants to disabled employees and trainees towards work-related extra costs. Grants towards setting up in self-employment are also available to disabled people.

Income guarantee for disabled workers

Every disabled worker (recognised by COTOREP) is guaranteed a minimum wage by the state (*garantie de ressources*), financed from tax revenues. This provision was introduced in 1975 to counter the effects of long-standing regulations which allow employers to reduce the wages of disabled employees in line with their working capacities. The legitimacy of wage reductions for disabled people seems to be generally accepted. Recent comparable proposals for young people with no employment experience were rejected, however.

The provision is used primarily for people in sheltered work. In 1995, only 7,000 people in open employment benefited, compared with 96,700 in CAT and sheltered workshops. In open employment it is intended to encourage employers to consider taking on disabled workers without also taking on any of the costs of reduced productivity. It is generally used in situations where the disabled person needs support in the workplace, such as help from co-workers or communication or mobility aids. The provision is not available in the public sector.

This earnings supplement to guarantee a minimum wage was until recently administered and paid only by the départemental office of the Ministry of Employment, responsible to the Prefect. In 1997, responsibility for disabled people working in open employment was transferred to AGEFIPH. The transfer has been criticised by some associations of disabled people as a mark of the withdrawal of state responsibility.

The employer pays the supplementary wage and related social security contributions and is reimbursed by the State on presentation of proof of payment. Demand typically is led by the employer, encouraged by local employment support teams. Some disabled workers are reluctant to comply, as doing so questions their social value (Velche, personal communication). Agreement between the employer and the disabled job-seeker may be facilitated by local employment support teams.

The decision to grant the supplement is discretionary, based on advice from COTOREP. The COTOREP committee examines the worker's level of disability in relation to the job held. The level of productivity is assumed to correlate with the assessed degree of disability.

The wage reduction (*abattement de salaire*) can be either a maximum of ten per cent of the normal wage when the worker is classified as moderately disabled or a maximum of 20 per cent when severely disabled. When the severity of the disability or health condition prevents full-time work, or work at a normal rhythm, the reduction can be up to a maximum of 50 per cent. In this case, beneficiaries normally work part-time. No supplement can be awarded if the worker's wage exceeds 130 per cent of the minimum wage. The way in which the wage compensation is calculated means that some workers end up with a lower wage than their non-disabled colleagues.

The supplement may be discontinued only if the worker's productivity increases. There is no information on unmet demand. The length of time taken by COTOREP to reach a decision may be an obstacle.

Combining invalidity pension with earnings from employment

Invalidity pensions (*pensions d'invalidité*) are part of the social security system and are mainly financed by employers' and employees' contributions but have been supplemented by a new tax-based source of revenue since 1990. Their administration is organised by the National Health Insurance Office of Salaried Workers which allocates resources to the local Social Security Boards (CPAM) which manage the pension fund. The pensions are paid by the CPAM (except for agricultural workers).

Invalidity pensions were introduced in 1945 when the social security system was established. (An earlier time-limited invalidity insurance system, established in 1930, applied only to trade and industry workers.) The main insurance schemes, the general and agricultural schemes, cover insured persons aged under 60 whose ability to work or earn is reduced by at least two thirds. In 1989, beneficiaries of these two schemes stood at 418,000 and 31,000 (Grammenos, 1995). Other schemes for state manual workers and local government employees require permanent unfitness for service; beneficiaries totalled 75,000 in 1989 (Grammenos, 1995). The account that follows refers to the general scheme only.

Invalidity pensions in the general scheme fall into two groups. 'First category' pensions compensate for loss of earnings of people presumed able to work but unable to earn more than a third of their previous wage. 'Second and third category' pensions provide income replacement for disabled people deemed totally unable to work. (Individuals in the third category are distinguished as those needing the assistance of a third person to carry out normal life functions.) Just under three in ten invalidity pensioners fall into the first category. The number of recipients of invalidity pensions of all categories has remained stable since 1980 at around 430,000 (432,000 in 1993). Numbers of pensioners of the first category have also remained static, standing at 124,000 in 1993.

Entitlement to first category pensions is restricted to people aged between 18 and 60 who are disabled as a consequence of accident or disease, excluding work-related accidents and diseases which are covered by a separate scheme. Progressive illnesses are covered by the sickness insurance scheme. The largest groups among pensioners of all categories in 1993 were people with mental illness (26 per cent), people with circulatory diseases (20 per cent) and those with osteo-muscular impairments (17 per cent).

Usually, first category benefits are awarded on transfer from the sickness insurance scheme after three years of illness. Transfer is managed by the authorities and beneficiaries do not themselves file applications. The CPAM's medical control practitioners decide when the worker is unable to recover the previous level of earnings. Eligibility decisions are based not only on remaining work capacity but also on age, physical and mental faculties, and vocational training level. A first category pensioner is regarded merely as *able* to work and there is no assumption that the person *ought* to work. Rather, the medical control practitioner may interpret failure to return to work as evidence that the individual is unable to work because of disability, and so decide that a second category classification would be more appropriate.

The process of transfer from sickness to invalidity pension is supported by a social worker. On transfer the person is given a social work service and a range of benefits in kind (Bolderson and Mabbett, 1997). The invalidity benefit thus may be seen as a kind of protracted sick-pay. There is no direct help for return to employment in this process. Entitlement is reviewed if health conditions, and thus the possibility of taking up work, are assessed by the control practitioner as having changed.

Eligibility for first category pensions depends on having worked in the previous 12 years and on having made social security contributions for at least 800 hours work in the previous four months (and 200 hours in the first three months).[3]

If earnings are insufficient, a minimum pension is awarded, affecting between a fifth and a quarter of invalidity pensioners (of all categories) in 1992 (Roussel and Velche, 1995). The level of the first category pension is set at 30 per cent of the average wage in the last ten years. The amount of the average first category pension, therefore, is low: in 1985, it was 28 per cent of the minimum wage (Montès, 1987).

The low level at which first category pensions are set suggests that they are intended to encourage return to work but this aim is not explicitly stated. It is not possible to tell if pensioners are encouraged to work by the provision. It may be deduced that after three years' sickness benefit, with no active intervention from vocational rehabilitation services, first category pensioners are ill-prepared for return to employment. However, the very low level of the pension leaves them little choice, as income from work is also necessary to sustain an adequate standard of living.

Invalidity pensioners in employment

Until the law of 1987, invalidity pensioners were not included among the disabled groups covered by special employment legislation and no action was taken to help them find jobs. Invalidity pensioners now count towards the attainment of the quota in establishments with over 20 staff. The data suggest that the law has had some effect on the employment position of first category pensioners. Numbers in firms subject to the employment obligation have grown from 15,000 in 1988 to 25,000 in 1994. Their proportion among total beneficiaries of the law increased from under seven per cent to ten per cent. No data are available about

---

[3] The award is calculated on 30 per cent of earnings during the previous 12 months, within the earnings limit. If the previous wage exceeds the social security ceiling (13,720 FF per month at end February 1997) this ceiling becomes the basis for calculation.

employment of disabled people in smaller establishments. Thus around one-fifth of the 124,000 recipients of partial pension are recorded as working in establishments with over 20 employees.

According to the most recent report on the execution of the law (Ministry of Labour and Social Affairs, 1996) half of the invalidity pensioners counted towards the quota, but only a quarter of the total are women. Not surprisingly, given the qualifying conditions for the pension, 85 per cent are over 40 compared with around 60 per cent of the total.

There is no information about their hours of work although it suggested that most first category pensioners are unable to work full-time because of their physical disabilities (Velche, personal communication).

In conclusion, it seems that the low level of the benefit forces invalidity pensioners to seek work and that their employment may be encouraged by the 1987 law in favour of employment of disabled people. It is possible that the other financial incentives to employers, such as the lump-sum integration grant, facilitate their employment but no information is available to verify this suggestion. The role of local employment support teams in helping them into work appears slight; in a sample of 1,200 people on the files of 15 EPSR only two per cent were invalidity pensioners (Velche et al., 1993). The sickness-oriented system for transferring to invalidity benefits may militate against the intervention of employment services.

Lump-sum integration grants

The only direct financial incentive to disabled people is a lump-sum integration grant (prime à l'embauche) paid to disabled people on taking up work. It offers help to enter and retain employment and is generally thought to encourage a positive attitude to looking for a job.

This measure was introduced as part of the programme run by the quasi-governmental agency AGEFIPH which became operational in 1989. The management board of AGEFIPH has discretion to propose measures to disburse the funds it gathers from employers who choose to meet their employment obligation under the law of 1987 by paying a levy. The grant is administered by AGEPIPH's regional offices, under the control of its national office.

Disabled people covered by the law of 1987 may benefit. Thus, degree of disability and work capacity are not relevant, and there are no restrictions related to earnings. To benefit, they must work at least 16 hours per week. A lump-sum recruitment grant is awarded simultaneously to the employer, in the private sector only. Thus, the measure is equally an incentive to employers.

The grants have proved exceptionally popular. In 1995, they supported the recruitment of over 33,000 disabled workers and over the first six years 156,000 were supported by the grant (AGEFIPH, 1996). Popularity may be related to the very high level of the grant since 1994: 40,000 FF to the employer for the first disabled worker hired; and 30,000 FF to the employee. In October 1995 a new system was introduced. By this point, the integration grants represented over 80 per cent of AGEFIPH's allocations and 63 per cent of the budget (AGEPIPH, 1996). The amounts were reduced to 15,000 FF for the employer and 10,000 FF for the employee. However, public assistance from CIE (see below) supplements more than 70 per cent of cases.

Applications are examined by AGIFIPH's technical services. Awards are discretionary and often given automatically. The only reasons for refusal are almost certainly incomplete applications and early dismissals or resignations.

Currently the grant is for permanent job contracts or for contracts of at least 12 months. Most grants are given for full-time permanent jobs. The grant is paid in two instalments to promote retention, with the second paid after 12 months if the contract is maintained. According to AGEFIPH, 70 per cent of new recruits were still in employment after 12 months and 55 per cent in the same job after four years.

There is no published information about the characteristics of disabled recipients of integration grants. Half of all the disabled people helped by AGEFIPH in 1995 had motor impairments, over a fifth had chronic illnesses and one-sixth sensory impairments. Only eight per cent had learning difficulties and two per cent were mentally ill.

The grant has particularly benefited smaller establishments of under 20 employees. Two-thirds of lump-sum grants were awarded for recruitment in small firms, relating to 65,000 disabled people in a three year period.

Evaluation of the lump-sum grant's incentive effects appears to have concentrated on employers. According to AGEFIPH, one in four employers would not have hired the disabled person without this incentive. However, critics suggest that the grant does not affect the employer's hiring decision as it is offered and accepted automatically. Employers are reported to have little interest in the grant per se, as it is difficult to plan its use in the enterprise (Velche, 1997). Interest on the part of employers appears to be declining since the level of the grant was greatly reduced.

There is no available information on the incentive effect on disabled workers. However, the level of take-up suggests that the lump-sum integration grant is effective in promoting both access to work and job retention. The employment support services appear to be instrumental in encouraging its use. They tend to stress the value of the grant to potential employers when seeking to place disabled people with them; once the employer's interest has been caught the 'package' is then proposed to the disabled job seeker. While the grant has had a substantial short-term effect, there is some uncertainty over its appeal in the longer-term if the reduced rate remains.

GRANTS FOR EXTRA COSTS OF WORK

There are two main systems for helping disabled people with the extra costs of work. One operates through the social assistance scheme and the second through AGEFIPH. Both offer grants for specific costs rather than allowances to be spent as the disabled person wishes.

Compensatory allowances for work-related costs

Disabled people in work may benefit from a compensatory allowance for work-related costs which arise from their specific disability (*allocation compensatrice pour frais professionnels*). This social assistance allowance was introduced in 1975. It is presumed to act as an incentive to take up employment. It appears to be little used.

The allowance is administered by the social assistance services at département level and payment is made from the département social assistance funds. The recipient must be recognised by COTOREP as a severely disabled person, between the ages of 16 and 60, with 80 per cent incapacity. Eligibility is conditional on earnings limits.

The award relates to the real costs incurred, subject to a ceiling limit of 4,424 FF per month (January 1996). The claimant must produce invoices which are scrutinised by the social assistance services. The decision is discretionary, depending on confirmation by COTOREP that the claimant's working activity leads to extra costs specifically related to the disability and its consequences. When first introduced, the allowance was awarded for up to two years but could be withdrawn if COTOREP decided there was no continuing justification of extra costs. However, following decentralisation of administration, COTOREP may periodically review the award only when it is given for a limited duration or when the recipient or the Préfect asks for a review.

There are no data on numbers claiming, refused or using the allowance, or on their characteristics, as the statistics do not distinguish between this allowance and the allowance for care attendance. The latter is mainly used by people not in work, most of whom are of retirement age. Between 1984 and 1993, total recipients increased by over 70 per cent to 261,000. However, in the same period recipients aged 60 and over rose by over 100 per cent to 180,000, demonstrating the increased use of the allowance for care attendance by retired people (Padieu and Sanchez, 1994). It is assumed that only a minority of the total 81,000 recipients of working age benefit from the compensatory allowance for extra costs of work.

Levels of use are assumed to be low because of the very restrictive conditions. There is no evidence that the allowance is effective as an incentive to take up work.

Grants for aids and access to work

Financial assistance available from AGEFIPH is mainly for job seekers, students, trainees and apprentices. It includes help to buy special equipment such as voice synthesizers, video-enlargers and braille recognition and tactile devices. The costs of temporary helpers such as interpreters and secretaries are also covered. AGEFIPH can also partly fund the costs of housing, car purchase or adaptation and transport to work. Such help is designed to complement the compensatory allowance. In 1995, 5,600 disabled people received help under the AGEFIPH programme.

SUBSIDIES TO EMPLOYERS

Since 1982 there has been an extensive system of state subsidies to employers to promote recruitment of disadvantaged groups. A large number of 'work contracts' have been created, including disabled people among the target groups. This type of provision is widely used to encourage recruitment of people who have difficulties in finding employment, with or without disabilities. Among them, the CIE (*contrat initiative-emploi*) introduced in 1995 is the most recent, replacing many of the previous contracts targeted at long-term unemployed job seekers. In addition, there is a extensive use of subsidised temporary community work in the public and voluntary sectors (CES).

CIE *(contrat initiative-emploi)*

This contract exempts private sector employers from paying national insurance contributions for 12 or 24 months and awards a lump-sum grant of 2,000 FF per month for the same period. Under the CRE system (*contrats de retour à l'emploi*) which CIE replaced, ten per cent of contracts were awarded to disabled people in 1994 (19,500 contracts). In 1995, 12,000 disabled people benefited from CIE and 13,000 from CRE.

The département offices of the Ministry of Employment administer the contracts. They ensure that the disabled employee meets the criteria. Disabled beneficiaries must be recognised by COTOREP or covered by the law of 1987. Degree of disability and level of earnings are not relevant. To benefit the disabled person must have been unemployed. The job must be at least 16 hours per week. Most recipients will earn the equivalent of the minimum wage.

The grant is paid in instalments: on recruitment; after three months; after 12 months; and after 24 months (or at the end of the contract if it is shorter). In the event of breakdown of the employment relationship, the employer is obliged to repay the grants and the national insurance reductions. The system is too recent to report on its effects on job retention.

CIE is popular with employers taking on disabled people because it can be used in conjunction with the lump-sum integration grant provided by AGEFIPH. Employers say that it is easier to plan a reduction of national insurance costs than it is to use a lump-sum grant (Velche, 1997).

CES *(contrat emploi-solidarité)*

The CES ('community-work contract') is conceived of as a temporary integration measure to help priority groups among the unemployed to find employment through a short-term, part-time job (MISEP, 1996). Contracts are given for work which is useful to the community, in the public and non-profit-making sectors only. Disabled people were included as a priority group in 1991.

Contracts are for part-time work for no more than 20 hours per week. The normal duration is three to 12 months but extension to 24 months is possible for people in particularly difficult situations and is generally accepted if disabled people need more time to adjust to working life. The employee receives the minimum wage. The employer subsidy is between 65 and 100 per cent of wage costs, depending on the category of worker. The employer is also relieved of payment of employers' social security contributions for the duration of the contract.

Comparatively large numbers of disabled people are supported in this form of temporary, part-time public service employment. The number of contracts grew from 9,400 in 1992 to 43,700 in 1995. Six per cent of recipients of CES are disabled people. We have no information on the destination of disabled people whose contracts expire.

COMMENTARY

Policy to promote recruitment and retention of disabled people in France is based principally on incentives to employers, both through programmes to reduce general long-term unemployment and through help in cash or kind provided by the levy redistribution fund specifically for disabled people. While help in kind is available to disabled people taking up employment, the idea that financial incentives might encourage them to seek work is very new. Indeed, the only example of such an incentive is the lump-sum integration grant provided by the levy redistribution fund. However, it is not easy to tell whether the lump-sum works as an incentive to disabled people, given that a parallel grant is simultaneously available to the employer.

The compensation-based benefit system is not designed to promote return to work, although it is suggested that the low level of the 'first category' invalidity pension forces recipients to seek an income from employment. It was only in 1987 that invalidity pensioners joined war invalids and people recognised by COTOREP as beneficiaries of compulsory employment legislation. Their exclusion may be attributed in part to the sickness-based system of invalidity pensions.

There is little explicit recognition of the employment needs of disabled people who are able to do some work but unable to work full-time. Most financial incentives are given for full-time jobs. Nor is there much recognition of the needs of disabled people with fluctuating conditions which limit their ability to work regular hours. The current labour market policy emphasis on encouraging flexible work may ultimately favour disabled people, however.

Until recently the traditional emphasis on incentives and on obligations to employ disabled people has not been complemented by measures to overcome the barriers which disabled people face in employment. However, AGEFIPH (the body which plans and administers the redistribution of the voluntary levies) has taken steps in this direction with programmes to sensitise employers to disabled people's needs and practical help to readjust work and workplace. Although State programmes exist, they are little used. The less restrictive eligibility criteria and application procedures seem to encourage take-up of AGEFIPH provision.

REFERENCES

AGEFIPH (1996) *Rapport d'activité 1995*, Bagneux: AGEFIPH.

Bolderson, H., Mabbett, D. and others (1997) *Delivering Social Security: A cross-national study*, Department of Social Security Research Report No 57, London: The Stationery Office.

European Commission (1995) EMPLOYMENT *Community Initiative: Summaries of the Member States Operational Programmes*, DGV, Brussels: European Commission.

European Commission (1996a) *Employment in Europe 1996*, COM(96)485, Luxembourg: Office for Official Publications of the European Communities.

European Commission (1996b) *The 1995 Multiannual Programmes for Employment of the EU Member States*, V/436/96, DGV: Brussels.

Glendinning, C. and McLaughlin, E. (1993) *Paying for Care: Lessons from Europe*, Social Security Advisory Committee Research Paper 5, London: HMSO.

Grammenos, S. (1995) *Disabled Persons Statistical Data, Second Edition*, Luxembourg: Office for Official Publications of the European Communities.

Ministry of Labour and Social Affairs (1996) *L'Emploi des Travailleurs Handicapés en 1994 et 1995: Rapport sur l'exécution de la loi du 10 juillet 1989 en faveur de l'emploi des travailleurs handicapés dans les enterprises*, Employment Delegation.

MISEP (1996) *Basic Information Report France: Institutions, procedures and measures*, Employment Observatory, Brussels: European Commission.

Montès, F. (1987) 'Les invalides en France', *Handicaps et Inadaptations, Les Cahiers du CTNERHI*, no.39, 1-40.

Padieu, C. and Sanchez, J.L. (1994) *L'action sociale: dix ans de décentralisation 1984-1994*, Paris: Odas Editeur.

Roussel, P. and Velche, D. (1995) *AAH et pension d'invalidité: Conditions d'attribution et characteristiques des bénéficiaires*, Paris: CTNERHI.

Velche, D. (1997) *Recherche des facteurs qui conduisent les entreprises de petite taille et de taille moyenne à accepter ou refuser, en France, l'accès ou le maintien à l'emploi de personnes présentant des incapacités*, Paris: CTNERHI.

Velche, D., Champenois, E., Bald, E., and Kevassay, S. (1993) *Etude sur l'activité des EPSR. Deuxième partie: Caractéristiques de la population suivie, actions menées et résultats obtenus par les équipes de préparation et de suite du reclassement*, Paris: CTNERHI.

CHAPTER FIVE

GERMANY[1]

The guiding principles of German disability policy are set out in the Social Code, established in 1975. This states that a person who has, or is threatened by, a physical, mental or psychological disability, has the right to the assistance necessary to

> avert, eliminate or ease the disability, prevent its aggravation, or reduce its effects, and ....to secure a place in the community, in particular in working life, in accordance with his or her inclinations and abilities.

This social right forms the legal basis for the interpretation of social legislation. Four principles are emphasised in policy statements: integration (allowing the disabled person to live as normally and independently as possible); finality (providing assistance regardless of the cause of disability or the responsible institution); intervention at the earliest opportunity; and the provision of assistance tailored to the needs of the individual. As part of the negotiations surrounding the reunification of Germany, disability organisations were successful in inserting a clause forbidding discrimination against disabled people into the constitution (Frehe, 1995). Although this is viewed as an important symbolic recognition of the aim of integration, it is too early to say whether it has made (or will make) any significant impact on policy or practice.

A commitment to integration leads to considerable emphasis on rehabilitation in employment policy. Compulsory employment, in the form of a quota system, also has a long tradition, and is central to German employment policies for disabled people. Not only is it instrumental in enabling disabled people to obtain (or more often, retain) employment, but the compensatory payments levied in cases of non-compliance provide funding for a range of measures in the field of employment policy.

In addition to the recession of the early 1990s, Germany has experienced unique labour market problems as a result of reunification, which have worsened the employment situation. As in other countries, the German labour market has also experienced a shift from manufacturing industry to a growing tertiary sector in recent years. This is one of the factors leading to a current emphasis on the role of (re)training, and investment in new technology, as labour market policies.

The disability benefit system in Germany is geared to the provision of pensions only where attempts at rehabilitation have been unsuccessful. Administratively, this has proved difficult to achieve, and in many cases, rehabilitation measures are undertaken only after pension receipt has already begun. Current changes in funding also threaten to undermine this principle. There have been recent reforms in the social assistance scheme aimed at improving incentives to work, and there is a strong emphasis on anti-fraud measures in the administration of social security benefits generally.

German disability policy is marked by a degree of corporatism which is strongly characteristic of the German welfare state as a whole. Employers and employees are formally represented on the boards of the various institutions administering benefits. One consequence of this is a

---

[1] Markus Körbel and Werner Friedrich, WSF Wirtschafts-und Socialforschung, were national informants for Germany.

system marked by occupational fragmentation, and strong insider/outsider divisions. The institutional divisions create strong fiscal and other pressures to refuse responsibility for a disabled individual, in ways which run counter to an identified need for co-ordinated attempts at rehabilitation.

THE LABOUR MARKET AND DISABLED PEOPLE

Labour market characteristics and trends

The labour market, and indirectly labour market policy, is influenced not only by the Federal Government, the Länder and other public law institutions such as the Employment Service, but also to a large extent by collective agreements between the social partners. There are current problems of structural unemployment, and a concern that high labour cost and inflexible working practices are stifling the development of new employment opportunities.

Economic activity rates are slightly higher in the new Länder than in West Germany, at 77.7 per cent (80.7 per cent men/74.7 per cent women) and 71.7 per cent (82.2 per cent men/59.5 per cent women) respectively (MISEP, 1994). The deterioration in the German labour market during 1992 and 1993, resulting both from reduced employment opportunities due to recession and the problem of restructuring following reunification, together with increasing numbers of labour market participants, have created a significant rise in underemployment. The high, and increasing, proportion of long-term unemployment is a particular cause for policy concern. Women and migrants are over-represented amongst the long-term unemployed.

Table G.1
Key labour market indicators in Germany, 1995

	Men	Women	Total
Employment rate (% age 15-64)	72.7	54.4	63.6
Self-employed (as % employed)	11.9	5.8	9.4
Part-time (% total employed)	3.6	33.8	16.3
Activity rate (% age 15-64)	78.4	60.4	69.5
Unemployment rate (% labour force)	7.1	9.8	8.2
Long-term unemployment (% unemployed)	45.9	51.3	48.7

Source: European Commission (1996) *Employment in Europe 1996*

Labour market policy

The most important objectives of federal employment and labour market policy are the maintenance of a high level of employment and the reduction of unemployment. These are viewed as primarily dependent on sustained economic growth and investment in improvement to production capacity. Policy instruments, however, are more concerned with improving the chances of the individual worker, for instance by vocational qualifications. For disabled people, the underlying principle is that of 'rehabilitation before pensions', leading to an emphasis on programmes of vocational rehabilitation.

Disabled people in the labour market[2]

Official statistics on the labour force participation of disabled people are based on the numbers officially registered as severely disabled. As registration is voluntary, these under-estimate the prevalence of disability in the population. Women are particularly likely to be under-represented. In 1993 in the former West Germany about 5.6 million people were registered as severely disabled. In East Germany, the number was 814,000. The proportion of severely disabled people stands at about eight per cent of a total population of 81.3 million. As is to be expected, the proportion rises with age, reaching 16.25 per cent for the over 55 age group (Table G.2).

Table G.2
Proportions of registered severely disabled people by age (December 1993)

Age	u/15	15-24	25-34	35-44	45-54	55-64	64+
%	0.86	1.36	1.96	3.06	7.00	16.25	25.72

Source: Ministry of Labour and Social Affairs, 1995

Disabled persons are legally defined as those who are limited in their capacity for integration into society, other than temporarily, because of the effects of a physical, mental or psychological condition which is contrary to the norm. 'Severely disabled persons' have an assessed degree of functional disability of at least 50 per cent, as measured by essentially medical procedures. In 1986 an amendment to the Severely Disabled Persons Act replaced the term 'a reduced earnings capacity' with degree of disability, to avoid implying a reduction in the person's fitness for work. However, a special ruling allows for equal status for people with a degree of disability of 30 to 50 per cent who are unable to find or retain suitable employment because of their disability.

About one-third of severely disabled people in Germany have organic disease and 'invisible' disabilities are prevalent (Winkler, 1996). Stork (1996) notes that people with psychological disorders seldom achieve the 50 per cent status required.

The labour market participation rate of disabled people is currently only half that of non-disabled people. By 1996, there were 190,000 severely disabled people unemployed in Germany. This is not perceived as a question of providing incentives to work, but as related to the issue of labour market demand and the need to create more employment opportunities. Analysis of data from the microcensus shows that disabled women are far less likely to be employed than either disabled men or non-disabled women.

Table G.3
Numbers of unemployed registered severely disabled people

Year	Number
1991	136,689
1992	155,082
1993	172,849
1994	178,317
1995	176,123

Source: Ministry of Labour and Social Affairs

[2] Information drawn from sources cited in Thornton and Lunt (1997).

Table G.3 shows the rise in the absolute number of registered disabled people who are officially unemployed. Data for West Germany shows that the labour market position of disabled people has steadily worsened in relation to unemployed people as a whole. In 1986 when the unemployment rate was nine per cent, the rate for disabled people was 11.9 per cent, and the gap has stood at over 5.5 percentage points since 1992. In 1995 disabled people had an unemployment rate of 15.8 per cent compared to 9.4 per cent overall.

In 1994, over 60 per cent of unemployed severely disabled people were aged 50 or over; 45 per cent were over 55. About two-thirds of unemployed severely disabled people have no formal qualifications. They are over-represented amongst the long-term unemployed, and are unlikely to find work. In 1993 only 20.6 per cent left unemployment to take up a job, whilst over three-quarters retired early, were excluded from benefit, withdrew from the labour market or claimed sickness benefits.

Disabled people in employment

There are about 1.14 million disabled people who are active in the labour market, of whom one million have jobs. About 150,000 are in sheltered employment.

Analysis of the German Socio-Economic Panel (Burkhauser and Daly, 1993) looked at the employment status of disabled men in Germany[3] and the USA. In 1988, 58.4 per cent of disabled men worked full-time, compared with 81.4 per cent of non-disabled men, and around 48 per cent of disabled men in the USA. Disabled men were less likely to work part-time (9.5 per cent, compared with 13.6 per cent for non-disabled men) and only 13.5 per cent of disabled men who were working part-time were receiving disability benefits. Disabled men were also six times as likely as their non-disabled peers to have no work at all (32.5 per cent, compared to five per cent).

Backes-Gellner and Frick (1990) found considerable evidence of job segregation amongst disabled people. Disabled people were more likely to be doing work for which they were over-qualified. Their sample (which included both men and women) was also much more involved in part-time work in the service sector; about 15 per cent of disabled people had such work, compared with two per cent of the male workforce and 27 per cent of the female workforce as a whole. While theoretically such employment carries equal legal rights, in reality it is charac-terised by lower rates of pay and poorer holiday and other entitlements.

Older disabled people usually retire early, taking advantages of a regulation allowing disabled people over 60 who have 35 years of contributions to retire on a full pension. This has caused substantial increases in the numbers of disabled people taking early retirement since the 1980s, and has been widely used by private sector firms wishing to restructure. Disabled workers are least likely to take early retirement in firms where job accommodations have been made for them (Frick and Frick, 1994).

EMPLOYMENT AND SOCIAL SECURITY POLICIES

Policies to promote employment of disabled people

Legal obligations and rights are set out within the framework of the Severely Disabled Persons Act (*Schwerbehindertergesetz*) 1974. This extended compulsory employment provisions, first introduced in 1919, previously applicable to people with war or industrial injuries, to all with a degree of disability of 50 per cent or more and to those with a capacity assessed at 30 to 50

---

[3] Defined as those reporting an illness or disability limiting work capacity in two successive years.

per cent who are unable to find work because of disability. The Act was amended in 1986, strengthening the role of representatives of severely disabled people in the workplace, and again in 1990, to provide uniform conditions as part of the Treaty of Unification.

Current legislation requires that public and private sector employers, with a workforce of 16 or more, ensure that at least six per cent are severely disabled people. (In calculating numbers for quota purposes certain disadvantaged individuals may be counted as more than one, and part-time employees can be treated as full-time where the reduction in hours is necessary because of disability.) Employers are liable to fines if the quota requirements are not met, but these are scarcely ever imposed (Thornton and Lunt, 1997). In 1982, the average quota attained was 5.9 per cent; by 1994 it had fallen to 4.0 per cent. Seventy-six per cent of firms were employing less than the full quota, and 37 per cent employed no disabled people at all. Firms with high rates of turnover are particularly likely to be failing to meet the quota. Small and medium sized enterprises are also reported as finding it particularly difficult to accommodate the needs of disabled employees. It should, however, be noted that full compliance with quota requirements is not possible, as there are insufficient numbers of registered severely disabled people.

Employers who do not fulfil the quota requirements are subject to a compensatory levy in respect of each unfilled compulsory place. The purpose of the levy is twofold; to act as an incentive, and to distribute the costs of disabled workers equally among firms. It appears to be fairly ineffective in the former role, mainly because at 200 DM per month (since 1990) the levy is too low to act as an incentive; many employers find it cheaper to pay the levy than to hire a disabled worker.

The quota system favours the retention of existing workers rather than the recruitment of severely disabled people. A number of sources (Oyen, 1989; Brandt, 1984; Sadowski and Frick, 1992) confirm that the majority of disabled employees in firms are long-serving members of staff who have become disabled; Sadowski and Frick estimate this figure at 82 per cent. Moreover, over two-thirds of firms do not recruit any disabled people from the open labour market (Brandt, 1984).

Severely disabled workers in employment have entitlement to an additional five days paid leave annually. They also enjoy special protection against unfair dismissal, which applies after six months employment in firms with a workforce of more than five people. This requires employers to obtain the approval of the relevant administrative authority (*Hauptfürsorgestelle*) before giving notice of dismissal. One unintended consequence of these provisions is that employers are reluctant to take on disabled people, especially in times of economic downturn, because they anticipate problems in dismissing them should the need arise. Analysis of the outcomes of these procedures, however, suggests that such fears are largely unfounded; disabled people usually leave employment in accordance with their employer's plans (Thornton and Lunt, 1997).

Institutional responsibilities

At Federal level, the Ministry of Labour and Social Affairs (BMA) is responsible for relief payments to war veterans, laws relating to disabled people and vocational integration of disabled people. The Federal Employment Service is supervised by the BMA and provides special careers advice and placement services for disabled and severely disabled people at its unemployment benefit offices. The welfare agencies of the Länder (Hauptfürsorgestellen) provide specialist services for vocational integration of severely disabled people.

Social security policies for disabled people

The German social insurance system is a complex, comprehensive system involving all levels of government as well as worker and employer federations. There are many separate insurance schemes covering different risks such as unemployment, retirement and disability. Several funding agencies are therefore responsible for the provision of both vocational rehabilitation measures and disability pensions.

The social insurance office is intended to have a key role in the early identification of an emerging disabling condition. This involves doctors to a significant degree. It is they who will first inform the local sickness insurance agency that a rehabilitation investigation is called for. This should happen within a matter of weeks from the first claim. The agency will in their turn advise the rehabilitation agency of the measures to be undertaken. The aim is to avoid long-term receipt of benefit wherever possible.

Since 1978, responsibility for rehabilitation has been divided between the Federal Institute of Employment and the Pension Insurance Agency. The Federal Rehabilitation Council has a co-ordination role in respect of rehabilitation measures, and is responsible for distribution of the compensatory levy fund. Its members comprise representatives of state governments, insurance and pension institutes, the employment institute as well as employer and trade union federations.

Social assistance is the responsibility of the Länder, guided by broad Federal legislation which states that it should be provided by the local authorities. Most expenditure is for special circumstances, covering disabled people and other groups.

Overview of social security benefits

The main benefits, including unemployment, age, incapacity and sickness benefits, are contributory. Each scheme also provides services such as rehabilitation. Those unable to work regularly at least half a day are the responsibility of the pension insurance system.

Sickness benefit

Employers are legally obliged to pay the full wage for the first six weeks of incapacity. Sickness benefit is then paid by the sickness insurance fund (KK) at a rate of 80 per cent of gross earnings, subject to a ceiling. Benefit can be paid for a maximum of 78 weeks in any three year period.

If a long-term illness is likely to require a disability benefit, as indicated by a statement of medical diagnosis after five weeks of illness, the KK will arrange for a further medical examination and will request the person to apply to their insurance organisation for a disability benefit. Failure to apply within ten weeks of this request will result in withdrawal of sickness benefit (Bolderson and Mabbett, 1997). Time required for processing, which includes obligatory enquiry into rehabilitation possibilities, means that receipt of sickness benefit may continue. After 18 months of sickness the person may need to apply for social assistance, pending a decision.

Disability benefits

The German social insurance system provides two types of disability insurance benefits; full (*Erwerbsunfähigkeitrent* - EU) (general) disability benefit and partial (*Berufsunfähigkeitrent* -

BU) (occupational) disability benefit. Both are covered by statutory pension insurance, which covers about 85 per cent of employed earners; civil servants and some low-income groups are excluded, and insurance payments are optional for the self-employed.

For the full benefit (EU), the claimant must be deemed incapable of earning a regular income from *any* employment for the foreseeable future (five years, as a rule of thumb). This includes people who are only capable of working irregularly, or whose earnings capacity is less than one-eighth of that of a comparable person. EU can be granted for an unlimited period or, if an improvement in health is anticipated, for a period of three years or more.

To be eligible for partial (occupational) disability benefit (BU), the insured person's earnings capacity must be assessed at less than 50 per cent[4] of a comparable person's, for reasons of ill-health or disability. In calculating earnings capacity, reference is made only to employment commensurate with the claimant's capacities, abilities and previous work experience. In practice, BU is granted usually for one year only, as recipients move automatically to EU.

Partial disability pensions are by definition available only to skilled and semi-skilled workers. There are large numbers of older unskilled workers who do not qualify and who are forced to rely on unemployment benefits and/or social assistance.

Table G.4 shows numbers of men and women receiving the two benefits in the years 1993 to 1995.

Table G.4
Recipients of BU and EU

	Berufsunfähigkeitsrente			*Erwerbsunfähigkeitsrente*		
	Women	*Men*	*Total*	*Women*	*Men*	*Total*
Germany						
1993	18,151	93,319	111,470	700,674	1,017,244	1,717,918
1994	19,777	95,543	115,320	719,644	1,011,547	1,731,191
1995	19,670	92,738	112,408	612,145	838,900	1,451,045

Source: *VDR: Verband der Rentenversicherungsträger*

Disability benefits are usually awarded to older workers, blurring the difference between disability, retirement and unemployment. In 1990 the average age of new recipients was 55; nearly two-fifths of all recipients had mental disorders (Frick and Sadowski, 1996).

Policy context

From 1984, measures to reduce eligibility for both benefits were introduced; instead of quali-fying on the basis of any five year period of employment, claimants must now have worked for at least 36 months during the past five years. This change led to a substantial drop in the numbers of women eligible, and overall a sizeable annual drop in new benefit recipients. Between 1985 and 1990, in West Germany the number of recipients of EU fell from over 2.3

---

[4] According to 'Cash Benefits for the Handicapped: A selective study of the schemes of some European countries in Operation', an unpublished DHSS study, June 1972, the 50 per cent test applied to salaried employees from 1911 but until after World War II manual workers had to be two-thirds incapable.

million to 1.7 million. Recipients of BU decreased in a similar proportion in the same period, from 150,000 to 112,000.

Since 1985 less than one in twenty new recipients has received a partial benefit, compared with one in three in 1965, mainly due to the increasing relevance of labour market considerations in the eligibility procedure (Frick and Sadowski, 1996). In the mid 1980s, legislation required that the labour market situation should be taken into account when assessing eligibility for EU and BU; as a result almost all recipients of BU who could not be placed in employment within a year received EU. This was exacerbated by the worsening labour market situation and financial problems in the public sector. A later decree requiring restrictions in the granting of BU led to a further decline in recipients.

The institutional demarcations between the pensions institutes, the sickness insurance funds and the Federal Employment Institute starkly demonstrate the difficulties of categorising people as incapacitated, employable (and hence entitled to unemployment benefits) or unemployable (and hence entitled to social assistance) (Bolderson and Mabbett, 1997).

There are incentives for institutions not to accept responsibility for a claim, and this can have unfortunate consequences for individuals, who are often passed from one office to another, and may lose out financially. For instance, it is not uncommon for a client who has not exhausted sickness benefit to be pressurised to apply for a disability pension, which provides a lower level of benefit, simply because this shifts the responsibility from the sickness insurance office to the pension institute (Bolderson and Mabbett, 1997). Claimants have little redress in the face of such pressures, as they lose benefit if they fail to make a claim within ten weeks of the direction to do so.

COMBINING DISABILITY BENEFITS AND WORK

There are only two possibilities for combining benefits with work; partial disability benefit and a system for retaining benefits during introduction to a job.

Partial disability benefits

It is possible to combine BU with employment but very few do so. No data are available. In fact, there is very little incentive to combine the benefit with income from work. Frick and Sadowski (1996) argue that incomes from a combination of BU and a non-commensurate job frequently exceed those paid in the original employment. Since 1 January 1996, this situation can no longer arise, as earnings limits for receipt of BU have been introduced. Bearing in mind that EU, which is payable after 12 months of unemployment, is paid at 33 per cent higher level, the incentives to work are minimal.

The lack of opportunities in the labour market also means that very few recipients engage in paid employment, and for the vast majority BU functions as an interim pension before receipt of EU after a year. Critics of the assessment system for BU and EU argue that decisions based on health limitations are often arbitrary, as they do not constitute an accurate measure of work impairment. In addition, the potential effects of rehabilitation programmes tend not to be taken into account, with the result that decisions tend to reflect mainly the current state of the labour market, a process described by some observers as a 'scientific lottery'.

Step-wise rehabilitation

It is possible for claimants of EU and BU to enter into a 'step-wise rehabilitation' which involves working a gradually increased number of hours over a specified period of time. A formal contract is drawn up between the employer and employee specifying the hours to be worked, start and end dates, and the level of salary to be paid. Earnings are deducted from benefits. Because benefit entitlement continues throughout the period of rehabilitation, there is no break in claiming, and benefit can be restored to the previous level if the attempt at rehabilitation does not succeed. This form of rehabilitation is regarded as being particularly successful. Employees report greatly increased levels of confidence when they return to the workplace (Dean, 1990).

BENEFITS FOR VOCATIONAL REHABILITATION

Until the end of 1996, all disabled people had a legal claim to vocational rehabilitation benefits. Formal acknowledgement as disabled under the Severely Disabled Persons Act was not required; in fact only about ten per cent of participants were severely disabled persons.

From the beginning of 1997, disabled workers no longer have a legal entitlement to vocational rehabilitation benefits. They are now discretionary except for those registered as severely disabled. This change has been made to accommodate serious budget deficits in the federal employment office. Decisions about whether someone is put forward for vocational training are now therefore primarily dependent on financial considerations. This is widely regarded as very damaging to the principle of 'rehabilitation before pension', a concept which had, however, not always operated in practice. Frick and Sadowski (1996) cite one study that found that 25 per cent of people had received rehabilitation measures only in the year they began receiving disability pension, and another that demonstrated that about 75 per cent of disability pensioners did not undergo a rehabilitation measure within the five years before their pension was awarded.

From the beginning of 1997, benefit levels paid by the responsible funds have been reduced to bring them into line with the amount of benefit paid by employment offices.

Benefits are laid down in the employment promotion act (AF). There are four different types of benefit which can be obtained during vocational rehabilitation, altogether known as 'payments/assistance for living' (Leistungen zum Lebensunterhalt).

Substitutionary benefits for living *(Unterhaltsgeld)*

Participants in full-time vocational training, whether disabled or not, can apply for this benefit, which is usually paid at 60 per cent of last wage (67 per cent if the claimant has at least one child).

Assistance or subsidies for professional training *(Berufsausbildungsbeihilfe)*

These are available to both disabled and non-disabled people who are living independently of their parents and live a long way from their parent's home (i.e. they could not reasonably be expected to live with their parents) or have previously worked for at least a year and are now unemployed, or are socially handicapped or educationally subnormal.

Interim benefit *(Übergangsgeld)*

This can be paid instead of Unterhaltsgeld, to disabled people taking part in vocational rehabilitation, at a rate of 68 per cent of the last wage (80 per cent if the claimant has at least one child).

Professional training benefits *(Ausbildungsgeld)*

These are available only to disabled people and are payable to those undertaking professional training, or vocational training if the claimant is under 22 years of age. All disabled people (defined as those with a permanent reduction in their chances of labour market integration) not entitled to interim benefits are eligible to professional training benefits.

In 1995 job centres were asked to reduce the number of awards of the two benefits specifically for disabled people (*Übergangsgeld and Ausbildungsgeld*) with the aim of reducing costs. One result of this was an increase in the number of disabled people claiming the general rehabilitation benefits. Altogether both absolute and proportionate numbers of people awarded vocational benefits declined in 1995 compared to the previous year. However, the overall aim of reducing total costs was not achieved, both because of increases in unit costs and because of a five per cent rise in the number of 'first integration measures' undertaken. These measures, including professional training, are more expensive than re-integration measures.

Table G.5
Costs of vocational rehabilitation measures

	1994	*1995*
Individual promotion	4.031 billion DM	4.165 billion DM
Costs for measures and courses	2.476 billion DM	2.680 million DM
Payments/assistance for living	1.364 million DM	1.433 million DM
- Ausbildungsgeld	200 million DM	242 billion DM
- Berufsausbildungsbeihilfe	62 billion DM	146 billion DM
- Übergangsgeld	997 billion DM	682 million DM
- Unterhaltsgeld	101 million DM	368 million DM
Other measures (e.g. wage subsidies)	0.191 million DM	0.052 billion DM

Source: Ministry of Labour and Social Affairs

Table G.6
Disabled people sponsored under vocational rehabilitation programmes

	1994	*1995*
Payments/assistance for living	99,700	93,200
- Ausbildungsgeld	55,100	49,900
- Berufsausbildungsbeihilfe	2,700	3,600
- Übergangsgeld	29,500	20,100
- Unterhaltsgeld	10,400	19,400
Percentage of disabled people	87%	80%

Source: Ministry of Labour and Social Affairs

Tax allowances for extra costs of disability

Disabled people are entitled to a tax allowance depending on the degree of disability, intended to provide compensation for additional living costs. This was introduced in 1974, and has not been uprated, so that its financial value is now regarded as negligible. The current annual tax reduction provided varies between 600 and 2,760 DM. People who are blind or require substantial personal assistance are entitled to a higher allowance of 7,200 DM a year.

This tax allowance is available to people with a disability assessed at more than 50 per cent (and to those with a disability assessed at between 25 and 50 per cent who fulfil additional criteria, such as limited mobility or disability pension entitlement). There are no limits on earnings or hours worked. Below 12,000 DM there is no benefit from this allowance, as income is tax exempt. Above this threshold, tax savings increase in line with income. Except for those entitled to the higher allowance, the sums provided (generally less than 200 DM per month) are too low to provide either an incentive to work, or a realistic contribution to additional costs. The total annual amount of the reduction is estimated at less than 50 million DM.

Tax allowances for travel to work

Disabled people are also entitled to tax refunds in respect of travel to work. Tax allowances of this type exist for all employees, but disabled people receive a more generous rate of refund - 0.52 DM per kilometre instead of 0.35. However, eligibility criteria are so tightly defined that very few disabled people qualify; even amongst those who are very severely disabled, only about 80 per cent are able to establish eligibility.

Other costs

Subsidies are also available to meet the costs of purchasing a car, or obtaining a driving licence, for work purposes, depending on income level, and for equipment or modifications to a car, regardless of income. These are only available to very severely disabled people, and are paid at fairly low levels, except for people who are blind or who require substantial personal assistance. The policy intention underlying their introduction was not to provide work incentives but to compensate for disadvantages faced by disabled people.

There are further benefits available to meet the costs of technical assistance in the workplace, of modifications to the workplace, and of the costs of a limited period of 'probationary employment'. Subsidies for employers to compensate for 'extraordinary strains' are also available when a disabled person would otherwise lose their job. In 1995 such payments were made in 6,980 cases in the old Länder and 1,409 cases in the new Länder, at a cost of 78.6 million DM.

The main wage subsidy is the *Eingliederungszuschuß* (integration subsidy) which is paid to the employer of a severely disabled person, as a specific scheme under the Severely Disabled Persons Act. There is in addition a general scheme in the employment promotion act, covering unemployed people who require integration into the labour market, which can include disabled people. The Federal Employment Office is responsible for the administration of the schemes, although payment, particularly for re-integration into the labour market, may be funded by other agencies such as pension and accident insurance funds.

Wage subsidies for disabled people

Wage subsidies are intended to compensate employers for the additional costs involved in hiring a disabled person, including the additional leave entitlement, referred to above. Compared with other disability policies, they are of minor significance.

Wage subsidy payments are financed entirely from the compensatory levy. Introduced in 1986, they are available to firms which are not subject to quota requirements (i.e. those with under 16 employees) and those who have already met their quota obligation, but not to employers who are failing to meet this obligation.

The subsidy may apply when an employer takes on an unemployed disabled person:

● whose employment causes extraordinary costs for the employer
● whose capability is less than 70 per cent of that of a 'normal employee'
● who has a mental or psychological disability assessed at more than 50 per cent
● who is aged 50 years or above
● who has been unemployed for over a year.

It also covers disabled people who have left sheltered workshops, education, professional training and probationary employment (*Proarbeitsverhältni*s).

Employers who take on a person from one of these groups receive a subsidy for three years, which tapers from 80 per cent in the first year to 60 per cent in the third. For those aged over 55 subsidy is also available for a further two years, again reducing ten per cent per year. Subsidies for professional training are paid at the rate of 80 per cent for the whole three year period, and may be paid at 100 per cent where the person has an exceptionally severe disability. All of these subsidies are available for part-time as well as for full-time work. Local schemes may also offer more generous rates of subsidy than the main scheme outlined above.

Employers are obliged to provide continuing employment for the disabled person after the expiry of the subsidy period, and must repay the subsidy received if they fail to meet this condition.

In 1996, 9,100 disabled people were granted integration subsidies; of those 1,700 were classified as having a reduced rate of output. The vast majority (7,000) were physically disabled. Two-thirds of the total were men.

Wage subsidies are generally regarded as ineffective; firms tend to view the subsidies as windfall profits, and the vast majority of grants are made to a small number of large companies. It is estimated that between 75 and 85 per cent of all placements would have occurred without subsidy (Frick, 1992; Burger and Schröder, 1995).

Subsidies for retention

There is separate provision, funded by the Compensatory Levy Fund, for employers who retain an existing employee whose work performance is diminished as a result of disability. This is not formally time-limited, although in practice entitlement is reviewed after a period of two years (Seyfried, 1995).

General wage subsidies

The employment promotion act provides a subsidy of 50 per cent for the first six months, followed by 18 months at 40 per cent, for employers who take on a qualifying unemployed person (deemed unable to find work in the open labour market). Severely disabled people are a priority group, along with the long-term unemployed, older workers and younger unemployed people with no vocational training.

In the first half of the 1990s, use of this job creation measure expanded considerably in the former East Germany. In 1995 almost a third of the total participants in the new Länder took part in projects in social services and in the protection of the environment where remuneration is closely linked to the level of unemployment allowances.

Table G.7
Average numbers in subsidised jobs, West and East Germany

Year	Number	
	West	*East*
1991	83,000	183,300
1994	57,400	280,200
1995	70,100	312,000

COMMENTARY

In general, research findings indicate that German employment policies are particularly effective in ensuring that severely disabled people and people who become disabled while in work retain their employment. The system appears to be less successful in fostering the recruitment of disabled people. Employers have legal obligations under the quota system to employ a percentage of disabled people, but they tend to meet these obligations by encouraging existing members of staff who become disabled to register. As Frick and Frick (1994) argue, this is highly functional for employers, since not only do they retain a trained worker, as against the 'risk' involved in hiring an unemployed disabled person, but they also find this instrumental in securing loyalty from employees. From the point of view of the individual employee, recognition of disability status also offers a legitimate pathway into early retirement.

Although the availability of BU offers the opportunity to recognise partial incapacity for work, it is not a true partial incapacity measure, because of its link to occupation. It is not available to large sections of the disabled population, because those who are unskilled are not entitled, and is insufficiently flexible. It is being paid to a declining number of people, because of adverse labour market conditions, and is currently viewed as irrelevant for all practical purposes. Overall, improved negotiation between the various agencies involved is seen as the best way to improve the employment situation of disabled people. However, in a climate of increasing financial cutbacks, there are strong institutional barriers to such co-operation.

The rehabilitation system in Germany also tends to fall short of its professed ideals. Although placement rates from prestige training and rehabilitation centres for disabled people remain high, overall only between 30 and 50 per cent of those undergoing rehabilitation measures are in employment a year later (Körbel, personal communication). The decision to remove entitlement to vocational rehabilitation measures from January 1997 will reduce the numbers taking part and lead to further problems for disabled people seeking employment in the general labour market. They will have a serious impact on the principle of 'rehabilitation before pension' and in the medium term are likely to result in increased public expenditure because of the increased number of people claiming disability pension for extended periods of time.

REFERENCES

Backes-Gellner, U. and Frick, B. (1990) 'Discrimination in employment in the Federal Republic of Germany', *Georgia Journal of International and Comparative Law*, 20, 89, 105-121.

Bolderson, H. and Mabbett, D. and others (1997) *Delivering Social Security: A cross-national study*, Social Security Research Report No 59, London: The Stationery Office.

Brandt, F. (1984) *Behinderte auf dem allgemeinen Arbeitsmarkt*, Bonn: Bundesministerium für Arbeit und Sozialordnung.

Burger, S. and Schröder, M. (1995) 'Labour market policy for disabled people in Germany: the shortcomings of legal intervention', 56-90 in Bengtsson, S. (ed) *Employment of People with Disabilities: Colloquium in connection with a research project*, Copenhagen: Social Forsknings Instituttet.

Burkhauser, R. and Daly, M. (1993) 'The importance of labor earnings for working age males with disabilities', Cross-National Studies in Aging, Program Paper No. 11, Syracuse University.

Dean, D. (1990) 'Vocational rehabilitation innovations for disabled person within the Federal Republic of Germany', in Berkowitz, M. (ed) *Forging Linkages: Modifying disability benefit programs to encourage employment*, New York: Rehabilitation International.

Frehe, H. (1995) 'Mandatory employment or equal opportunities? Employment policy in Germany', in Leichsenring, K. and Strümpel, C. (eds) *Mandatory Employment or Equal Opportunities? Employment policies for people with disabilities in the UN-European Region*, Vienna: European Centre for Social Welfare Policy and Research.

Frick, B. (1992) 'Gruppenspezifische Lohnsubventionen und Arbeitsvermittlung Schwerbehinderter', 149-182 in Sadowski, D., Brühl, N. and Kütten, R. (eds) *Regionale Sozialpolitik*, Frankfurt/New York: Campus.

Frick, B. and Frick, J. (1994) 'Labour Market Policy and the Convergence of Interests: The 'Benefits' of the German Handicapped Act for Employers and Employees' in Schwarze, J. *et al.* (eds) *Labour Market Dynamics in Present Day Germany*, Frankfurt: Campus Verlag.

Frick, B. and Sadowski, D. (1996) 'A German perspective on disability policy', in Aarts, L., Burkhauser, R. and de Jong, P. (eds) *Curing the Dutch Disease*, Aldershot: Avebury.

MISEP (1994) *Basic Information Report Federal Republic of Germany: Institutions, Procedures and Measures*, Employment Observatory, Brussels: European Commission.

Oyen, R. (1989) *Berufsbildung, Arbeitsmarktchancen und Betriebliche Integration Behinderter: Überblick über die empirische Forschung der 80er Jahre*, Stuttgart: Verlag W. Kohlhammer.

Sadowski, D. and Frick, B. (1992) *Die Beschäftigung Schwerbehinderter: Betriebswirtschaftliche Analysen und politische Empfehlungen*, Schulz-Kirchner Verlag.

Seyfried, E. (1995) 'Social enterprises in Germany', *International Journal of Practical Approaches to Disability*, 19, 2, 20-22.

Stork, E. (1996) '20 Jahre Schwerbehindertengesetz: Aspekte einer Entwicklung', *Behindertenrecht*, 1, 12-22.

Thornton, P. and Lunt, N. (1997) *Employment Policies for Disabled People in Eighteen Countries: A review*, York: Social Policy Research Unit.

Winkler, A. (1996) 'Integration of persons with disabilities into the labour market and state intervention: crucial design features and the effectiveness of compulsory employment policy from a German perspective', in *Rehabilitation of partially disabled workers in the workforce in various European countries: decisive factors seen from an international perspective*, Papers from an expert meeting held in Utrecht 4 and 5 November.

CHAPTER SIX

NETHERLANDS[1]

OVERVIEW

In the Netherlands, policies to promote employment of partially disabled people have been driven by political and public concern over high sickness absence rates and increasing numbers receiving disability benefits. The financial consequences of the latter, in the context of low labour market participation, provoked a series of radical reforms to the social security system. These were accompanied by a series of new obligations on, and incentives to, the economic actors to assist the return to work of disability benefit recipients and to prevent workers who become disabled from entering the benefit system.

The concept of partial capacity for work is fundamental to Dutch income and labour policy. As disability is a wage-related concept, degree of incapacity is expressed in terms of loss of earnings capacity. Partial capacity benefits were first designed in 1967 to complement earnings from work. However, the way in which the system was implemented has meant that only about 13 per cent of beneficiaries are in open employment. The 1993 reforms aiming to reduce overall expenditure on disability benefits have had a temporary effect on numbers entering and leaving benefit, but a lesser effect on return to work with partial benefits.

Radical reforms to the disability insurance system are expected to be introduced in January 1998. Employers will for the first time contribute to the disability insurance fund and will be financially responsible for income replacement in the case of sickness or disability for the first five years. Currently, employers are responsible for sickness benefit for the first year. The employer is encouraged to ensure against the risk in the private insurance market. Under the proposals, premiums will be differentiated according to the employer's record in retaining and taking on disabled workers.

Financial incentives to disabled people were introduced on a small-scale in 1995 and 1996. They include an arrangement to try out work unpaid for three months and receive the same level of benefit. It is too early to report the effects of the most recent incentives but a measure introduced in 1995 reached less than five per cent of its target group, older workers. Subsidies to employers towards wage costs and the extra costs of employing disabled people are also a recent innovation, as yet little used. The policy assumption in March 1997 was that further incentives were required to promote (re)integration, alongside measures to reduce the disincentive effect of 'red-tape'.

THE LABOUR MARKET AND DISABLED PEOPLE

Labour market characteristics and trends

In the Netherlands the population in the age range of 15 to 64 years is growing faster than in most European Union countries and stands at about 10.5 million. The level of labour market participation among people aged 15 to 64, although increasing steadily, is considered low for both men and women. The proportion employed part-time was 37.4 per cent in 1995, by far the highest in the EU member states. A large percentage of the population withdraws from work at a relatively early age. Over two-thirds of all employees work in the service sector.

---

[1] Edwin de Vos, NIA-TNO Amsterdam, was national informant for the Netherlands.

Table N.1
Key labour market indicators in the Netherlands, 1995

	Men	Women	Total
Employment rate (% age 15-64)	74.5	53.2	64.0
Self-employed (as % employed)	13.3	8.6	11.4
Part-time (% total employed)	16.8	67.2	37.4
Activity rate (% age 15-64)	79.3	58.5	69.1
Unemployment rate (% labour force)	6.0	9.1	12.5
Long-term unemployment (% unemployed)	52.4	41.1	46.7

Source: European Commission (1996) *Employment in Europe 1996*

Labour market policy

The government expects to solve employment problems and reduce the public expenditure burden by re-shaping a highly institutionalised system into a more market-like arrangement through privatisation, deregulation and shifting of responsibility to individual economic actors (MISEP, 1995).

Central government policies to facilitate the growth of regular employment follow three lines: lowering the cost of labour, for unskilled work in particular; stimulating the flexibility of the labour market; and differentiation of working hours and work patterns. Extra jobs are being created for the long-term unemployed. Work incentives have been introduced in the social security sector. The public employment service role has withdrawn to public placement and brokerage and a pluralistic approach is being fostered through contracting out public services to independent organisations (MISEP, 1995).

The legal minimum wage level has been almost stable for five years and was not increased in 1994 and 1995. Wage scales are generally determined by collective agreements. In most sectors the lowest wage scale starts at a level that is far above the minimum wage level; and the vast majority of workers receive wages which are substantially higher than the minimum wage (de Koning *et al.*, 1996). In order to encourage recruitment of long-term unemployed people and disabled workers there are special dispensations to allow payment of wages at below the minimum or collectively agreed levels but the dispensation for disabled people is little used. Wage-cost subsidies to employers have recently been introduced on a relatively small scale for employment of disabled people and the long-term unemployed.

The role of the state versus the free market is intensely debated in the Netherlands. Considerable discussion, and proposals for legislative reform, have focused on the future of collective agreements over labour conditions, regulation of dismissal and hours of work, the role of public employment services, and income protection (Knegt (ed), 1995).

Disabled people in the labour market

For a combination of reasons, it is difficult to assess the extent of labour market participation of disabled people. The Netherlands has no registration or other routine system for identifying disabled people in the working age population. Estimates based on general population surveys relate mainly to people with physical impairments and chronic illness. There has been no population research among people with learning disabilities and the only data relate to those who use facilities designed for them and are registered.

The proportion of disabled people in employment is based on estimates. While 75 per cent of non-impaired 18 to 55 year olds are employed, an estimated 40 per cent of moderately impaired and one-third of seriously impaired *physically* disabled people do paid work (Timmermanns and Schoemakers-Salkinoja, 1996). Around half of men and a fifth of women of working age with chronic illness are estimated to be in work (de Vos *et al.*, 1995).

A minute proportion of people with learning disabilities work in mainstream, competitive employment. In 1993, about 31,500 were in sheltered employment, or waiting for a sheltered job, out of an estimated working population of less than 34,000. People with physical impairments make up rather less than half of the employees in sheltered work. Most of those disabled at birth or in childhood work in sheltered employment.

Actual numbers of disabled people in open employment are difficult to determine, even where there is legal definition and an obligation to record. The number in employment under the terms of the WAGW (see below) is estimated at between 96,000 and 150,000.[2] Recording of disabled employees by their employers is not enforced but from 1998 employers will be required to create permanent registers. Although a main aim of the system of benefits for partial capacity for work is to support employment, official figures do not reveal numbers of beneficiaries in work. In 1995, a total 640,000 received a full benefit (which theoretically can be combined with work) and 220,000 a partial benefit. Research estimates that 16 per cent of male recipients (96,000) and ten per cent female recipients (32,000) were in open employment in 1993 (de Vos *et al.*, 1995).[3]

A rough estimate of the officially defined working population of disabled people is in the order of 250,000. There are, of course, disabled people in work who are not recognised by the law. Research has estimated large numbers of employees with chronic illness (450,000 men and 200,000 women) of whom only a small minority (11 per cent of men and six per cent of women) are recognised as disabled in the benefits system (de Vos *et al.*, 1995). People with mental health problems are under-represented in employment and, as noted, people with learning disabilities almost entirely absent. Historically, open employment measures have been aimed at people with physical impairments.

Numbers of unemployed disabled people are not known. Since 1981 regional employment offices have not been required to record disabled people in a special category of those registered as seeking work. Among recipients of the two main disability benefits (WAO and AAW) in 1991, 55,000 were 'wanting a job' and 29,000 were 'looking for work' (Grammenos, 1995). Research estimates based on 1993 data put the total wanting work at between 135,000 and 200,000, however (de Vos *et al.*, 1995).

Research has concluded that two factors are mainly correlated with low labour market participation: personal care needs; and reduced stamina. It is postulated that those groups are often unable to cope with the demands of the organisation, such as fixed timetables or work tempo, as they do not fit into existing work regimes.

---

[2] The number of disabled people in employment for whom adaptations have been funded (one qualification under the WAGW) is only 6,000.

[3] The estimated total of 128,000 shows an increase on figures cited by Grammenos (1995) of 104,000 and 116,000 for 1990 and 1991 respectively.

Occupational situation of disabled people

Although there is no firm evidence on occupations held by disabled people or their economic situation, it is generally recognised that the majority hold low paid, 'heavy' jobs for which no qualifications are needed, mainly in industry and the service sector. Disabled people seldom work in agriculture or in the hotel and restaurant trade. They are under-represented in government employment (den Uijl *et al.*, 1996). Hours of work are not known but it is suggested that disabled people tend to work long-hours.

EMPLOYMENT AND SOCIAL SECURITY POLICIES FOR DISABLED PEOPLE

The Dutch 'labour and income' system means that policies for employment and for income replacement are inseparable. Under the social security legislation a person is termed 'unfit for work' when capacity to obtain an income from labour is diminished. The Ministry of Social Affairs and Employment is responsible for both labour market policy and income security.

Social security provision for disabled people

All residents are insured under the national insurance scheme. The scheme provides a disablement pension under the General Disablement Pensions Act (AAW) for non-employed people disabled from an early age[4] and for self-employed people who become disabled. The social assistance scheme provides for a minimum income under the National Assistance Act. There is special provision for supplementing the income of unemployed and formerly self-employed partially disabled people, to bring it up to the minimum guaranteed income level. That scheme is funded through tax revenues.

Separate employees' insurance schemes provide benefits to full-time and part-time employees at times of sickness and long-term disability. No distinction is made between occupational injury or disease and illness which is not work-related. Those who are sick and do not resume work after 52 weeks receive total or partial benefits under the Disability Benefits Act (WAO). The reduction in the capacity to earn the former income determines 'disability' and not the impairment. (Thus, someone who previously held a large salary will be judged more disabled than someone with the same impairments who earned less.) There are seven categories of disability to indicate full and partial incapacity.

Until 1994, sickness benefits were granted from the first day of work incapacity, with no period of compulsory wage payment. However, legislation now requires employers to bear 70 per cent of the wage costs during the first 52 weeks of work incapacity and the Sickness Benefits Act (ZW) is now effective only for the small proportion of the workforce working under special conditions, for maternity leave and for people who receive a benefit from the unemployment insurance scheme (WW).

WW is of increasing relevance to disabled people now that disability benefits, because of tighter eligibility criteria, are tending to provide partial income maintenance which has to be supplemented by unemployment benefits or, as a last resort, social welfare.

---

[4] Younger disabled people with no employment record. Those disabled from an early age must have become disabled before the age 18 or, if they have never worked, before age 28.

Institutional responsibilities

The Central Employment Board, on which the employers' federation, the central employees' federation and central government have equal policy-making responsibility, rules over 28 similarly constituted Regional Employment Boards which, in turn, operate the Employment Service (ES). The ES concentrates on vocational guidance and training, brokerage and placement and other assistance to unemployed jobseekers. From 1998, the ES will have total responsibility for services to partially disabled workers.

The social assistance scheme is administered by local authority social services departments. AAW, unlike others benefits in the national insurance scheme, is administered along with the employees' disability insurance scheme. The WAO and the other employee insurance schemes were run, until March 1997, by 18 bi-partite Industrial Insurance Boards (IIB), each established for a specific branch of industry. Some of the boards joined together to use a single administrative organisation, the GAK. From March 1997 accountability for delivery of benefits was transferred to the GAK and the other, smaller, administrative organisations (AdO).

The IIB had considerable autonomy and, until the 'Tica' was established in 1995, no legal co-ordinating body. A temporary body, Tica had powers to direct the administration of schemes and was charged with developing a strategy for regionalisation and co-operation with the employment offices. The Ctsv (Social Security Advisory Board), an independent body with far-reaching powers, supervised Tica . On 1 March 1997, a new act on the organisation of social insurance came into force. The IIB are to be reformed into regional boards. The Ctsv will continue to control social insurance, but the Lisv (National Institute for Social Security) will be responsible for implementation and practice. From 1998, the Employment Service will have total legal responsibility, devolved from the Lisv, for the integration of disabled workers. Meanwhile, the GAK and the other AdOs are responsible for administration and delivery.

The AdOs assess capacity for work, the level of disability benefit and opportunities for employment. Teams consist of a vocational expert, a national insurance medical practitioner and a legal assessor. The vocational expert investigates work possibilities with local employers, may call in training and other experts, designs a re-integration programme, helps obtain employment and solves adaptational problems. As well as assessing work disability, the AdO aims to reduce obstacles to the disabled person's chance of work and to support the person in the process of finding a job.

Disability benefits and employment policy developments

In 1947 the first regulations for the placement of disabled workers introduced voluntary registration as a 'less able-bodied' person, an obligation on public and private sector organisations with over 25 employees to meet a quota and an obligation on the employer to adapt the workplace and working tools to the disabled person. Disabled people were defined as 'those whose prospects of earning their living are substantially restricted by reason of infirmity, sickness or mental or physical differences'.

The obligation to meet a quota had little effect; the definition was too vague, and the option of registering was never widely used (Krug, 1990). Financial support from central government for sheltered workshops became the main policy instrument (Krug, 1990). The number of employees soared to 82,000 by 1984. In the late 1980s and early 1990s the government acted to contain the growing costs. By the end of 1995 there were 85,000 full-time equivalent employees, equalling 1.5 per cent of total employment. The waiting list had grown to over

20,000. New legislation from January 1998 will limit access to those who are able to work *only* under the adjusted conditions of sheltered workshops.

Since the mid 1980s, disability employment policy has aimed to contain the growth in recipients of disability benefits, widely acknowledged as a social problem. When the WAO - the act insuring workers against the risk of unfitness for work on account of disability or accident - was introduced in 1967 it was assumed that beneficiaries would not exceed 100,000 but by 1968 they reached 163,500. Between 1970 and 1980 the number of employees drawing benefit under the WAO increased by 240 per cent. The introduction of the AAW in 1976 added to the increase in benefits.

The 1986 Handicapped Workers Employment Act (WAGW) placed an obligation on employers, employers' organisations and workers' organisations, in public and private sectors, to facilitate the employment of people receiving disability benefits. The WAGW abandoned the registration requirement and extended coverage of the law to all those receiving a WAO benefit or a AAW disability pension. Also covered were those disabled employees for whom special provisions had been made, or needed to be made, to enable them to carry out their work. The aim was to achieve a quota of between three per cent and five per cent within three years, by voluntary effort. The quota was not reached and, in the face of employer opposition, was not legally imposed.

Simultaneous reductions in the level of benefits failed to reduce demand. By 1989 the number of beneficiaries had reached 846,000. Explanations for the growth include the increase in the number of insured persons; a broader view of what constitutes sickness, including a greatly increased recognition of psychological disturbances (by 1991 one in three of those eligible were so diagnosed); a widening gap between the skills of previously employed disabled people and the demands of industry; increased competition for jobs; the tolerant application of eligibility rules; and the relatively high level of benefit.

There was little emphasis on preparing disabled people for (re)entry to work. The emphasis on employment protection and the use of disability benefits as a route out of the labour market kept to a minimum the supply of and demand for rehabilitation services. In 1991, public expenditure as a percentage of GDP on labour market measures for disabled people was minimal, at less than 0.01 per cent (Aarts *et al.*, 1996a). The administrative organisations charged with supporting the disabled person in job-finding, as well as with assessing disability for benefits purposes, integrated less than half of their caseload into work.

Policy developments in the 1990s

The 1990s saw a new policy emphasis on increasing individual responsibility and freedom of choice. Moves to make the social security system more selective and market-oriented marked a radical shift from the Dutch solidarity principle of collective responsibility. Policy now has two main thrusts: reducing inflow to the WAO and AAW by tightened eligibility criteria and new measures to retain disabled people in employment; and increasing outflow through benefit reassessments and incentives to both disabled people and employers.

The 1990s have brought considerable legislative change.

● the Reduction of the Number of Benefit Claimants Act 1992 (TAV) aimed to stimulate employers and employees to prevent sick leave and to keep partially disabled people at work, or ensure their return to work. It introduced variation in employers' contributions to sickness benefit insurance according to the firm's sickness absence rates

- the Act to Restrict Claims on Disablement Benefit 1993 (TBA) included a more strict assessment of disability, time-limited and age-related payments, and compulsory re-examination of recipients under the age of 50

- the Reduction of Sickness Absence Act 1994 required the employer to pay at least 70 per cent of the salary for the six weeks[5] if a worker is absent through sickness or incapacity, to take responsibility for counselling aimed at encouraging the sick employee back to work, and to contract with private providers of occupational health services. This was followed in January 1996 by the extension of employer responsibility for coverage of sick pay to a maximum of 52 weeks. However, also in 1996, the wage payment obligation was lifted in the case of sickness of partially disabled employees within the first four years of their employment

- the Amendment to the Labour Conditions Act in 1994 stipulated that all employers must pursue a labour conditions policy which aims to prevent absence through sickness and must use private occupational safety and health services.

These acts also introduced a range of financial incentives to disabled workers and to employers to supplement earnings or subsidise wage costs and to help with costs of adaptations, supervision, personal assistance and training. These operate on a small scale only. Measures for vocational rehabilitation such as training, adaptations and employer subsidies are mainly funded within the framework of the insurance funds but the proportion of expenditure devoted to these measures is very small. Under consideration are proposals for a uniform rehabilitation fund, fed through transfer from the social insurance funds, and for more effective allocation procedures.

A further round of reforms will extend market economy principles to the WAO. The so-called 'Pemba' proposals, expected to be introduced on 1 January 1998, will integrate the AAW and WAO. The financing structures will change, introducing financial incentives for employers to adopt prevention and re-integration policies. Under the new arrangements, employers will contribute to the disability insurance fund and contributions will be differentiated, depending on the number of employees assessed as fully or partially disabled. Employers will have the choice of insuring this risk for five years through a private insurance company or deciding to pay the disability benefit themselves.

When the reforms appeared to have an effect in meeting their economic aims, as measured by reduced absence from work, reduced inflow to and increased outflow from disability benefits, the social goal of improving the integration of partially or formerly disabled people increased in prominence (Beljaars and Prins, 1997). A new Re-integration Act is planned to include further incentives to employers and employees. Measures under consideration include tax reductions for employers who employ a required number of disabled workers; employer-held re-integration budgets to increase flexibility and reduce bureaucratic delays; and a scheme of rehabilitation vouchers held by the disabled person.

In summary, policy at the beginning of 1997 had three main strands:

- legal obligations to promote and maintain the employment of disabled people, and to prevent the occurrence of disability

- financial incentives directed at employers and employees

- measures to reduce individual reliance on and access to disability benefits.

---

[5] Two weeks in the case of companies with up to 15 employees.

The main work/benefit combination is retention of a partial WAO/AAW benefit on (re)entry to work after a period of 52 weeks of sickness absence. In addition there is an in-work supplement to WAO/AAW, introduced in 1996 to bridge the shortfall in earnings resulting from the new system of assessing lost earnings capacity and designed as an incentive to the disabled worker. Several other smaller work incentives have been introduced for specified groups of disabled people, for example older people who have received disability benefits for more than two years.

Partial capacity benefits (WAO/AAW)

The concept of partial capacity for work permeates the Dutch income and labour policy. The WAO and AAW provide either a full benefit or a partial benefit set at one of seven levels reflecting degree of reduced earnings capacity.[6] Table N.2 shows numbers of disabled beneficiaries of the WAO and AAW schemes in 1993 and estimates for 1996.

Table N.2
Beneficiaries of WAO and AAW

	1993	1996*
WAO employees (including civil servants)	707,400	696,900
AAW self-employed	52,900	55,900
AAW disabled before age 18	75,500	102,400

* Ctsv estimate

Around one-quarter of beneficiaries receive a partial disability benefit and 63,000 received a combination of WAO/AAW and WW (unemployment benefit). Statistical data (Grammenos, 1995) indicate that around one-third of people with physical impairments (affecting skeletal and support apparatus) receive partial benefits, compared with only about one-tenth of those with intellectual and psychiatric impairments and 15 per cent of those with sensory impairments.

Combining partial capacity benefit and work

Although the main aim of the system of benefits for partial capacity for work is to support employment, official figures do not reveal numbers of beneficiaries in work. Research estimated in 1995 that 16 per cent of male disability benefit recipients (96,000) and ten per cent of female recipients (32,000) were in open employment in 1993 (de Vos *et al.*, 1995).

When the WAO was introduced in 1967 rehabilitation was the prime objective (de Vroom and Rovers, 1997). Programme administrators were expected to help people find work commensurate with their residual capacities, in hope that employees who became disabled could remain full members of the workforce despite their impairments (Aarts *et al.*, 1996b). A number of factors thwarted the reintegrative aims of the WAO (de Vroom and Rovers, 1997; Aarts *et al.*, 1996b). Disabled and partially disabled people were rarely able to find paid employment because of job shortages and the increasing supply of young people and married women in the labour market. The responsible institutions - generally considered inefficient - failed to

---

[6] According to 'Cash Benefits for the Handicapped: A selective study of the schemes of some European countries in operation', an unpublished DHSS study, June 1972, the wide range of assessments built into the system is the result of the integration of the industrial injuries scheme with the general scheme in 1966.

promote complementary measures, such as job accommodations and training, provided for under the national disability insurance programme. The system was not designed for the unexpectedly large number of people found to be disabled for psychological reasons. Consequently the re-integration function of the WAO 'failed entirely' (de Vroom and Rovers, 1997).

The concept of partial benefit commensurate with earning capacity was not rigorously applied (Aarts *et al.*, 1996b). The difficulties a disabled person might face in finding commensurate employment - 'the labour market consideration'- were assumed, by an administrative decision in 1973, to result from discrimination rather than just economic conditions and impairment (Aarts *et al.*, 1996b). The threshold at which a person became entitled to a full benefit was sufficiently low for rigorous assessment of earnings capacity to be unnecessary and the administrators are generally thought to have adopted over-lax practices. Thus, partially disabled applicants tended to be treated as if they were fully disabled. By 1986 as few as 12 per cent of new disability beneficiaries were awarded partial benefits.

The most important change in 1987 was that labour market considerations were no longer to be taken into account in establishing the level of disability. It had been estimated that up to 50 per cent of recipients were hidden unemployed. Benefits to non-working partially disabled people became a mixture of disability and unemployment benefits, proportionate to degree of disability. Despite the WAGW requirements on employers to make accommodations, among other employment promotion measures, the old practices continued and people were still declared fully disabled on a large scale (de Vroom and Rovers, 1997). It soon became clear that the impact of the 1987 reforms would be much smaller than the estimated 50 per cent reduction in disability beneficiaries and in 1989 the government adjusted its estimate to a mere ten per cent (Aarts *et al.*, 1996b).

The TBA Act (Restriction of Claims on the Disability Benefits Regulations) came into effect on 1 August 1993 and its provisions remain at the time of writing. The TBA limited eligibility for WAO and AAW to five years, changed the criteria by which lost earnings were assessed, introduced age-related rates, reduced the overall level of payment and introduced reassessment of existing claimants.

Assessing eligibility for partial capacity benefit

Workers who claim unfitness for work because of illness or infirmity (conditions which are not defined in the social security legislation) have to undergo a medical and technical assessment. A trained health insurance specialist carries out a medical examination, often complemented by tests by clinical specialists, to reach a clinical diagnosis and an estimate of the person's physical and/or mental restrictions and remaining capabilities. The level of work disability is determined by a technical procedure. A computerised system matches restrictions and capabilities against the job demands of several thousand occupations. If a fit is found with at least three occupations, the person is deemed able to work. Whether the jobs are vacant is not relevant, as long as there are at least ten real jobs for all of the three occupations. However, if the loss of earning capacity is high enough, the person can be labelled as officially disabled: the level of disability is dependent on the difference between the income from the last job held and that of the second best paid of the three best paid jobs.

This use of the 'acceptable employment' criterion differs from the pre-1993 concept of 'suitable work' in that education and previous occupation are no longer taken into account.

81

Calculation of benefit[7]

There are six partial disability categories, ranging from 15 to 25 per cent up to 80 per cent disabled. The category 80 to 100 per cent is considered to be full incapacity. Benefits are provided as a percentage of previous earnings in each category, progressing in steps from 14 to 70 per cent.[8] Previously, benefit was 70 per cent of last earned salary up to age 65.

Under the new arrangements,[9] the WAO benefit is split into two periods. In the first period, duration depends on the employee's age: nil for beneficiaries under age 32, rising by six months for each five year age band up to age 57.[10] When the first period is exhausted, the disabled person may claim a follow-up benefit for the second period. This time the amount of the benefit is calculated according to the minimum wage and the pervious wage, with an age-related supplement. As before, the benefit payable depends on the degree of disability.

As with the WAO, the amount of AAW benefit depends on the degree of incapacity for work but those with incapacity of less than 25 per cent are excluded from the AAW.[11]

Effects of the changes to WAO/AAW benefits

The changes to the benefit arrangements, along with the employer obligations and incentives outlined above, were expected to increase numbers leaving the benefit or moving to a lower rate of benefit and numbers resuming work or increasing their hours of work.

---

[7] *Example of a calculation of a WAO benefit:* Before she became work incapacitated, Mrs Apple earned ƒ 3,500 a month. After the WAO assessment, the AdO concludes that, with less heavy work than she used to do, she is capable of earning ƒ 2,500. Within the framework of the WAO assessment, this amount is referred to as 'remaining earning capacity'.

The WAO benefit is fixed as follows:

$\dfrac{3,500 - 2,500}{3,500} \times 100\% = 28\%$ work incapacitated,

so she is categorized as being 25% - 35% work incapacitated. Her benefit amounts to 21% of the daily wage. Mrs Apple's daily wage = ƒ 160.92 (ƒ 3,500 : 21.75). So Mrs Apple's benefit is ƒ 33.79 per working day.

[8] *Degree of disability and amount of benefit*

Degree	Amount
15 to 25%	14% of 100/108 x daily wage
25 to 35%	21% ....
35 to 45%	28%
45 to 55%	35%
55 to 65%	42%
65 to 80%	50.75%
80% or more	70%

[9] For further details, see Ministry of Social Affairs and Employment (1997).

[10] Age when qualifying and duration of first period in years

Age	Years
up to 32	0
33 - 37	0.5
38 - 42	1
43 - 47	1.5
48 - 52	2
53 -57	2.5
58	6
59 and over	until aged 65

[11] The amount of the benefit is based on a statutory 'basic rate' approximating to the gross minimum wage. The rate per day is age-related between ages 18 and 23: the rate for someone aged 23 is more than twice that for someone aged 18. AAW benefits are also granted for five years.

WAO/AAW claimants younger than 45 on 1 August 1993 were medically reassessed in 1994, 1995 or 1996 on the new criterion of 'suitable employment' and since then have received only temporary benefits. In 1994 and 1995 respectively 53,000 and 38,000 people were reassessed (de Vroom and Rovers, 1997).

The number of benefits terminated after the introduction of the 1993 legislation increased from 85,000 in 1993 to 105,000 in 1994 and 1995, almost entirely due to the re-examination of beneficiaries (Beljaars and Prins, 1997). It had been expected that about 21 per cent of recipients would leave benefit or receive a lower payment: 50 per cent of those had been expected to resume work or extend their working hours. However, an interim evaluation, relating to two cohorts aged under 35 (in 1994) and 35 to 40 years (in 1995), found that 52 per cent and 35 per cent respectively left the benefit or received a lower benefit (Beljaars and Prins, 1997).

Fewer people than expected had resumed or increased work one year after reassessment. Only 22 per cent of those re-evaluated as fully or partially able to work had increased their employment; further analyses show higher rates of work resumption in the group not working before reassessment than in the group that (partially) worked (Beljaars and Prins, 1997). Of the rest deemed fully or partially capable of work, one year on about half received unemployment and social assistance benefits and half received no benefits at all.

After a drop in total recipients of more than 60,000 between the end of 1993 and the end of 1995, the last four months of 1996 showed an upward trend, with increasing intake and decreasing outflow.

WAO benefit wage supplement

A person who is entitled to a WAO benefit may be granted a supplement to that benefit, for a maximum of four years' employment, if he or she accepts employment at a lower wage than his or her theoretical earning capacity. This statutory regulation came into force on 1 April 1996. The supplement is designed as a work incentive for the partially disabled employee. Since the TBA reforms of 1993 there can be a substantial difference between theoretical earnings (upon which WAO benefit is based) and real earnings. As this difference might hinder acceptance of paid work, the wage supplement was introduced to bridge the gap temporarily. There is no similar provision for groups other than partially disabled people.

The partially disabled person, who must be in employment, must apply for the wage supplement, although the AdO which grants the supplement may take the initiative to prompt the person involved to accept employment. The employee has to apply to the AdO which administers the benefit within two months of starting the employment. A late application may be accepted if the AdO agrees that the reason is valid. As the supplement is part of the WAO benefit, the same regulations, such as the obligation to give information, apply. The supplement is paid to the employee as part of the WAO benefit.

According to rules formulated by the Lisv, and not based on legislation, employment may be in either the public or private sector and may be with a new employer or adapted work at an adapted payment with the original employer. The job must be permanent or a temporary contract of at least six months. It must average at least 15 hours per week, unless the average working week was shorter before disability, and must be of a minimum of eight hours a week. If an employee starts part-time work while still capable of working full time a wage supplement is possible but will be reduced proportionately.

The employee must receive at least the minimum wage or the wage stipulated by collective agreement, or a lower wage when wage dispensation has been granted. As there is no non-accumulation clause, the provision may supplement low wages which result from other measures such as wage dispensation. The supplement is adjusted in such a way that the combination of supplement, WAO benefit, wage and any other benefit (such as sickness benefit) can never be higher than the wage of an equivalent non-disabled earner.

The supplement may amount to a maximum of 20 per cent of the theoretical earnings capacity.[12] It is granted for a maximum of four years, tapering from 100 per cent in the first year to 25 per cent in the fourth year. The period of benefit ends precisely four years after the first claim even if the employee has not been constantly employed during this period. The supplement continues during episodes of illness, however. Entitlement is renewed annually.

In fixing the budgets for the various AdOs, the Lisv assumed the number of wage supplements at five per cent of the population of people with a partial disability. The government expects about 10,000 people to receive a wage supplement at an annual cost of 50 million NGL. Awards cannot exceed the budget for the calendar year.[13] The first information on use and expenditure since April 1996 is available in the second half of 1997.

Other incentives to work

There are several separate work incentive measures for disabled people in special circumstances. All have relatively small budgets attached. One is described below.

Incentives to employment for disabled persons aged 50 and over

Older (50 years and over) disabled individuals who have received benefits for at least two years may receive an annual incentive benefit if they resume either full-time or part-time work. The benefit amounts to 60 per cent of the benefit that was saved. Given the age distribution of WAO beneficiaries, the target group for this benefit is large at around 500,000. Since it was introduced in 1995, a total of 325 has been achieved out of an anticipated 7,300.

BENEFITS FOR REHABILITATION

Here we describe two measures which aim to encourage disabled people into training and into trial employment and one measure which provides disabled workers with grants for adaptation of work.

Postponement of estimation of degree of disability after training

As a disabled person's employability can increase after completion of training, in theory the assessed degree of disability should reduce. This measure allows a WAO/AAW beneficiary to retain the original disability benefit for a full year after completion of training while searching for suitable employment. It is intended as an incentive to pursue training.

---

[12] The amount of the supplement is expressed as a percentage of the difference between the higher benefit which would be obtained according to the theoretical earnings capacity and the lower actual benefit.

[13] As the Lisv calculated the budgets for the AdOs on the basis of the maximum percentage supplement and the maximum earnings capacity, there is some scope for AdOs to vary their budgets.

Re-integration benefit for trial employment

The goal of this new re-integration instrument is to give an employee with a partial disability, who receives both a AAW/WAO benefit and a WW benefit, the opportunity to do unpaid work for a trial period of three months at the most, for a new employer in the private or public sector. During this trial employment the employee receives a re-integration benefit from the AdO which guarantees the same income. The measure was introduced in 1996. The rationale is to avoid the risk of an employer selecting an employee without a work incapacity in preference to one with, no matter how skilled and motivated the latter is and even if the financial risk of employing the latter is limited. The incentive is aimed at both the employer and the employee. Trial employment with the current employer is excluded; thus the target group is limited to people with a partial capacity for work who have an employer who cannot help them.

The re-integration benefit replaces the WW benefit, which ends as soon as the employee starts the unpaid work. As the level of the re-integration benefit is equal to the level of the WW benefit the employee should not lose out financially. Working on the basis of trial employment is entirely voluntary. The employee may always refuse an offer by the AdO or the potential employer without negative consequences for the WW benefit or the AAW/WAO benefit. During the trial employment, the AAW/WAO benefit will not be discontinued or revised.

The AdO cannot legally grant a re-integration benefit if the work is not suitable for the employee and will refuse it if it is evident that the trial employment will harm the employee's health. Nor can the benefit be granted legally if the employer has not closed a liability insurance for the employee. It will not be granted if it can be fairly assumed that the employee would have been taken on for the job in any case.

After the trial employment has ended, the employer is not obliged to hire the employee. If the employee is not taken on, the WW benefit is resumed to supplement the AAW/WAO benefit. If the employer decides to hire the employee after the trial employment period the various other re-integration measures may be used.

If the employee interrupts or ends the unpaid work prematurely, the re-integration benefit is stopped. Holidays are not possible. However, if the employee falls ill during the trial employment, he/she receives a benefit on the basis of the ZW (Sickness Act). As soon as unpaid work is resumed, the maximum period of three months is extended by the period of sickness, so that the employee is able to work with a re-integration benefit for a period of three months in total.

An employee wishing to do unpaid work on the basis of trial employment, personally has to apply to the AdO which pays the AAW/WAO. This is thought to prove that the employee is well motivated to go back to work. An employer wanting to use this instrument cannot direct the request to the AdO but must encourage the employee to do so. The Lisv advises the AdOs not to wait passively for requests but to use the instrument actively, in the direction of both employers and employees. In principle, the employee has to submit the request four weeks before the trial employment begins but there is some flexibility to consider later requests.

The Lisv has fixed a budget of nine million NLG, based on AdO estimates and an overall assumption that the number of trial employments would be five per cent of the population 'WW and AAW/WAO combined'. Take-up is not known yet because of the date of commencement. In reporting on take-up to the Lisv, the AdOs must provide evidence of the result of the trial employment and whether or not it was followed by regular employment.

GRANTS FOR EXTRA COSTS OF WORK

The AAW allows employees to recover from the AdO the costs of special measures for adapting the work to their needs. These adaptations are not bound to one workplace and can be taken elsewhere. Examples include financial means for transport to and from work, special shoes, and education costs. Table N.3 shows the number and costs of those grants.

As AAW grants may be given for more years, the total workers with special measures is higher (but numbers are unknown).

Table N.3
Grants paid to employees

Year	Numbers	Total NLG education	Total NLG not including education
1994	4900	1100	3800
1995	660	7000	2500

Source: de Vos *et al.*, 1996

There are also subsidies paid to the employer rather than to the disabled person which are described in the following section.

SUBSIDIES TO EMPLOYERS

Several subsidies are available to employers towards the costs of employing a disabled worker. These divide between relief of part of wage and sickness costs and compensation for the extra costs incurred in employing a worker who is disabled. Some of the latter are indirect benefits to disabled workers.

Wage subsidies

The WAGW specifies that a disabled employee is entitled to the same wages as a non-disabled worker with a comparable job and the same working hours. However, the employer may get permission from the AdO to pay lower wages if the disabled employee's productivity is much less than usual. In 1995, the estimated number of permissions granted was 540 (540 in 1993, and 480 in 1994). The total number of people working with dispensation is higher, because dispensation can be given for several years. In 1993, for example, there were 850 running dispensations (de Vos and Smitkam, 1997).

All employers in the private sector who take on a partially disabled person can apply for a *wage-cost subsidy* under the TAV. This amounts to a maximum of 20 per cent of the salary and can be paid for no longer than four years. In 1994 and 1995 respectively 3,135 and 2,661 subsidies were granted (de Vos and Smitkam, 1997).

Relief of obligation to supplement sickness benefit

If persons who have been declared partially unfit for work do return to work, but fall ill, their sickness benefit is increased to 100 per cent of the salary which they would otherwise receive. This means that the employer no longer has to supplement the sickness benefit previously set at 70 per cent. This is only for employers in the market sector and only for new employers. Numbers granted were 230 in 1994 and 420 in 1995 (de Vos and Smitkam, 1997).

Compensation for costs incurred

Supervision subsidy, introduced in 1992, awards a maximum of NLG 4,000, only if it is evident that extra time and effort is necessary to integrate into the workplace a potential employee who is disabled. In 1994 and 1995, respectively 2,179 and 1,753 subsidies were granted (de Vos and Smitkam, 1997).

Allowance for personal assistance on the job was introduced in 1994. It applies to those who can work in mainstream employment only if some personal assistance is provided. The employer may receive a compensation for 15 per cent of the hours worked by the disabled person. Some job coaching experiments, for people with mental disabilities, have made use of this allowance (Krug, 1995). In 1995 there was personal assistance for 0.01 per cent of the total working population in the private sector (de Vos and Smitkam, 1997).

Subsidies for workplace improvements: the AAW provides the financial means for employers to recover the costs of adapting the workplace to the needs of employees (as required by the WAGW). The AdOs decide on the adaptations needed. In 1994 and 1995 respectively, 730 and 660 grants were made (de Vos *et al.*, 1995).

Effects of financial measures

Research has found that these measures have had very little effect, especially the labour cost subsidies and relief of the obligation to pay 70 per cent of wages if the worker falls ill. Subsidies are temporary and may be insufficient to overcome employers' reluctance to hire less productive workers (den Uijl et al., 1996). Employers rarely claim compensation for education and work adaptation costs. It has been found that few employers have objections to such installations (Timmermans and Schoemakers-Salkinoja, 1996) and in fact 80 to 90 per cent of adaptations are paid for by employers without recourse to special funding (de Vos *et al.*, 1995 and 1996).

Lack of awareness among employees and among employers, who must apply, reluctance to accept there is a need, red-tape and frequent changes in fragmented legislation have been contributory factors in the very low take-up (den Uijl *et al.*, 1996). The main obstacle is found to be 'risk selection' among employers who prefer healthy employers as opposed to those at risk of dropping out because of ill health. The risk outweighs the positive benefits of wage subsidies and other financial compensations (den Uijl *et al.*, 1996).

COMMENTARY

Although the concept of partial capacity for work is fundamental to the Dutch labour and income system, income support and employment policies have had limited success in returning recipients of partial disability benefits to work. Recent measures to reduce individual reliance on and access to disability benefits have not resulted in the expected numbers resuming work or extending their working hours, although larger than expected numbers left the benefit or received a lower benefit. One effect appears to have been to increase dependence on unemployment and social assistance benefits, and some ex-recipients appear to have disappeared from the benefit system altogether.

In addition to measures to restrict access to disability benefits, the current Dutch approach contains a mix of financial incentives to partially disabled people and employers to promote recruitment, economic incentives to employers to promote retention, and legal obligations to prevent absence through sickness. All of these measures have been introduced since 1992, following legislation in the 1980s which had limited success in obliging all parties in the employment sector to facilitate employment of disability benefit recipients. Proposed further legislation will increase financial incentives, rather than obligations, notably through extension of market economy principles to disability insurance.

Take-up of financial incentives has been limited, so far, in part because of lack of awareness, frequent changes in fragmented legislation and bureaucratic obstacles. However, the main obstacle to recruitment is employers' preference for healthy employees as opposed to those perceived to present a risk because of ill health. Further measures are proposed to circumvent these problems but anti-discrimination legislation is improbable in the short term because of the complexity of existing Dutch legislation.

The effectiveness of employment support and vocational rehabilitation services has come under scrutiny. The same agency assesses eligibility for disability benefits and opportunities for (re)integration but the tendency towards awarding full benefits has reduced use of services for return to work. Market competition between agencies is currently thought to offer a solution.

The system of partial capacity benefits in the Netherlands is designed to complement lost earnings and, as such, does not primarily reflect capacity to work. The Netherlands has the highest rate of part-time employment in the EU but it is not clear how far the benefit supports part-time work or accommodates the needs of people with fluctuating capacity for work. The low take-up of wage dispensations, and the very large sheltered employment sector suggest that the number of people in open employment with reduced productivity is low. It is known that almost no people with learning disabilities are in open, competitive employment.

REFERENCES

Aarts, L., Burkhauser, R. and de Jong, P, (1996a) 'A Cross National Comparison of Disability Policies: Germany, Sweden and the Netherlands vs the United States', in *Rehabilitation of partially disabled workers in the workforce in various European countries: decisive factors seen from an international perspective*, Papers from an expert meeting held in Utrecht 4 and 5 November, 1996.

Aarts, L., Burkhauser, R. and de Jong, P. (1996b) *Curing the Dutch Disease*, Aldershot: Avebury.

Beljaars, P. and Prins, R. (1997) 'Combatting a Dutch disease: recent reforms in sickness and disability arrangements in the Netherlands', *ABP World* (magazine of the Dutch Pension Fund for the Public Sector), 97/1.

De Koning, J., van Nes, P. and Gesthuizen, C. (1996) *Labour Market Studies: Netherlands*, Employment and Labour Market Series No 1, Luxembourg: Office for Official Publications of the European Communities.

Den Uijl, S., Bahlmann, J., Klosse, S. and Schippers, J. (1996) 'Re-integration of partially disabled employees' in *Rehabilitation of partially disabled workers in the workforce in various*

European countries: decisive factors seen from an international perspective, Papers from an expert meeting held in Utrecht 4 and 5 November, 1996.

De Vos, E.L., Kremer, A.M. and others (1995) *Werkaanspassing bij reintegratie na ziekte* (Adaptations of the work and workplace for job retention after sick leave), Leiden: TN-PG / Den Hague: Vuga.

De Vos, E.L., Nijboer, I.D. and others (1996) *Werkaanspassing en arbeidshandicap* (Disabled employees and adaptations of work and workplace), Leiden: TNO-PG.

De Vos, E.L. and Smitkam, C.J. (1997) *Instrumenten bij werkhervatting na ziekte* (Instruments (legal) for job-retention after sickleave), Amsterdam: NIA-TNO; Den Haag: Vuga.

De Vroom, J. and Rovers, M. (1997) 'Development of the disability regulations in the Netherlands', *Social Policy Journal of New Zealand*, 8, 78-96.

European Commission (1996) *Employment in Europe 1996*, COM(96)485, Luxembourg: Office for Official Publications of the European Communities.

Grammenos, S. (1995) *Disabled Persons Statistical Data: Second Edition*, Luxembourg: Office for Official Publications of the European Communities.

Knegt, R. (ed), Van der Heijden, P. et al. (1995) *Instituties van de Arbeidsmarkt: een restrospectieve studie*, (English summary, pp 227-232) Hugo Sinzheimer Instituut, Den Haag, V43 OSA.

Krug, R. M. (1990) 'Sheltered employment for handicapped people: trends and issues in the Netherlands', paper presented at the International Expert Meeting on Vocational Rehabilitation and Sheltered Employment held at Velm, Vienna, 6-10 November 1990, Paper No.4, Vienna: European Centre.

Ministry of Social Affairs and Employment (1997) *A Short Survey of Social Security in the Netherlands*, i 514, January, Central Directorate for Public Relations, Library and Documentation of the Ministry of Social Affairs and Employment in The Hague, and others.

MISEP (1995) *Basic Information Report Netherlands: Institutions, procedures and measures*, Employment Observatory, Brussels: European Commission.

Timmermans, J. and Schoemakers-Salkinoja, I. (1996) Rapportage Gehandicapten 1995, (Analytical Summary in English, pp 179-191) Rijswijk: Sociaal en Cultureel Planbureau.

CHAPTER 7

SWEDEN[1]

OVERVIEW

Sweden's traditional commitment to full employment has come under increasing pressure in recent years, but remains fundamental to its economic policy, which is based on growth and the maintenance of macro-economic stability. The centrality of employment in Swedish social policy is reflected in its linkages with other programmes, especially social security. Employment policies are viewed as taking priority over the provision of handouts. Such an approach is illustrated by recent attempts to reduce the numbers receiving long-term sickness benefits and disability pensions.

The aim of Swedish disability policy is full participation and equality for all its citizens; people with functional disabilities must have the same opportunities as others. Disability is seen as a relationship between a person and the environment and not a personal characteristic caused by injury or illness. Policies for the employment of disabled people are part of general labour market policies. The concept of occupational disability means that a condition which does not limit work capacity cannot be regarded as an occupational handicap. Social security and labour market policy assumes a partial work capacity in most cases and enables part benefits to be combined with part-time work.

Facilitating early return to work has become a major policy objective with an important economic rationale (Westerhäll, 1996). In addition to diverting funds from sickness benefit to rehabilitation measures and cash benefits, there have also been moves to improve co-ordination of medical and vocational measures, by making this a direct responsibility of the social insurance offices. More responsibility has been placed on employers and individuals to achieve more rapid return to work. Current debate concerning labour market policy, however, appears to focus primarily on measures for immigrants, young people and the long-term unemployed.

Historically, many disabled people have been employed in special programmes, either through the sheltered workshops run by Samhall, or in subsidised employment in the labour market. There is currently a renewed emphasis on transitions to open employment in the general labour market.

THE LABOUR MARKET AND DISABLED PEOPLE

Labour market characteristics and trends

The working age population in Sweden is 5.5 million. Labour force participation rates have remained high for the entire post-war period, reaching 85 per cent by the start of the decade. Labour force participation has declined amongst men aged 55-64, but less so than in other countries; only Japan has a significantly higher participation rate in this age group. Female labour force participation rates began to increase in the 1960s and by the 1980s were the highest in the world, and very similar to those of men, with a difference of only four percentage points. Labour force participation amongst young people has declined markedly during the early 1990s, mainly as a result of extended periods in education. Immigrants, particularly recent and non-European immigrants, have much lower rates of labour market participation than the rest of the active population.

---

[1] Eskil Wadensjö, Swedish Institute for Social Research, Stockholm University, was national informant for Sweden.

90

Compared to other EU countries, Sweden has a smaller proportion of self-employed people, mainly because the agricultural sector is smaller. Levels of part-time work, at 25 per cent, are significantly higher than the EU average of 16 per cent. Although Sweden is characterised by high levels of economic activity for both men and women, women are much more likely to be working part-time.

Until the early 1990s, Sweden was characterised by a high and increasing rate of employment and had very low levels of unemployment by international standards. The manufacturing, engineering and construction industries were the most severely affected by the recession of the early 1990s. By 1994-1995 there were signs of recovery in the manufacturing and engineering sectors, but not in construction. The public sector, which has historically been a major employer in Sweden, is now contracting and the number of people employed is expected to continue falling over the next few years. Compared with other EU countries, regional differences in wages rates and unemployment are small in Sweden (Swedish Institute for Social Research/ECOTEC, 1997).

Table S.1 provides summary information on the labour market for 1995. Levels of unemployment fell slightly during 1995, after a steep rise in the early 1990s, but remain at almost three times their 1991 level. Long-term unemployment as a proportion of total unemployment has also risen sharply, almost doubling between 1994 and 1995. Men are currently more likely than women to remain long-term unemployed. In the longer term, however, women's employment rates are likely to fall relative to men's, because of cuts in the public sector, where the majority of women are employed.

Table S.1:
Key labour market indicators in Sweden, 1995

	Men	Women	Total
Employment rate (% age 15-64)	72.6	71.6	72.1
Self-employed (as % employed)	16.3	5.9	11.3
Part-time (% total employed)	10.5	43.0	25.8
Activity rate (% age 15-64)	80.8	77.2	79.4
Unemployment rate (% labour force)	10.1	8.2	9.2
Long-term unemployment (% unemployed)	23.4	15.9	20.2

Source: European Commission (1996) Employment in Europe 1996

Labour market policy

Labour market policy in Sweden is geared to the maintenance of full employment. This has been impossible to sustain during the recessions of the 1990s but remains a long-term goal. To this end active labour market policies are pursued. During the early 1990s, approximately five per cent of the labour force were engaged in labour market programmes, which played a large part in reducing the unemployment rate.

State subsidies have been available to employers who contribute to an increase in employment. Unemployed people are also offered training and education with a view to increasing their opportunities of employment. These include special measures aimed at those who are occupationally handicapped and mobility impaired. The principle of encouraging work activity, including training, vocational rehabilitation and work experience, rather than allowing individuals to receive benefit in a passive way, is an important aspect of Swedish labour market policy. It is linked to time-limited receipt of benefits and a duty to accept suitable work or labour market programmes when they are offered.

In response to the rising levels of unemployment during the 1990s, there have also been moves to enhance geographical and occupational mobility, enhance skill levels, and facilitate expansion and recruitment by firms. There are no minimum wage rules in Sweden. Measures such as job-sharing, deregulation and growth in low-paid occupational sectors have, however, generally been resisted, although there are widely divergent views amongst unions and employers about the possible benefits of such measures, with employers tending to favour their introduction. From April 1995, there has been a particular emphasis on policies designed to assist the long-term unemployed, who are now the main priority group for the Employment Service (Swedish Institute for Social Research/ECOTEC, 1997).

Labour market institutions

Labour market policy in Sweden, with some exceptions, is organised within Arbetsmarknadverket (AMV), the Labour Market Administration. This is a government body with three levels; the National Labour Market Board at national level, 23 offices at county level, and local offices. The National Labour Market Board, together with the government and the Riksdag, the Swedish Parliament, outlines the general framework of labour market policy and determines the rules of the different programmes, as well as deciding on budget allocations for programmes in different counties. In addition to around 380 employment offices, there are 100 employability institutes (Ami); about half of these offer specialist counselling and vocational preparations for occupationally disabled people, and 20 of them offer services solely for disabled people.

Disabled people in the labour market

The Swedish definition of disability, as laid down in government documents and Acts of Parliament, does not regard disability as a characteristic of a person, caused by injury or illness, but as a relationship between a person and the environment. This is similar to the definition of handicap formulated by the WHO which also locates disability in environmental factors, rather than in the individual.

Labour market measures for disabled people are based on the concept of occupational disability. A person is regarded as occupationally disabled if he or she has, or is expected to have, difficulties in obtaining or retaining gainful employment as a result of an impairment, medical condition or illness of a physical, mental, intellectual or social nature. Occupationally disabled people qualify for particular types of support, and various grants and subsidies are made available to their employers. A person may only be regarded as occupationally disabled if an impediment exists in respect of a particular type of work; a medical condition which does not limit work capacity cannot be regarded as an occupational handicap. A broader definition of occupational disability which refers to the relationship between an individual's physical, mental, intellectual and socio-medical[2] condition and the organisation of the work environment more generally is used by Samhall, the government-owned group of companies responsible for sheltered employment.

Figures from 1991 suggest that 70 per cent of those registered occupationally disabled have a physical disability, with a further 18.5 per cent being classed as having socio-medical disabilities

---

[2] Usually drug and alcohol-related problems.

and the remainder accounted for by those with mental and intellectual disabilities (National Labour Market Board, 1991). Participation rates amongst disabled and older workers are generally high in Sweden. Wadensjö and Palmer (1996) attribute this to three factors: the work principle; full employment; and opportunities to combine work and partial compensation. The work principle, which has been at the root of Swedish social and labour market policy for many decades, is argued to influence not only laws and regulations, but the social attitudes and habits of the population.

The number of occupationally disabled people who are unemployed has increased rapidly in recent years, from a monthly average of 20,200 in 1991/2 to 54,200 in 1995, although the rise has been less rapid than amongst the population as a whole. Current projections suggest that disabled people will continue to experience great difficulty in the labour market over the next five years (European Commission, 1995).

Occupational situation of disabled people

Data from the 1988/1989 disability survey (SOU, 1991) show that although many disabled people have earnings similar to their non-disabled peers, people who have either mobility problems or severely impaired working capacity earn rather less than average; between 128,000 SEK and 129,000 SEK per year, compared to a mean of 148,000 SEK for the population as a whole. Disabled people are more likely to have poor working conditions such as being exposed to high levels of noise, heavy lifting or monotonous and repetitive tasks; for instance, 29 per cent of those with mobility disabilities reported having to lift heavy loads on a daily basis. This is a reminder of the causal links between manual work and physical disabilities for many workers.

EMPLOYMENT AND SOCIAL SECURITY POLICIES

Policies to promote the employment of disabled people

Disability policy has been integral to labour market policy since the 1940s. Many of the main provisions in respect of disabled people and employment were developed during the 1960s and 1970s. However, the current trend is to devolve responsibility for the rehabilitation of disabled workers to employers and the social insurance offices, reducing the role of labour market regulations.

There are currently two main areas in which employers are obliged to make provision for disabled people. The Work Environment Act (SFS 1977:1160, amended SFS 1991:677) creates a legal requirement for employers to adapt working conditions to individuals' physical and mental requirements, together with a duty to establish a scheme for job modification and rehabilitation. There is also a legal duty to remove architectural barriers in workplaces and other public buildings, so that they are accessible to those with reduced mobility and/or a decreased sense of orientation.

Secondly, for employees who become disabled, the employer is primarily responsible, legally, for identifying and determining the need for rehabilitation, financing and implementation of any necessary measures. The employer's rehabilitation inquiry may result in: modification of the workplace; changes in working tasks or redeployment; changes in working hours; job testing and job training; or education.

Labour market policy consists primarily of programmes tailored to an individual, seeking to secure employment via employment agencies and mobility grants, or to improve job skills by programmes of education and training. A special effort is made to promote the participation of those under 30 receiving disability pensions. Until 1991, their rehabilitation was dealt with by a special project, which has now been integrated into the main work of the Employment Service/AMI institutes.

A number of job creation measures exist in Sweden, some of which are aimed specifically at disabled people. AMU, labour market training centres, provide vocational training for disabled and non-disabled people alike; one recent estimate suggested that almost a quarter of participants were disabled (Thornton and Lunt, 1997). There have also been attempts in recent years to improve the number of young disabled people, especially those receiving disability pensions, who are placed by Labour Market Services. Supported employment was established on a trial basis in 1993.

Government policy requires that the percentage of 'occupationally handicapped' workers in labour market measures must be higher than their representative percentage in the population of unemployed jobseekers. Thus in the last quarter of 1995, 11.2 per cent of those enrolled in labour market measures (excluding wages subsidies and sheltered employment) were 'occupationally handicapped', as against 10.3 per cent of unemployed jobseekers as a whole.

Swedish labour market policy for disabled people, while based on the concept of 'work for all' has until now explicitly rejected a model involving compulsion. There is a growing recognition that the present legal framework may be insufficient to secure the employment rights of disabled people. The use of a quota system, because it would require registration of disability, is regarded as an unwarranted intrusion into the lives of disabled people, a view shared by disability organisations and employers, as well as by government agencies. The office of Disability Ombudsman was established in 1994 to monitor issues concerning the rights and interests of people with functional disabilities. The Disability Ombudsman aims to remedy legislative deficiencies by presenting proposals for legal amendment to government. Models of non-discrimination legislation are now being considered by Government.

Social security policy for disabled people

Although labour market programmes are undoubtedly important for disabled people, by far the largest programme, both in terms of costs and the number of recipients, is the disability pension scheme. The other two related programs are sickness insurance and work injury insurance.

In the 1980s absence from work due to sickness increased considerably, with the number of recipients of sickness and disability benefits for more than one year rising from 311,000 to 436,000[3] in the decade. The policy response in the 1990s was to reduce compensation levels for sickness benefit, give employers a legal responsibility for rehabilitation, give a co-ordination role to social insurance offices, practically abolish the right to work injury benefit, and restrict the disability pension by abolishing the labour market consideration (Westerhäll, 1996). The government has established cost reduction targets for sickness and disability payments (Wadensjö and Palmer, 1996).

Sickness insurance
Sickness insurance is universal and all workers resident in Sweden are entitled to compensation for earnings lost due to sickness or injury. There is no limit to the number of days an individual can receive sickness benefit but the social insurance administration recommends that local claims administrators investigate a move to the disability benefit system after 12 months.

---

[3] The population of working age in 1990 was 5.4 million.

Reforms in the 1990s reduced income replacement rates (from 90 per cent in 1990 to 75 per cent in 1996, after the third day of absence), required employers to pay for the first two weeks, and introduced a cap on supplementary compensation to statutory sickness benefits paid by occupational insurance or employers.

Work injury insurance

Job-related injuries and illnesses entitling a claimant to income replacement for more than 180 days are covered by a separate work injury insurance branch. Following intense debate as successful claims escalated in the 1980s, the law was changed in 1993 so that the burden of proof now rests with the injured worker. The temporary replacement rate was brought into line with sickness benefit, and social security no longer distinguishes between general sickness and work injury, except in cases leading to permanent income loss. As a result of these changes, work injury claims declined by almost 50 per cent between 1990 and 1995 (Eriksen and Palmer, 1996).

Disability insurance

Disability pensions date back to 1913. People aged 16 to 64 are eligible for a temporary or permanent disability insurance benefit if their work capacity is seriously reduced by a physical or mental impairment or illness.[4] The decision to transfer clients after about a year from sickness benefit to disability pension is at the discretion of individual adjustors and the timing is in practice flexible.

Disability pension, like retirement pension, consists of two parts. The first tier is universal. Eligibility is not conditional on past employment but is based on citizenship or long-term residency. This basic pension *(folkpension),* calculated by reference to a 'base amount', is the same for all claimants. The second part is an earnings-related supplement (ATP) introduced in 1960, based on the average of the best 15 years earnings (reduced proportionally for those who have spent less than 30 years in the labour market). Those with a low ATP pension receive a special supplement. Calculations are based on assumed earnings from the onset of disability to age 65. The ATP is funded by a special payroll tax. The basic pension was also intended to be funded from earmarked taxes, but its costs are now met out of general taxation.

Because of the very high rates of labour market participation, few claimants are not eligible for the ATP supplement. Those ineligible are likely to be people with congenital disabilities and other disabilities acquired at an early age (Wadensjö and Palmer, 1996). Benefit may be awarded at full, three-quarter, half or quarter rate (until July 1993, the rates were a half or two-thirds). On average full disability benefit replaces about 65 per cent of lost earnings. Occupational schemes provide on average an additional 10 per cent compensation.

From 1997 capacity for work is the only basis for entitlement to disability benefits; people with work capacity (whether or not in their previous occupation) are to be treated as unemployed. Previously labour market considerations had been taken in to account. From 1972 to 1991 a full disability pension could be granted to older workers (usually 60 or over) who had exhausted entitlement to unemployment benefits, regardless of medical condition, and from 1970 to the 1997 changed labour market factors were taken into account together with medical aspects.

It is administrative practice to grant only temporary pensions to those aged under 60, on the assumption that the person will recover and return to work. In reality, the recovery rate stands

---

4 From 1977, alcoholism was included (Lonsdale, 1993).

at only one per cent for those over 30, so that disability is to all intents and purposes a permanent status (Wadensjö and Palmer, 1996).

Institutional responsibilities

Policy in respect of employment and social security for disabled people is mainly made by central government, with some input by the National Social Insurance Board. Social insurance societies at municipal level are responsible for administration, payment of benefit and advice, under the supervision of the National Social Insurance Board.

COMBINING DISABILITY BENEFITS AND WORK

Swedish social security and labour market policy assumes that disability or diminished work capacity is partial in most cases and that many of those unable to work full-time can work part-time (Wadensjö and Palmer, 1996). All income support and labour market programmes have a part-time option and partial benefits can be combined with part-time enrolment in a labour market programme or with part-time employment; combining part retirement pension with part-time work is very common among those aged over 60 (Wadensjö and Palmer, 1996).

Partial disability pension is the single benefit-work combination specifically for disabled people. There are no specific in-work social security benefits. Grants can be paid to disabled people setting up a business full time.

Partial disability pension

The partial disability pension was introduced in 1960; the main aim being to recognise the varying degrees of disability, and facilitate a combination of pension receipt with other activities, whether paid or unpaid. At that time most recipients were women, who carried out household duties while receiving partial disability pension. The current policy intention is to enable people with reduced capacity to take and retain part-time employment, thereby increasing their integration into society. The partial disability scheme has not been evaluated.

Assessment

There is not any one clear concept underlying the assessment of partial capacity; it is decided on an individual basis, taking into account a large number of factors. The Organisation of the Social Insurance Societies issues a 50 page guidance booklet which is intended to provide a framework for decisions by local social insurance societies. This is being revised at the time of writing, and is to be made available to the public. In this context, it should be noted that very few social insurance decisions in Sweden are the subject of appeals and court cases, so that there are not the case law precedents which exist in many other countries.

Residual capacity for work is the point of departure in disability assessment procedures (Wadensjö and Palmer, 1996). Responsibility rests with an insurance officer. Grants are based on the judgments of several experts: the claimant's physician, an insurance medical adviser, the insurance office's rehabilitation expert and the vocational expert, as well as on the employer's experience.

Partial awards may be at three-quarter, half, or quarter rates; before 1993, rates were two-thirds or a half. Award of a partial pension may result from an initial assessment of the disabled person's capacity, or may be triggered by a decision to take up part-time work. Benefit is reduced according to the number of hours worked, and is independent of the level of earnings received. Temporary awards of pension will lead to a review of capacity when they expire. It is also possible for the social insurance office to initiate a review, although this happens very seldom.

Recipients of partial disability pensions

About one in four disability pensions is partial. It can be seen from Table S.2 that partial disability pensions, as well as full pensions, are more commonly held by women.

Table S.2:
Disability pension recipients by sex (1996)

	Full	*3/4*	*2/3*	*1/2*	*1/4*	*Total*
Men	149,697	3,496	1,118	29,714	3,291	187,316
Women	166,081	4,128	1,563	51,069	8,729	231,570
All	315,778	7,624	2,681	80,783	12,020	418,886

Source: Rfv *Statistikinformation* Is - I 1997:5

Receipt of disability pensions, both full and partial, increases with age. In the younger age groups, up to the age of 30, partial pensions are uncommon. The ratio of partial disability pensions to full is highest between the ages of 45 and 54 (see Table S.3).

Table S.3:
Disability pensions by age group - rate per 1000 registered insured (December 1994)

Age	*Full*	*3/4*	*2/3*	*1/2*	*1/4*	*All*
16-19	7.8	0	0	0	0	7.8
20-24	7.9	0	0	0.5	0.1	8.6
25-29	9.4	0.1	0	1.7	0.3	11.5
30-34	15.1	0.3	0.1	3.9	0.5	19.9
35-39	24.1	0.5	0.2	7.6	0.9	33.3
40-44	36.3	0.7	0.5	12.4	1.3	51.2
45-49	52.4	1.0	0.8	18.1	1.8	74.1
50-54	80.4	1.5	1.3	26.2	2.2	111.6
55-59	153.4	2.3	2.1	39.8	3.1	200.7
60-64	301.4	2.7	3.6	44.2	1.9	353.8
All	60	0.8	0.8	14.2	1.2	76.9

Source: Rfv *Statistikinformation*

The statistics do not indicate what proportion of those receiving partial disability pensions actually have part-time employment. The greater use of partial benefits by women may result from the greater opportunities for part-time work available within the female labour market, as well as including those who combine unpaid domestic work with receipt of disability pension. It is considered that almost all men with a part disability pension also have part-time work but that is not so for women (Wadensjö, personal communication).

As those with partial pensions who do not work are not generally entitled to other benefits, such as unemployment, social assistance or housing benefits, the award of a partial pension represents a cut in real income, and a saving in social security expenditure.

Combining work with pension does not lead to any additional entitlements, nor are any lost, although increased income will have an effect on means-tested benefits for housing and social assistance where these have been received. Within certain time limits, it is possible to return to the previous benefit without undergoing examination. Once this period has expired, a fresh claim for benefit must be made.

Trends in disability pensions

The total number of new disability pensions increased gradually from the mid 1970s to the mid 1980s, and declined slightly in the period between 1987 and 1990, when unemployment levels were very low. There was a very large increase in the number of new disability pensions between 1991 and 1993, which resulted not only from the economic recession of the early 1990s but from changes in the handling of claims for sickness benefit, which obliged firms to carry out rehabilitation investigations, rather than allowing employees to claim sickness benefits for indefinite periods of time. A large number of claims were also received in advance of proposed changes in entitlement conditions which had been announced. Following this peak, new awards fell between 1994 and 1996. Not only had eligibility criteria been tightened, but many potential claimants had been identified at an earlier stage, and were already receiving benefits. In 1996, the total numbers of disability pensioners declined for the first time in many years. There are no published statistics on the number of unsuccessful claims for disability benefits.

Table S.4:
New disability and temporary disability pensions (men)

Year	Full	3/4	2/3	1/2	1/4	Total
1990	17,793		262	5,588		23,643
1991	17,721		311	5,781		23,813
1992	20,982		469	6,831		28,282
1993	22,312	323	326	6,994	450	30,405
1994	15,872	907	20	5,582	1,036	23,417
1995	12,140	636	9	4,935	919	18,639
1996	12,304	637	5	4,424	934	18,304

Source: Rfv *Statistikinformation*

Table S.5:
New disability and temporary disability pensions (women)

Year	Full	3/4	2/3	1/2	1/4	Total
1990	18,273		351	8,226		26,850
1991	17,064		407	8,270		25,741
1992	19,343		617	10,140		30,100
1993	19,578	301	420	10,473	1,288	32,060
1994	13,723	774	18	7,820	2,779	25,114
1995	11,048	623	9	6,675	2,210	20,565
1996	11,424	661	6	6,568	2,282	20,941

Source: Rfv *Statistikinformation*

As Tables S.4 and S.5 show, the proportion of new partial pensions has increased, particularly among women.

BENEFITS FOR REHABILITATION

Rehabilitation has been given a very high priority since the early 1990s. Responsibility for occupational rehabilitation is shared by the labour market authorities[5], the social insurance office and the employer. Responsibility for co-ordination rests with the social insurance office. The same office assesses an employee's entitlement to sickness benefit and to rehabilitation benefit. The office is responsible for planning the rehabilitation of disability benefit recipients who are not employed.

People are paid rehabilitation benefits whilst undergoing an agreed programme of rehabilitation. Rehabilitation measures may be, for example, work rehabilitation programmes, an investigation at an 'Ami' and labour market training. Rehabilitation benefit can be paid for planned training on the job, with the person's employer or some other employer, with the agreement of the person, the employer, the physician in charge and the social insurance office. Training can start with a few hours a day and increase gradually, so that the individual can test and enhance working capacity, without the pressure of piece-rates or normal working hours (Westerhäll, 1996).

Benefits for vocational rehabilitation are paid at the same rate as the benefit payable before the period of rehabilitation, whether sickness, unemployment or disability benefits. A special rehabilitation benefit, payable at a higher rate than sickness benefit, was introduced in 1992. This was intended to provide incentives to participate in rehabilitation and promote an early return to work. However, it has been reduced in value and is now paid at the same level as sickness benefit, removing this financial incentive. Rehabilitation benefits can be paid at partial rates where an individual is engaged in the programme part time. When the programme ends they are expected to obtain employment, claim unemployment benefits or return to sickness benefit.

Tables S.6 shows the growth in take-up of rehabilitation cash benefits from 1992 to 1994, expressed as days per person with sickness benefit. Women use the benefit more than men.

---

[5] Decisions regarding vocational rehabilitation as a labour market programme are made by the labour market administration.

Table S.6:
Days with rehabilitation cash benefit, per person with sickness allowance, 1992-1994

Year	Men	Women	Total
1992	0.61	0.73	0.67
1993	0.89	0.99	0.94
1994	1.11	1.21	1.16

Source: RSV *Socialförsäkring* 1993 and 1994, Stockholm, 1996

Education capacity is the key factor in successful rehabilitation, as there are few opportunities in the Swedish labour market for those who are disabled and have only a low level of education. Poorly educated individuals are over-represented amongst the long-term unemployed.

EXTRA COSTS OF WORK

Grants may be made to disabled people and to their employers to cover the costs of technical aids, which range from simple machines such as text telephones to robots specially designed to carry out specific tasks. In the case of individually designed aids, these can be transferred to a new workplace when an employee changes jobs. Grants are available to disabled people to cover the purchase and modification of a car (or other vehicle) which is required for work purposes. Provision can also be made for the employment of a personal assistant to provide necessary assistance, such as signing or reading, to the disabled person at work.

WAGE SUBSIDIES

Provision of wage subsidies is in line with the general principle of favouring employment rather than cash support. The policy intention underlying wage subsidies is to compensate employers for the additional costs of recruiting a disabled employee, by acting as a subsidy for reduced productivity. Originally such subsidies were paid at differential rates to employers in the public sector, who received subsidies of 90 to 100 per cent as against 25 to 75 per cent in the private sector. Since July 1991 they have been available equally to all employers, at rates negotiated between the employers and the Labour Market Administration.

There are three main wage subsidy schemes. Open employment with wage subsidy is organised in all sectors of the economy. The government-owned Samhall group of companies provides employment in its sheltered workshops. In addition, sheltered work is available in the public sector (OSA) for those with mental and psychological disabilities. Together with temporary work, these three programmes accounted for around two in five disabled jobseekers obtaining work in 1995 (SOU, 1997).

Table S.7:
Participants in labour market programmes for disabled people (thousands)

Year	Samhall	Work with wage subsidy	Sheltered work in public sector
1980	21.6	29.3	0
1981	22.6	31.6	0
1982	23.4	33.9	0
1983	24.6	35.9	0
1984	25.3	37.3	0
1985	26.4	39.3	1.8
1986	27.6	41.2	4.8
1987	28.2	42.8	5.5
1988	28.7	44.4	5.8
1989	30.2	43.9	5.7
1990	30.6	45.0	5.7
1991	29.7	44.5	5.4
1992	29.1	42.6	5.5
1993	28.3	42.6	5.7
1994	28.5	46.4	5.4
1995	29.2	49.6	5.6
1996	28.3	46.2	5.2

Source: Åsa Olli, Arbetsmarknadspolitiskt Kalendarium, EFA and information from the Labour Market Board

Wage subsidies are paid to a maximum of 80 per cent of wages (based on a maximum wage of 13,700 SEK per month) plus corresponding insurance contributions. For severely disabled people, subsidy can be paid to 100 per cent of this maximum wage. Where subsidy is extended beyond the initial four year period, it is limited to 80 per cent in all cases.

Wage subsidies are discretionary. There is no formal limit to the number of subsidised employees who may be taken on by a single employer. The level of subsidy paid depends on the severity of disability. It is not fixed but is negotiated between the employee, the employer and the placement officer. The aim is for subsidy to be phased out gradually as work capacity increases. In 1994/5 the average subsidy level was 72.5 per cent. This represented a reduction in the average level of subsidy, although subsidies were paid to a larger number of people; overall, expenditure savings were achieved. Subsidy is available for part-time work as well as for full-time work. Many of those working part-time with wage subsidy are employed by Samhall.

Workers who are employed either with wage subsidy or by Samhall or OSA receive collectively agreed wages on the same basis as other employees (there is no minimum wage in Sweden). In practice, since disabled employees do not work night shifts or overtime, or carry out piece-rate work, their actual earnings are lower than those of their non-disabled colleagues. Those in blue-collar industries receive around 85 per cent of the average wage paid to members of the blue collar union (Wadensjö, personal communication).

In theory, wage subsidies are intended to be temporary. Initial awards are only for a maximum of four years. However, they can be renewed after the expiry of this period and in practice, people tend to remain in the programme where they are placed for substantial periods of time. There is no incentive for either employee or employer to end the arrangement. Of those leaving work with wage subsidy, around 20 per cent go on to obtain work without subsidy on the open market.

There have been few formal evaluations of wage subsidy and related programmes, but those carried out have generally been positive. The high labour force participation rate of disabled workers in Sweden is generally taken as evidence that they act as effective incentives to work. For a disabled person, the financial effects of taking subsidised or non-subsidised employment are identical; the key factor is likely to be the impact on the availability of suitable employment.

Wage subsidies are viewed with some ambivalence by disabled people and their organisations, as they are felt to be demeaning where an employee is able to carry out a job as well as a non-disabled person. On the other hand, they undoubtedly provide a positive incentive for employers to recruit disabled people.

Employment in Samhall does not always operate well as a transitional measure; disabled people find it difficult to move from there into open employment, possibly because of employer prejudice, although the numbers have improved somewhat in recent years from 650 in 1992 to 1,372 (4.2 per cent of the workforce) in 1995 (MISEP, 1995). Some possibilities of individuals being seconded to other companies whilst having their wages paid by Samhall have been developed in order to improve this situation. The aim is to enable potential employers to obtain a picture of an individual's capabilities before making a commitment to employing them. Samhall also offers a 12-month return guarantee for its former employees and the evidence is that many workers (around 30 per cent) do indeed return during this period (Thornton and Lunt, 1997).

COMMENTARY

The idea of providing individual financial incentives to work is not typical of Swedish labour market or social security policy. Work is viewed as a normative aspiration for disabled and non-disabled people alike, and benefit claimants can be required to participate in labour market programmes. There is therefore more emphasis on creating job opportunities using policy instruments such as subsidies to employers.

As there is no data available on the numbers of people receiving partial disability pensions in Sweden who are in employment, it is difficult to estimate their effects with any accuracy. The possibility of paying benefits in recognition of partial capacity reduces replacement rates and removes any potential disincentive to work. However, in the absence of employment opportunities, and in the context of rising unemployment amongst occupationally disabled people, such benefits offer at best a partial solution to the employment problems of disabled people. Policies affecting labour market demand are arguably much more important. The number of recipients of partial benefits is a quarter of the number of recipients of wage subsidies in open employment.

There appears to be a growing recognition of the need for legislation to counter discrimination against disabled people seeking employment. This is likely to gain importance with the increasing emphasis on seeking to integrate disabled people into the open labour market, rather than employing them on special programmes.

New policies to prevent job-loss through illness or disability, and thus reduce entry to the disability benefit system, have had a mixed success. Early intervention for job retention and return to work is likely to remain a policy priority.

REFERENCES

Eriksen, T. and Palmer, E. (1996) 'The concept of work capacity', paper to the Third International Research Seminar on 'Issues in Social Security', FKF/FISS.

European Commission (1995) *EMPLOYMENT Community Initiative: Summaries of the Member States Operational Programmes*, DGV, Brussels: European Commission.

European Commission (1996) *Employment in Europe 1996*, COM(96)485, Luxembourg: Office for Official Publications of the European Communities.

Lonsdale, S. (1993) *Invalidity Benefit: An international comparison*, Department of Social Security Analytical Services Division, Social Research Branch, London: Department of Social Security.

MISEP (1995) *Basic Information Report Sweden: Institutions, procedures and measures*, Employment Observatory, Brussels: European Commission.

National Labour Market Board (1991) 'Employment Counselling in Sweden', Number 3.

SOU (1991) *Disability, Welfare, Justice*, A Report by the 1989 Disability Commission, 1991: 46.

SOU (1997) *Aktivt lönebidrag: Ett effektivare stöd för arbetshandikappade*, 1997: 5.

Swedish Institute for Social Research and ECOTEC (1997) *Labour Market Studies: Sweden*, Luxembourg, Office for Official Publications of the European Communities.

Thornton, P. and Lunt, N. (1997) *Employment Polices for Disabled People in Eighteen Countries: A review*, York: Social Policy Research Unit.

Wadensjö, E. and Palmer, E. (1996) 'Curing the Dutch disease from a Swedish perspective', in Aarts, L., Burkhauser, R. and de Jong, P. (eds) *Curing the Dutch Disease*, Avebury: Gower.

Westerhäll, L. (1996) 'The rehabilitation of partially disabled workers in Sweden', in *Rehabilitation of Partially Disabled Workers in the Workforce in Various European Countries: decisive factors seen from an international perspective*, Papers from expert meeting held in Utrecht 4 and 5 November 1996.

CHAPTER 8

UNITED KINGDOM

Labour market strategy in the period from 1979 sought to reduce regulatory controls on industry, encourage incentives to work and promote individual choice and enterprise. Minimum wages were almost completely deregulated. A quarter of the workforce are in part-time jobs, on average one-third less well-paid. With a rise in low paid jobs wage inequality has increased.

The belief that out-of-work benefits are a disincentive to work has heavily influenced the UK social security system. The level of benefits, relative to earnings, has been reduced. Equally, it has been assumed that people need financial incentives to take up low paid work, and means-tested supplements to low wages have been introduced. Reforms to disability benefits policy reflected those two assumptions. Incapacity benefit is targeted at those who are medically assessed as incapable of work and those found ineligible are expected to claim Jobseeker's Allowance. An in-work partial incapacity benefit (Disability Working Allowance) has been introduced as an incentive to take up paid work and to meet the needs of people with limited working capacity. Links between benefit payment and active job-search for the unemployed have been strengthened and employment services for ex-recipients of out-of-work disability benefits have been augmented. Policy responsibility for social security and for employment rests with two separate government departments, both in Great Britain and in Northern Ireland.

Disability employment policies have focused on persuading employers of the advantages of employing disabled people and on practical services to disabled people for access to employment. At the end of 1996, the Disability Discrimination Act came into force. It confers a right not to be treated less favourably because of disability, unless there is a justification, and employers of 20 or more may have to make reasonable adjustment where the workplace or working arrangements place a disabled person at a substantial disadvantage. There is no specific financial support to employers to make adaptations; rather the support is tailored to the needs of the disabled worker.

THE LABOUR MARKET AND DISABLED PEOPLE

Labour market characteristics and trends

The working age population in the United Kingdom is 37.5 million. The overall labour market participation rate (76.6 per cent in 1995) is well above the EU average and has varied only slightly over the past ten years. The activity rate for women has remained constant at around 67 per cent since 1990.

The UK labour market is considered distinctive because of the growth of 'atypical' forms of employment. Part-time work grew most rapidly in the 1960s, however, and in the last ten years growth has been slower. In 1995, 24 per cent were employed part-time, with 44 per cent of women employees in part-time jobs. In the EU member states only the Netherlands has a much higher rate of part-time working and Sweden's is on a par with the UK. The distribution of hours worked is very wide in the UK. Part-time work is less well paid: on average, part-time employees earn two-thirds of the hourly earnings of full-time employees. Equal employment protection was extended to part-time workers in 1995, following a ruling that part-time women workers were unfairly discriminated against. There is a two year qualifying period for access to employment protection rights, however.

The share of temporary work, although growing, is relatively low. Self-employment rose sharply in the 1980s but in the 1990s the share of self-employment has remained static at around 13 per cent.

The rate of unemployment in 1995 was estimated at 8.8 per cent, below the EU average. Half of the unemployed are long-term unemployed. Regional differences in unemployment rates are narrower than any time in last 70 years (Robinson, 1997).

Table UK.1:
Key employment indicators in the United Kingdom, 1995

	Men	*Women*	*Total*
Employment rate (% age 15-64)	77.0	62.8	70.0
Self-employed (as % employed)	17.8	7.0	13.0
Part-time (% total employed)	7.7	44.3	24.1
Activity rate (% age 15-64)	85.7	67.5	76.6
Unemployment rate (% labour force)	10.1	7.0	8.8
Long-term unemployment (% unemployed)	49.6	32.3	43.5

Source: European Commission (1996a) *Employment in Europe 1996*

Labour market policy

Policies in place before 1 May 1997 demonstrated a continued commitment to a "flexible" labour market free from restrictive working practices, regulation and wage determination. Removing burdens on businesses was a prime concern. A series of reforms led to almost total deregulation of minimum wages and a reduction of the role of collective bargaining in wage determination. The UK is the only country in the study without significant minimum wage regulation. With deregulation of wage agreements, there has been a shift towards company or plant-level agreements, with more pay determination based on individual performance. A trend in the UK not evident elsewhere in Europe is an increase in low paid jobs and widening disparities in incomes (Robinson, 1997).

Promotion of individual responsibility and incentive to work were central themes of successive Conservative governments from 1979, alongside reducing the costs of the welfare state. A stated priority for action was 'an improved benefits system, which offers both strong encouragement to unemployed people to make efforts to find work and improved incentives to work' (European Commission, 1996b). Programmes for the unemployed, including long-term disabled people, focused on reducing the value of benefits, restricting eligibility, tightening their administration and introducing new programmes to assist access to work. Links between benefit payment and active job search were strengthened.[1] Changes to incapacity benefits in 1995 exemplify the dual policy aim of minimising opportunities for labour market withdrawal and encouraging greater labour market participation through active measures.

---

[1] An example is the Jobseeker's Allowance, introduced in 1996 to replace unemployment benefit and income support. To be eligible, an unemployed person must enter into a Jobseeker's Agreement which details the action s/he will take to find work.

The low wages available in 'entry-level' jobs taken by the unemployed mean that some individuals can be little or no better off in work than out of work and claiming benefits. In-work earnings supplements seek to avoid this 'unemployment trap' for families with dependent children. They were first introduced in 1971. A similar in-work benefit was introduced for disabled people in 1992. The policy is based on the assumption that heightened income is the main incentive to work. In 1996 and 1997 pilot programmes were introduced for groups for whom the unemployment trap is a less significant difficulty.

Within the range of benefits and services to promote access to employment, there are some financial incentives to unemployed people, such as lump-sum entry payments. Subsidised programmes of community work with public and voluntary sector employers have been wound down. Recruitment subsidies to private sector employers were re-introduced with the Workstart scheme which offers a payment phased over one year for recruitment of a long-term unemployed person. An evaluation of Workstart pilots found that considerable investment in placement was required.

Disabled people in the labour market

A new definition of a disabled person was introduced by the 1995 Disability Discrimination Act (DDA) in relation to employment and access to goods and services. A person has a disability if he or she has a physical or mental impairment which has a substantial and long-term adverse effect on ability to carry out normal day-to-day activities. Severe disfigurement is also included as a disability, as are progressive conditions which have some effect even though it is not yet a substantial adverse effect. Coverage is extended to someone who has had a disability in the past. The results of a new base-line survey of disabled people's participation in the labour force, using this definition of disability, are expected in 1997.

There are several sources of data about disabled people in the population and their economic situation drawn from sample surveys. The data most commonly used are from the Labour Force Survey (LFS). The LFS give extensive information, up-dated quarterly, about the characteristics of disabled people in the labour market in Great Britain.[2]

According to the Autumn 1996 LFS (Office for National Statistics, 1997) in Great Britain there were five million people of working age (15 per cent) with work-limiting conditions[3] and 2.4 million of those were economically active. Economically active disabled people represent 8.8 per cent of the labour force. Their activity rate is half that of the rest of the population. People with mental health problems are much less likely to be economically active than those with physical impairment or sensory impairments. The activity rates of disabled and non-disabled people increasingly diverge as age increases.

Nearly one-fifth of economically active disabled people were unemployed according to the ILO definition (unemployed, ready to start work in a fortnight, having looked for work in the last four weeks) in Autumn 1996, compared with under a tenth of non-disabled people. Unemployed disabled people are more likely to be unemployed for more than a year; half were long-term unemployed. People with learning difficulties and people with depression are most likely to be unemployed.

---

[2] In Northern Ireland there are approximately 75,000 disabled people of working age. Of those 19,600 are believed to be in paid employment; 33,500 are unable to work; 8,900 are looking after home and family; 4,100 are looking for work and 2,600 are available but not actively seeking work (European Commission, 1995).

[3] Respondents to the Labour Force Survey are asked whether they have a health problem or disability, expected to last for more than 12 months, which limits the kind of paid work they can do.

Employment Situation of Disabled People

Four in ten disabled men and one-third of disabled women are in employment, according to the Autumn 1996 LFS. A quarter of employed disabled people work part-time, 560,000 in total. Disabled men are significantly more likely than non-disabled men to work part time. More disabled women work part time than full time. Disabled people tend to be over-represented in partly skilled and unskilled manual jobs and under-represented in professional and intermediate occupations, although the distribution across industrial sectors is similar to that for non-disabled people.

The sheltered employment sector is small, compared with most countries in the study. Segregated sheltered workshops still exist but the trend for more severely disabled people is towards supported placements in open employment. In 1995 there were around 12,000 disabled people placed in workshops and 10,000 in supported placements.

EMPLOYMENT POLICIES FOR DISABLED PEOPLE

Past governments' commitment to non-interference in the labour market and promotion of individual enterprise have favoured policies of persuasion rather than compulsion. Their policy position was encapsulated by the declaration that 'the most effective way to promote job opportunities for people with disabilities is to get employers to recognise the abilities of disabled people and the business case for employing them' (Employment Department, 1994).

The long-standing legal obligation[4] on employers to employ registered disabled people to meet a quota, and to reserve designated posts, was repealed in 1996, along with special protection against dismissal. These measures were not enforced and were widely disregarded. The Disability Discrimination Act of 1995 (DDA) allows disabled people to take civil action against employers; there are no arrangements for investigation and regulation of employment practices. The DDA requires employers to take into account reasonable changes to the workplace or working arrangements so that an applicant or employee is not at a disadvantage compared with non-disabled people.

Financial incentives directed at employers have never played a significant part in UK disability employment policy which, since 1944, has assumed that disabled people in competitive employment should be employed on merit and not be demeaned by subsidies (Thornton and Lunt, 1995). The other main strategies directed at employers have been encouragement, dating from the late 1970s, to adopt voluntarily good practices in recruitment and employment, backed by codes of practice and schemes to acknowledge 'good employers'; and campaigns to raise public awareness of the abilities of disabled people and to persuade employers of 'the business case' for recruiting them.

Practical programmes are directed mainly at individual disabled people. Increasingly, disabled people receive mainstream education and training for work, and are expected to use employment support services open to all unemployed people. Programmes are directed in the main at improving access to employment, and thus reducing unemployment and benefit dependency. Job retention is not a major policy issue, although several measures designed primarily to improve access also support retention.

There are four main forms of special assistance for disabled people who need extra help in mainstream employment:

---

[4] Disabled Persons (Employment) Act 1944 in Great Britain; 1945 Act in Northern Ireland.

- vocational preparation and placement services, since 1991 increasingly contracted by local Placement, Assessment and Counselling Teams (PACTs) to independent specialist agencies, for disabled people who need help beyond that available in mainstream employment services
- the Supported Employment programme which, under the Supported Placements scheme, places severely disabled people with host employers, and can arrange supplements to the wages of those with reduced productivity
- since 1994, a co-ordinated programme of financial assistance and practical aids to disabled individuals to help overcome obstacles on the job or in getting to work, known as Access to Work (replacing several separate schemes targeted mainly at employers)
- from 1992, Disability Working Allowance, a new social security benefit to top up low earnings, designed as an incentive for partially disabled employees and self-employed people.

From June 1997, access to Employment Services programmes and services has been governed by the DDA definition of a disabled person; that is, a person with 'a physical or mental impairment which has a substantial and long-term adverse effect on his ability to carry out normal day-to-day activities' (Section 1).

Responsible bodies

Since the merger of the long-established Employment Department with the Education Department in 1995, responsibility for most elements of employment policy in England and Wales rests with the Department for Education and Employment (DfEE). A similar merger took place within the Scottish Office. Since May 1997, policy responsibility for the DDA has rested with DfEE, which hosts the Minister with responsibility for disabled people's issues.

Services are delivered by an executive agency, the Employment Service (ES) which covers England, Wales and Scotland (Great Britain). In Northern Ireland, a Training and Employment Agency relates to the Department of Economic Development which is accountable to the Secretary of State for Northern Ireland; the Agency's offices provide services which correspond to those in Great Britain although they are sometimes delivered in different ways.

The ES has joint responsibility with the Benefits Agency (BA), which is controlled by the Department of Social Security (DSS), for administering employment-related benefits. The BA administers social security benefits, including Disability Working Allowance, under the control of the DSS in Great Britain. (In Northern Ireland the Social Security Agency relates to the Northern Ireland Department of Health and Social Security.) ES was established in 1987 to link the payment of benefits with provision of employment support services to unemployed people. ES offices provide placement services (although only an estimated one-third of vacancies are notified to Jobcentres) and ensure that beneficiaries conform to the conditions attached to benefit receipt. ES delivers directly, or through contracts with independent providers, a range of assistance for priority groups of unemployed (or 'jobseekers') including disabled people. It operates Access to Work, oversees Supported Employment and offers support to unemployed disabled people within its mainstream services. It also oversees PACTS and PACT members, known as Disability Employment Advisers, who are based in Jobcentres.

Policy responsibilities for training for the unemployed, vocational training for young people, employer-based training and support for enterprises in Great Britain rest with local employer-led private companies (TECs and, in Scotland, LECs). These are responsible for about two-fifths of the ES budget, spent mostly on the two main training programmes. TECs and LECs sub-contract training services to a range of public, private and voluntary sector providers.

In the UK a 'bewildering array of benefits' is available to disabled people of working age; benefits were introduced at different times, for different purposes and for different groups of disabled people (Rowlingson and Berthoud, 1996). As in other countries, compensation for injury through war and military service is a long-standing element and is not covered here.

Three income replacement benefits exist for categories of disabled people incapable of work; as described in the next section certain recipients may undertake some work under very restrictive conditions. Unemployed disabled people who do not receive any of these three benefits may receive Jobseeker's Allowance. There is no out-of-work benefit for those with partial capacity for work, although claimants of Jobseeker's Allowance may be allowed to restrict their availability for work on grounds of physical or mental limitations. There are two benefits which may be held in and out of work; an industrial injuries disablement benefit and a benefit for extra costs of disability. Finally, there is an in-work partial capacity benefit, Disability Working Allowance. These are described briefly below. Not described here are means-tested reductions for disabled people for housing rental costs (Housing Benefit) and local property taxes (Council Tax).

Incapacity Benefit

In 1971, a contributory benefit to replace lost earnings arising from long-term incapacity for work was added to the range of national insurance benefits established in 1944, as a response to a growth in long-term sickness claims. In 1995, invalidity benefit was amalgamated with sickness benefit to become Incapacity Benefit (IB). The benefit is not means-tested but is taxable. It is paid at two short-term rates in the first year and thereafter at a higher long-term rate. Two separate age additions are payable depending on the age of onset of incapacity, with the higher of the two paid if the age of onset is below 35, and the lower for ages between 35 and 44. There are also additions for adult and child dependants. At August 1996 there were 1.78 million recipients (*Hansard*, cols 324-5, 13/3/97).

Severe Disablement Allowance

In 1984 a severe disablement allowance (SDA), funded from tax revenues, was introduced for severely disabled people of working age who have never worked or have insufficient national insurance contributions; SDA replaced two separate benefits. The amount of this allowance is lower than the insurance-based benefit. Anyone who became disabled for work under the age of 20 need only be incapable for 28 weeks to qualify. Others must prove that they have been 80 per cent disabled for at least 28 weeks. At August 1996, there were 355,000 recipients (*Hansard*, cols 324-5, 13/3/97). Around 80 per cent of SDA recipients are of working age (there is no upper age-limit for receiving the allowance once it has been awarded). More women than men of working age receive SDA due to the transfer of women to SDA from the former Housewives Non-Contributory Invalidity Pension. Rather less than half have intellectual disabilities (Grammenos, 1995).

Income support

Disabled people who are ineligible for the insurance benefit (IB) or for SDA may apply for Income Support (IS), the means-tested general social assistance benefit available for those not working 16 hours or more a week. IB and SDA recipients can also receive IS. It is designed to bring income up to a minimum level. IS may be the only income source or a top-up to other benefits. IS premiums are paid to groups not required to be available for work; pensioners, lone parents and disabled people under the age of 60. The disability premium (ISdp) is awarded if certain other 'qualifying' disability benefits are being received or if the claimant has been incapable of work for at least 52 weeks. In 1995 around one in eight

(739,000) recipients were disabled; of those, 231,000 also received SDA (Department of Social Security, 1996).

Jobseeker's Allowance

Disabled people not receiving IB, SDA or IS who are unemployed for more than six months may receive the income-based Jobseeker's Allowance. There is no test of disability for this benefit and numbers of disabled recipients are not available.

Industrial Injuries Disablement Benefit

Industrial Injuries Disablement Benefit is a non-means-tested pension for people who become disabled as a result of accident at work or industrial disease. It does not depend on having a national insurance contribution record and is tax free. The amount of the pension normally depends on the extent of disability and not on occupation or lost earnings. Supplements based on reduced earnings capacity are being phased out. Some beneficiaries may be entitled to an additional constant attendance allowance. The benefit can be paid to people in or out of work and in addition to any earnings replacement benefit. The number of recipients in 1995 was 237,000 and over 60 per cent of recipients were of working age (Department of Social Security, 1996).

Disability Living Allowance

Disability Living Allowance (DLA) helps to meet the extra costs of long-term disability, including mobility costs. It is a non-means-tested benefit for people who become disabled before the age of 65. It is tax free and does not depend on having a national insurance record. DLA was introduced in 1992, at the same time as Disability Working Allowance (DWA), replacing two separate extra costs benefits. It is meant for people who need help with personal care, with getting around, or both. The 'care' component is paid at three rates and the 'mobility' component at two rates. At February 1996 there were 1,231,000 recipients of working age, rather over half of whom were men. It is not explicitly intended to support people in employment but there are no restrictions on receiving the benefit in work. The benefit can be received in conjunction with the other benefits described here.

Disability Working Allowance

Disability Working Allowance (DWA) was introduced in 1992. It is a means-tested benefit which may be claimed by disabled people in paid work averaging at least 16 hours a week. As DWA is the only benefit specifically designed for disabled people in work, it is reported in detail later in this report. It is necessary to note here that eligibility for DWA depends on receipt on benefits already described.

Recent policy developments

Public expenditure on benefits for sick or disabled people now accounts for almost one-quarter of the total spent on social security benefits, is second only to that for people of retirement age and is considerably more significant than provision for the unemployed. Spending on Incapacity Benefit (and the former Invalidity Benefit) rose from £2.13 billion in 1976-77 to £7.97 billion in 1994-95 (House of Commons Social Security Committee, 1997a). The number of people on the main benefit increased by 250 per cent between 1977 and 1995. Growth in expenditure was attributed to weak controls on access to and continued receipt of the benefit, considered by Government of the time to be ill focused and subject to abuse. Reforms which came into force in 1995 sought to re-focus provision on people who were 'genuinely' incapable of work through sickness or disability, by tightening eligibility criteria and reducing the level of benefit.

The introduction of Incapacity Benefit (IB) in April 1995 was accompanied by a tighter test for assessing capacity to work, the 'all work' test. Government projections were that 200,000 existing beneficiaries would lose entitlement through the all work test and that a further 50,000 new claimants each year would be found capable of work. Annual savings of £1,720 million by 1997-8 were projected. Savings would also be assisted by the reduced rates of payment, resulting from abolition of earnings-related additions, changes to dependency and age allowances, and increase in the qualifying period for long-term benefit.

In the first year 100,000, less than half the predicted number, were found capable of work following the all work test. The shortfall can be attributed in part to delays in medical assessments and in handling of cases by the Benefits Agency, despite new recruitment of doctors and staff retraining. Four out of ten appealed against disallowance. There were considerable delays in the appeals.

It had been anticipated that 200,000 ex-recipients would claim unemployment benefit (now Jobseeker's Allowance) in 1995-96 and 40,000 did so (*Hansard*, cols 171-3, 26/11/96). It was estimated that a third of those found capable of work under the all work test and not entitled to unemployment benefit would be newly entitled to income support (*Hansard*, col. 247, 31/10/96).

Extra resources were allocated to the Employment Services to help ex-recipients of incapacity benefits into work. Around two-fifths of ex-recipients were expected to make use of mainstream job finding programmes (Jobplan, Jobclub and Job Introduction Guarantee) but in 1995-96 less than 500 started on each of the three main programmes. Of the 40,000 expected to receive PACT support, under a quarter underwent PACT assessment (*Hansard*, cols 171-3, 26/11/96; cols 78-9, 29/10/96). Numbers recorded as entering work via the Employment Service have been low; in 1995-96, rather over 1000 started work with mainstream ES help and a rather larger number with PACT help.

Assessment procedures
A new approach to assessing eligibility was a central element of reforms to disability benefits in the first half of the 1990s which culminated in the introduction of IB in 1995. The introduction of self-assessment marked a departure from medical examination towards recognition of the practical effects of disability. Self-reporting procedures may be involved in applying for any of the disability benefits (except for Industrial Injuries Disablement Benefit for which the extent of disability is assessed in percentage terms, based on a medical assessment).

Eligibility tests for income replacement disability benefits are now based initially on self-assessment of functional capacity. The 'own occupation' test applies for the first 28 weeks of a claim of incapacity to work and assesses the person's ability to do their usual work, supported by a medical certificate issued by their own doctor. After 28 weeks, those who continue to claim are subject to the 'all work' test (those with no usual occupation are subject to the all work test immediately). This assesses capacity to do any work determined by 'functional ability' to carry out activities.[5] Limits on ability are scored; a total of 15 points qualifies. Claimants complete a questionnaire and statements are supplied by medical practitioners and specialists. Claimants may be asked to undergo a medical examination if required by the decision makers (the Benefits Agency Medical Service).

---

[5] Walking, climbing stairs, sitting, standing, rising from sitting, bending and kneeling, manual dexterity, lifting and carrying, reaching, speech, hearing, vision and continence. Susceptibility to fits is also scored. The mental health assessment covers ability to complete tasks, cope with daily living, deal with other people and cope with pressure. For people with a diagnosed mental health problem, scores from this latter part of the test are combined with physical assessment scores.

Implications for people with partial capacity for work

The IB 'all work test' contains no reference to labour market conditions. Under the previous arrangements for Invalidity Benefit, incapacity for work had been judged by reference to medical condition in the context of factors such as age, skills and experience. Although most claimants have found the self-assessment test easy to complete, concern has been expressed about the difficulty of capturing fluctuating conditions (Davoud, 1996). Research indicates that the new rules exclude from incapacity benefit some disabled people with partial capacity for work, notably those who are unable to work a full day or week because of disability, those who need extra rests during a full working day and those likely to need substantial amounts of time off work for treatment and sick leave (Birkin and Meehan, 1997).

COMBINING BENEFITS WITH WORK

There are limited opportunities for recipients of IB, SDA and ISdp to combine their benefit with income from work. The only benefit specifically designed for this purpose is the Disability Working Allowance.[6]

Combining IB and SDA with work

Recipients of IB and SDA may undertake 'exempt work' on the advice of a medical doctor if it 'helps to improve, or prevent deterioration in, the disease or bodily or mental impairment' which causes incapacity for work. The rules allow the claimant to do some work without being considered as capable of work, thus avoiding disqualification from incapacity benefit. Exempt work is limited to 16 hours per week. It is also subject to an earnings limit of £46.50 per week (from April 1997). Earning above that limit is taken as evidence of fitness for work and means complete loss of incapacity benefit. (Claimants may also undertake up to 16 hours a week of voluntary work which pays reasonable expenses only.)

The rules for 'exempt work', introduced in April 1995, are more restrictive than those for 'therapeutic earnings' which it replaced. The original 'therapeutic earnings' rule was applied when disabled people undertook rehabilitative work under hospital supervision (Robbins, 1982). Guidance on use of the therapeutic earnings allowance was minimal: it allowed work for which the claimant had 'good cause'. The more precise conditions for exempt work appear to rule out people whose condition is static. Therapeutic work, on the other hand, was seen as having potential to help people with an eventual return to work regardless of the stability of their condition, as well as to offer some therapeutic activity for those not expected to leave benefit.

No data are routinely collected on take-up. According to research, therapeutic earnings exemption was used by only around two per cent of eligible recipients and less than a fifth knew about it (Lonsdale et al., 1993). Further analysis of the OPCS survey of disabled adults aged under 60 found two per cent of Invalidity Benefit recipients and one per cent of SDA recipients in work (cited in Rowlingson and Berthoud, 1996).

There is thought to be potential for greater use of the exempt work rule as part of a staged return to work programme, as used to some extent by Supported Employment agencies for people with learning disabilities (Davoud, 1996). Other commentators have suggested that

---

[6] Industrial Injuries Disablement Benefit may be combined with earnings from employment without restriction but published statistics do not show numbers of recipients in work. A stratified sample survey of successful and unsuccessful claimants found that one-third of successful claimants who had suffered industrial accidents were in employment but only one in ten of those who suffered from an occupational disease (Tremlett and Dundon-Smith, 1995).

'therapeutic work' is seen by disabled people as patronising and consequently deters participation (DIG, 1996) although this view is not supported by past evidence from research (Robbins, 1982).

Combining Income Support with work

Recipients of income support disability premium can work up to 16 hours a week if they declare their earnings. They may earn up to £15 per week before their benefit is affected. There is a special exemption to work up to 24 hours if the person's earnings are less than three-quarters of those of someone without a disability.

Disability Working Allowance

DWA was introduced in April 1992. It was conceived as bridging the too stark choice between relying on benefits and relying on earnings. The benefit is intended primarily to encourage disabled people off benefits and into work, by topping up low wages or self-employed earnings and so making work more financially rewarding. It was introduced following recommendations from the Social Security Advisory Committee (SSAC) that the benefit structure should provide incentives for disabled people to achieve independence through employment (SSAC, 1988) and the subsequent government review of disability benefits (DSS, 1990). DWA is aimed particularly at people on long-term incapacity benefits, to help them get back to work (DSS, 1996).

DWA was designed also in response to the identified absence of help for disabled people who can do some work but are not fully able to support themselves (SSAC, 1988; DSS, 1990). As partial capacity provision, DWA has two main aims:

- short-term rehabilitation - to enable disabled people returning to work to progress towards full-time work, through, for example, providing an opportunity to develop stamina or to build up skills or experience in a lower-paid job; and
- long-term support for disabled people who cannot work full-time because of a disability or who can work full-time but at reduced capacity (*Inside ES*, August 1996, cited in Davoud, 1996) .

In addition the benefit is designed to encourage disabled people to give work a try, without risk to their former rate of IB if return to work is unsuccessful within two years (as long as the person is still incapable of work).

DWA is strictly an in-work benefit. It was modelled on Family Credit, a means-tested benefit for families with children working 24 hours[7] or more a week. Like Family Credit, DWA supplements low wages (or earnings from self-employment) only and is not a general wage subsidy. Claimants of DWA must be in a paid job, of an average of 16 hours a week or more, which is expected to last at least five weeks. To qualify, disabled people in work must be receiving DLA[8] (or similar payable under war pensions or Industrial Injuries Disablement Benefit), or have received IB, SDA or the disability premium with IS, Housing Benefit or Council Tax Benefit in the eight weeks prior to starting work.[9] Qualification thus depends on current or past receipt of contributory, non-contributory and means-tested benefits.

---

[7] The hours threshold for Family Credit has since been lowered to 16 hours.
[8] Higher rate of the mobility component or the higher or middle rates of the care component.
[9] Some other minor qualifying benefits also apply.

The broad target group is people 'whose disability puts them at a disadvantage in getting a job'. Initial claims should be supported by a self-declaration that the claimant has a physical or mental disability which has that effect, guided by a list of functional disabilities. For subsequent claims, a self-assessment test may be required. This 'disability test' lists 20 areas (in mobility, dexterity and so on) where claimants may have a difficulty, and if any one applies the claimant is eligible. Renewal forms ask the claimant to specify the disability which places them at a disadvantage and to name a professional who will confirm the assessment. Those getting DLA at the higher rate or SDA previously are assumed to satisfy the disability test.

DWA is means-tested according to capital assets (a minimum of £3,000 and a maximum of £16,000) and the family's net earnings after tax and national insurance contributions (but disregarding some benefits which include DLA, IS, Housing Benefit and Council Tax Benefit).[10] The weekly payment depends on whether claimants are single or couples and whether they have children; credits are payable for children. An earnings taper applies; for every £1.00 earned above the threshold, £0.70 is deducted.

Once awarded, DWA is normally paid for the next 26 weeks regardless of any changes in income and most other circumstances. There is a supplement to the highest rate payable for people working at least 30 hours a week (introduced in 1995 at £10 and since up-rated). A rule introduced in 1995 allowed DWA recipients (with savings of less than £8,000) to receive free National Health Service prescriptions, dental treatment, sight tests and wigs and so on, as well as refunded costs of travel to hospital treatment and help with costs of glasses. These are in addition to the existing 'passported' benefits for DWA[11] and bring DWA into line with Family Credit.

Trends in claims and awards
Compared with initial Government expectations, the results to date have been disappointing. It was estimated that about 150,000 claims per year would be received and that 100,000 six-month awards would be made, giving an average caseload of about 50,000 people. By October 1996 in Great Britain[12], there were 11,350 recipients and in the four years from November 1992 a total of almost 17,500 new awards had been made. Take-up was initially slow; at the end of the first year there were 2,800 recipients (April 1993). By January 1994 there were 3,700 and 5,200 a year later. Numbers rose steadily in the two years to January 1997, however, as the Table UK.2 shows.

---

[10] A claimant is also allowed up to £60 of formal child-care costs for children aged under 11.

[11] Social Fund, maternity and funeral grant payments, minor works grants, free legal advice and assistance, and assisted prison visits.

[12] All official statistics cited here exclude Northern Ireland.

Table UK.2:
Recipients of Disability Working Allowance, January 1995 to January 1997

Quarter	Number
1995	
January	5,202
April	5,685
July	6,544
October	7,644
1996	
January	8,340
April	9,365
July	10,519
October	11,352
1997	
January	11,942

Source: *Disability Working Allowance Statistics Quarterly Enquiry,* various

Initial obstacles were the low number of claims (35,000) and the high proportion of rejected claims (77 per cent) in the first 18 months. At that time, nearly four out of five claims were rejected because the applicant had not started work or because they did not receive a qualifying benefit. The proportion of successful claims has since risen.[13] Those two obstacles to successful claims dominate the overall figures on reasons for disallowances between November 1992 and October 1996; in one-third of disallowances the qualifying benefit test was not satisfied and in a quarter of cases the claimant was not in paid work (*DWA Statistics Quarterly Enquiry October 1996*).

Characteristics of recipients
The *DWA Statistics Quarterly Enquiry October 1996* shows the characteristics of DWA recipients. Three-fifths were male, one-third of the total were aged between 30 and 39 and two-fifths aged 50 and over, and two-fifths had children. About 60 per cent were single people. Information on types of disability is available only for renewed and repeat awards. Bearing in mind that claimants may declare more that one type of disability, it is nevertheless interesting to note that 'exhaustion and pain' accounts for over 40 per cent of all types declared and confirmed in renewal rewards made in the four years to October 1996.

Information from the same source on claimants' employment situation shows that over a third of all awards between November 1992 and October 1996 were to people in self-employment. In January 1996, the average number of hours worked was 27 per week, nearly half worked for between 16 and 24 hours and just under three in ten worked for 36 or more hours (*Hansard*, cols 320-1, 1/7/96). At that time, around two-fifths (3,400) received the premium for working 30 hours or more (*Hansard*, col. 321, 1/7/96).

Evaluation
As noted, DWA was mainly aimed at getting long-term recipients of invalidity and incapacity benefit back to work. Table UK.3, which gives the main qualifying benefit in all new awards

---

[13] Sources from *Hansard*, cited by Finn (1994).

made in four years of DWA, shows that in only one-fifth of new awards was invalidity or incapacity benefit the main qualifying benefit.

Table UK.3:
Main qualifying benefit of new DWA awards between November 1992 and October 1996

Type of benefit	Number of awards
Disability Living Allowance (higher rate)	6,997
Disability Living Allowance (lower rate)	3,065
Invalidity Benefit	2,076
Severe Disablement Allowance	1,252
Disability Premium in IS/HB/CCB	2,337
Incapacity Benefit (higher rate short-term)	417
Incapacity Benefit (long-term)	1,312
All qualifying benefits	17,456

Source: *Disability Working Allowance Statistics Quarterly Enquiry October 1996*, Table 9

DWA's effect on enabling people to move off incapacity benefits was initially negligible. Movement from the main incapacity benefits to full-time work was in any case low, according to a sample survey conducted as part of the major DWA evaluation commissioned by DSS; in the period from Spring 1992 to Autumn 1995, only two per cent of the 1.5 million working-age recipients of one of the three main incapacity benefits moved off these benefits and into full-time work, almost all without the help of DWA (Rowlingson and Berthoud, 1996). The data in Table UK.3 indicate that when SDA is also taken into account, at least 5,000 people left benefit and entered or re-entered work and were awarded DWA in the four year period. (A number of ISdp recipients will have also taken up work.)

The figures in Table UK.3 do not show how many new recipients were already in work. It had been assumed that 70 per cent of the estimated 50,000 claimants would be people who had taken jobs in response to the benefit; the rest were expected to be already in work. The evaluation found that in October 1993 only 200 of the 3,500 DWA claimants had been encouraged into work by the benefit and that most recipients were already in work when they heard of it. As in well over half of new awards in the four years to October 1996 the main qualifying benefit was Disability Living Allowance, it may be assumed that rather less than half of new recipients were returning to work after a period out of work.

As Rowlingson and Berthoud (1996) note, it is important to distinguish between the short-term rehabilitative functions of DWA and its function as a long-term supplement to low wages. Rehabilitative aims were not the main focus of their evaluation of the use of DWA but the study found that people whose conditions had improved (some almost to the point of ineligibility) were much more likely to have found jobs. It is not possible to tell from the published statistics how far DWA has enabled recipients to progress in employment and move off benefit. The DWA evaluation study found that only a very small proportion of the study cohort had done so, and only about two per cent because their own income (as opposed to the family unit's) was too high for DWA.

The evidence suggests that DWA's main role has been to sustain claimants in work for extended periods through subsidising their low earnings. Rowlingson and Berthoud (1996) found that about half of those who claimed DWA in the first half of 1993 were still in work and eligible for the benefit in the Autumn of 1995; and around two-fifths of all those still in work two and a half years after they first claimed said that they would not now be in a job without DWA. In the four years to October 1996, 60 per cent of awards were renewals suggesting that the benefit does have an effect as a long-term wage supplement (*DWA Statistics Quarterly Enquiry October 1996*).

The evidence on repeat awards (that is, where there has been a break in employment since the previous award) shows only 1,700 instances in four years, suggesting that the provision is not much used to enable people with partial capacity to move out of and back into employment.

In explaining the initial limited take-up of DWA, commentators focused on the qualifying requirements, the family-based means-test, the complex overlap with other benefits and the possibility that some claimants may be no better off on DWA (House of Commons Social Security Committee, 1993) and the strict rules for the guaranteed return to IB within two years (Finn, 1994). These features of the benefit continue to attract criticism (Davoud, 1996; DIG, 1996). There is evidence that awareness of the benefit has been low (Rowlingson and Berthoud, 1996). An argument from the DWA evaluation is that there is an in-built contradiction in the system whereby having recently received an incapacity benefit, which demonstrates *inability to work*, is a qualifying condition for an *in-work* benefit. Rowlingson and Berthoud also argue that the premise that disabled men on the margin of work want short working weeks is false. A further identified obstacle to take-up of DWA is the requirement that claimants should be in work within eight weeks of leaving the qualifying benefits IB and SDA (Davoud, 1996; DIG, 1996).

BENEFITS FOR REHABILITATION

Disabled people can join mainstream Training for Work without the usual required period of six months' unemployment, proving that they are endorsed as disabled by Employment Services. Disabled people undertaking Training for Work can receive the Training Allowance, which is equivalent to any benefit they are entitled to, with a £10.00 per week addition. Eligibility for IB is retained for two years (as is the case when taking up DWA). People can train part time if they have a disability or have domestic responsibilities that prevent them from training full time. Under the outcome-based funding arrangements, there are financial incentives to providers to take on disabled people but screening out of people with the greatest needs is a suspected problem (Davoud, 1996; DIG, 1996).

Employment Service employment rehabilitation programmes can be undertaken by claiming a Rehabilitation Allowance but in most cases should be accompanied by a claim for Income Support (Davoud, 1996).

WAGE SUPPLEMENTS, SUBSIDIES AND GRANTS

Supplements and subsidies to wages are not a significant feature of UK provision. A consolidated programme of grants towards costs associated with employment of disabled people has recently been developed.

Wage supplements

Wage supplements for reduced productivity in open employment have only recently begun to operate on more than a modest scale, and only within the special context of the Employment Service *Supported Placement Scheme* which has extended the notion of 'sheltered' work into open employment. Employers are not compensated directly for reduced productivity under the Supported Placements Scheme; rather, the employer pays only a portion of the wage and the state, through an agency, pays the remainder.

The criteria for entry are that a disabled person, who complies with the DDA definition, should be 30 to 80 per cent productive relative to a non-disabled person and that they cannot otherwise obtain or retain employment on account of the severity of their disability (*Hansard*, col. 227, 27/6/96). Most of those in supported employment agency schemes have learning difficulties. Those whose wages are supplemented under this scheme may also receive DWA.

Wage subsidies

Until recently, the idea that employers should receive incentives in the form of wage subsidies has not been favoured in the UK. The few schemes giving direct financial support to employers of disabled people have not been promoted as financial incentives to take on disabled workers. Rather, they are said to offer an opportunity to discover disabled people's skills and potential, and to deal with any practical concerns, so building on the argument that it makes economic sense to employ disabled people.

Currently, only one small scheme, administered by the Employment Service, provides direct financial assistance to an employer. Under the *Job Introduction Scheme*, a private sector employer who takes on a disabled worker is paid a weekly grant of £45.00 towards the wages during a 'trial period', usually of six weeks but exceptionally extendable to a maximum of 13 weeks. The job can be full-time or part-time but it must be expected to last for at least six months after the 'trial period' has ended. The employer is expected to pay the normal rate for the job. The value of the weekly grant, has not kept pace with inflation since it was introduced in 1977 at £30 and the Job Introduction Scheme is under review.

Grants for access to work

In the past, financial support for employers was designed in the main to contribute towards the costs of adapting the working environment to meet the needs of a specified employee. However, take-up was always poor. Schemes once targeted at the employer, such as the Adaptions to Premises and Equipment Scheme, have now been incorporated in the overall *Access to Work* programme designed around the disabled employee. When introduced in 1994, there was no cost to the employer. However, 1996 changes made employers liable for part of the cost of help to existing disabled employees.

Access to Work (ATW), administered by the Employment Service, can pay for physical alterations to the workplace, special equipment or adaptations to existing equipment, deaf awareness training for co-workers, job coaches to help familiarity with new tasks, adaptations of a vehicle or help with transport to work costs, a communicator at interview, and other practical needs. ATW will pay for 100 per cent of approved costs for unemployed disabled people or those changing employer, and 100 per cent of travel to work and communicator at interview costs, regardless of status. For those in work, employers pay the first £300 each year and, thereafter, ATW will meet up to 80 per cent of the costs.[14] All the costs in excess of £1,000 over three years will be met.

The original aim of ATW was to increase numbers of disabled people in employment; it was intended that half of entrants would be unemployed. However, a survey one year after its introduction found 92 per cent already in work when they applied (Beinart *et al.*, 1996). In the quarter ending September 1996, Access to Work supported 4,233 people in work with continuous help, helped a further 456 new users in work, and helped 334 people to obtain work (*Hansard*, col. 80, 11/11/96).

COMMENTARY

In the UK, the pattern of policies and programmes was shaped over 20 years or so by the belief that unemployed people respond to individual incentives to work and that benefit levels induce a culture of dependency. Hence, the UK witnessed an emphasis on social security benefits which top up low wages and cuts in the value of unemployment and invalidity benefits, coupled with tighter eligibility criteria. At the same time, governments' commitment to non-interference in the labour market and promotion of individual competitiveness accentuated the post-war trend away from policies which imposed obligations on employers to promote the employment situation of disabled people. The idea that financial incentives might change practices in the recruitment and employment of disabled people has not been part of the UK approach. Thus, UK policies have been almost entirely directed at the 'supply side' of the employment equation.

Disability Working Allowance (DWA) has so far had limited success as a route into work for people with partial capacity for work. Re-entry to work from benefit may be adversely affected by the rule that requires DWA to be claimed in work and within eight weeks of leaving long-term incapacity benefit. It is clear that ex-recipients of IB are not using Employment Service provision at the expected level. They are likely to be out of touch with the current labour market and may find it hard to identify what they might want from employment finding services (Birkin and Meehan, 1997). Co-ordination between benefit agency and employment staff in benefit eligibility decisions has been advocated (Davoud, 1996), as has early in-depth exploration of ex-IB jobseekers employment goals and job search needs (Birkin and Meehan, 1997). In the UK, there is no special provision in the benefit system to give extra financial support to disabled people in the process of rehabilitation.

DWA has had more impact as a long-term wage supplement for people in low-paid work with limited earnings capacity. Take-up of the benefit has been much higher among people already in work, as has been the case with the Access to Work scheme. There is some evidence that DWA may be meeting the needs of certain groups of people with partial capacity for work in particular; people who report exhaustion and pain, and disabled women who choose to work part-time. Its rehabilitative functions are hard to determine, however.

Unlike provision in most other study countries, partial capacity provision in the UK does not allow recipients to move in and out of work while retaining the benefit. There is no provision for people with limited capacity to work who are unable to find suitable work, other than mainstream benefits, and for them the 'sick or fit' distinction remains (House of Commons Social Security Committee, 1997b).

---

[14] Changes to the threshold in second and subsequent years were announced in June 1997.

REFERENCES

Beinart, S., Smith, P. and Sprogton, K. (1996) *The Access to Work Programme: A survey of recipients, employers, employment service managers and staff,* London: SCPR.

Birkin, R. and Meehan, M. (1997) 'The Employment Needs of Jobseekers Entering the Jobmarket as a Result of the Introduction of Incapacity Benefit', Customer Report 539/2, Occupational Psychology Division, Employment Services.

Davoud, N. (1996) *Welfare to Work: Disability perspective,* Report from the London North CEPD Incapacity Benefit Working Group, London: North London Committee for the Employment of People with Disabilities.

Department of Social Security (1990) *The Way Ahead,* London: HMSO.

Department of Social Security (1996) *Social Security Statistics 1996,* London: The Stationery Office.

Department of Social Security Analytical Services Division (1997) *Disability Working Allowance Statistics Quarterly Enquiry October 1996,* London: DSS.

Disablement Income Group (DIG) (1996) 'Barriers and Bridges: Benefit barriers preventing disabled people from moving into work and some policy options for overcoming them', paper prepared for a Joseph Rowntree Foundation Seminar, 12 November 1996.

Employment Department (1994) *The United Kingdom Response,* Response by the United Kingdom Government to the European Commission's Green Paper on European Social Policy, London: Employment Department.

European Commission (1995) *Employment Community Initiative: Summaries of Member States Operational Programmes,* DGV, Brussels: European Commission.

European Commission (1996a) *Employment in Europe 1996,* Luxembourg: Office for Official Publications of the European Communities.

European Commission (1996b) *The 1995 Multiannual Programmes for Employment of the EU Member States,* V/436/96, DGV: Brussels.

Finn, D. (1994) 'Disability Working Allowance: A route out of dependency?', *Working Brief,* 50, 10.

Grammenos, S. (1995) *Disabled Persons Statistical Data: Second Edition,* Luxembourg: Office for Official Publications of the European Community.

House of Commons Social Security Committee (1993) *Disability Benefits: The delivery of Disability Living Allowance and Disability Working Allowance,* Third Report, Session 1992-93, London: HMSO.

House of Commons Social Security Committee (1997a) *Incapacity Benefit: Minutes of Evidence and Appendices to the Minutes of Evidence,* Session 1996-97, London: The Stationery Office.

House of Commons Social Security Committee (1997b) 'Draft Report (Incapacity Benefit)' in *Minutes of Proceedings from 23 October 1996 to 12 March 1997*, Session 1996-97, London: The Stationery Office.

Lonsdale, S., Lessof, C. and Ferris, G. (1993) *Invalidity Benefit: A survey of recipients*, Department of Social Security Research Report No. 19, London: HMSO.

Office for National Statistics (1997) 'Labour market participation amongst people with long-term health problems/disabilities', *Labour Force Survey Key Facts, March 1997*.

Robbins, D. (1982) *The Chance to Work: Improving employment prospects for disabled people*, London: Disablement Income Group.

Robinson, P. (1997) *Labour Market Studies: United Kingdom*, Employment and Labour Market Series No 1, Luxembourg: Office for Official Publications of the European Communities.

Rowlingson, K. and Berthoud, R. (1996) *Disability, Benefits and Employment: An evaluation of Disability Working Allowance*, Department of Social Security Research Report No. 54, London: The Stationery Office.

Social Security Advisory Committee (1988) *Benefits for Disabled People: A strategy for change*, London: HMSO.

Thornton, P. and Lunt, N. (1995) *Employment for Disabled People: Social obligation or individual responsibility?*, Social Policy Reports Number 2, York: Social Policy Research Unit.

Tremlett, N. and Dundon-Smith, D. (1995) *Survey of Claimants of Industrial Injuries Disablement Benefit*, London: SCPR.

CHAPTER 9
COUNTRY SUMMARIES

In the last decade there have been extensive changes in policies to promote economic integration of disabled people. Commonwealth disability discrimination legislation was enacted in 1992, as part of the then government's social justice agenda for disabled people. The current approach to income and services reflects the principles behind the Disability Services Act (DSA) of 1986 that disabled people have the same fundamental rights as other people and that services should be oriented towards realising those rights. The DSA most notably aimed to shift the funding emphasis from segregated employment to forms of open employment which bring disabled employees the same relative levels of pay and conditions as other workers. There are short-term wage subsidies and other incentives to employers to take into competitive employment disabled and other unemployed people.

Disabled people in the labour market

The Disability Reform Package, introduced in 1991, derived from the philosophy of the government of the time, expressed in its 'active society' framework, which argued that people had more chance of achieving independence and self-determination if they had better access to the labour market. The rise in unemployment in the 1990s made it difficult for disabled people to obtain and maintain employment and budget cuts to mainstream labour market programmes will increase competition for jobs. There is a marked growth in part-time and casual employment.

Social security policy for disabled people

Benefits for disabled people came under review by an inter-departmental Disability Task Force in the late 1980s which published the influential Disability Reform Package. It aimed at the creation of a more active system of support linked to the benefit system, which encourages disabled people to maximise their employment potential through rehabilitation, training and labour market programmes. The reforms were radical, given a long history of reliance on an 'all or nothing' invalid pension and exclusion of disabled pensioners from Commonwealth employment services programmes.

The social security system in Australia has no social insurance. Benefits are means-tested, paid at a flat-rate and withdrawn when income or assets exceed defined maximum levels. Thus, benefit receipt can be combined with work. Three main social security benefits allow a combination of substantial disability and work.

Disability Support Pension (DSP) was introduced in 1991, replacing Invalid Pension. To qualify, a person must have a physical, intellectual or psychiatric impairment of at least 20 per cent (or be permanently blind), and a 'continuing inability to work', defined as being prevented by the impairment, within the next two years, from doing any work and undertaking education, vocational or on-the-job-training likely to reskill the person for work. 'Any work' in this context means work for at least 30 hours per week at 'award' wages (i.e. the minimum industry- and job-based rates laid down by the Industrial Relations Commission). Thus DSP recipients may do some part-time work. Moving into and out of work, within the parameters of benefit eligibility, does not affect entitlement. Six per cent of beneficiaries have earnings from work; nearly three-quarters are in casual or temporary work. Eligibility for benefits is assessed by assessment officers in regional DSS offices. Specialist Disability Support Officers identify DSP recipients who might benefit from a new Workforce Transition Package of training, rehabilitation or job search assistance, and convene Disability Panels, made up of representatives of several government Departments including the Department of Employment (DEETYA).

Disability Wage Supplement (DWS) was introduced in 1994, and provides supplementary assistance to people participating in the Supported Wage System, administered by the Department of Health and Family Services (DHFS). The Supported Wage System allows the payment of an agreed wage to a disabled person at a pro-rata level of the normal award rate, based on a nationally consistent assessment of the person's skills and productive capacities. Initial assessment, on-the-job support and workplace modifications to help maximise performance are also available through DHFS. To be eligible for DWS, claimants must also satisfy the rules for DSP. There are rules covering movement back onto DSP from DWS, which allow for easy transition without further assessment within a specified period. There is little use of DWS.

Mobility Allowance provides help for people in employment, vocational training or voluntary work, who are unable to use public transport without substantial assistance because of a physical, psychiatric or intellectual disability. Recipients must undertake job search as part of an agreed activity plan, or receive an unemployment allowance. The number of recipients increased substantially between 1993 and 1996.

Pension recipients and Mobility Allowance recipients are automatically issued with *concession cards* which give access to Commonwealth health care concessions and to some State concessions for transport, public utilities, telephone charges and rates; they also receive a quarterly *Pharmaceutical Allowance*. Lump-sum *Employment Entry Payments* for unemployed and disabled people were abolished in March 1997.

Benefits for vocational rehabilitation

There are no longer any specific benefits for rehabilitation in Australia. Rehabilitation Allowance was merged with the new Disability Support Pension in 1991, as part of the Disability Reform Package. All recipients of DSP can retain their benefit while participating in any rehabilitation work or training.

Subsidies and grants

Wage subsidy schemes broadly aim to give employers incentives to take on people whom they otherwise would not, in the hope of demonstrating that they can be valuable workers, and therefore worth retaining. Temporary wage subsidy schemes specifically for disabled people are *Work Experience Program for People with Disabilities (WEPD)*, which provides fully subsidised places for DSP recipients placed in work through Disability Panels, and the *Disabled Apprentice Wage Subsidy*. Under the WEPD scheme, wages are fully reimbursed, up to limit, for people referred by a Disability Panel, for around 12 weeks for full-time and 20 weeks for part-time positions. Employers can be reimbursed up to a ceiling for costs of adaptations. Employers of disabled people are eligible for temporary subsidies (for 13 to 26 weeks) under the *Jobstart scheme*, introduced in 1991, which provides the largest number of subsidised placements and which is primarily oriented to people who are long-term unemployed or otherwise disadvantaged in the labour market. Employers of people unemployed for over 18 months receive a lump-sum establishment fee under *Jobstart*.

Research found WEPD to be the most highly regarded of the DEETYA programs for disabled people and appeared to lead to particularly satisfactory outcomes when used to lead on to a

Jobstart placement. Earlier experience of wage subsidy schemes for disabled people suggested that they were not particularly effective, possibly because output rather than price variables were more influential in determining employment. It is difficult to identify the results for disabled people in the limited data on the impact of *Jobstart* and the other more recent schemes, but it does appear that overall, the wage subsidy schemes have had some effect in terms of higher rates of 'positive outcome' for DRP *Jobstart* participants.

Workplace Modification Allowance provides a grant to private sector employers who employ disabled participants to cover the cost of essential equipment, or of modifying the workplace to enable disabled people to undertake employment.

Evaluation

Evaluation of the specific policy of enabling people with partial incapacity to combine benefits and work has to be seen within the wider context of the raft of reforms introduced since the late 1980s, but especially the Disability Reform Package. The Disability Task Force's 1995 evaluation of the DRP judged it to be a success overall, though with shortcomings in some areas. Certainly, the package has had the effect of increasing the numbers of DSP recipients with some earnings, and in increasing the level of these earnings. The work transition package has been important and some community groups have regarded this as one of the most successful elements of the DRP. The policy changes, however, have not translated into fewer DSP recipients, partly because of demographic and other factors increasing claim levels and partly because of a downturn in demand for labour. Also, DSP arrangements are not really designed to get people completely off benefit *per se*, but rather to allow work, backed up by a social security payment, and reasonably smooth transitions off or back on to benefit as the need demands. Overall, Australian policies to break down the rigid barriers between disability and paid work may be said to have had modest, but not insignificant, success.

FINLAND

Labour market policy is directed to dealing with the effects of the severe economic recession experienced by Finland in the first half of the 1990s. In the three years from 1990, economic output declined by 12 per cent, the worst drop recorded in any OECD country in recent decades. Unemployment grew rapidly from 3.4 per cent in 1990 to a peak of 18.4 per cent in 1994. It has now fallen back slightly, to 17.2 per cent in 1995. Finland has always had a comparatively high level of labour market participation and of full-time working, and most women in employment are in full-time jobs.

Social security expenditure on unemployment measures has risen eight-fold in the last decade and unemployment expenditure is now more than double the cost of active labour market operations. This has led to attempts to rectify the imbalance between income maintenance schemes and the use of active labour market programmes. Particular priority groups are the long-term unemployed, young people, and disabled people. Finland has always favoured active policies, including advice, training, placement and rehabilitation. The employment needs of people with limited capacity for work have been recognised since 1973 in social security legislation with the provision of a partial disability employment pension. Across all benefits, however, recent policy changes have acted to tighten eligibility criteria and reduce the value of awards in an attempt to contain public expenditure and to encourage more people to take up employment.

Disabled people in the labour market

The inclusion of disabled people within Finnish society and securing equal opportunities are widely accepted policy goals. Unemployed disabled people are served by a range of mainstream employment services; wage subsidised employment is an increasingly common destination. In 1990, there were 43,000 registered disabled jobseekers, around eight per cent of all jobseekers. Since then the proportion of disabled jobseekers to all jobseekers has fallen due to the sharp rise in unemployment, despite numbers of disabled jobseekers having risen to 58,000 in 1994. At the end of 1994, while the overall unemployment was around 18 per cent, it was estimated to be almost twice as high among disabled people.

Social security policy for disabled people

Social security policy and provision for disabled people is under review in Finland. There are currently two income maintenance social security benefits that can be combined with work; partial employment disability pension and individual early retirement pension. There are also two types of benefit which cover the extra costs of working; disability allowance and local authority disability benefits. These benefits have their own administrative and funding arrangements.

Partial employment disability pension is an insurance benefit for those with an employment history. It was introduced in 1973 with the explicit aim of keeping people in some form of work for as long as possible, reflecting the general policy objective of promoting employment but also as a means of reducing expenditure on employment pensions. The aim is to help people who, due to illness, permanent disability or injuries, are unable to carry out their usual work. The claimant can move to part-time work or change job or become unemployed searching for new work. The number of recipients in employment is not recorded but is thought to be low, in view of the limited opportunities in the labour market and for part-time work in particular. Administration of partial employment disability pensions is the responsibility of the Employment Pensions Institutes. This partial pension (which corresponds to half of the full employment pension) is awarded if the ability to work is reduced by between 40 per cent and 59 per cent. (The claimant is eligible for a full pension if their reduced capacity is assessed at 60 per cent or more.) Changes to the period used for the calculations for partial pension awards are being phased in from 1996; by 2006 awards will be based on the wages of the claimant over the previous ten years. The effect will be a decrease in the level of awards.

Individual early retirement pension is a benefit for people aged 58 or over who cease work for health reasons. Although it was not initially intended to act as an in-work benefit, in practice some people combine its receipt with employment. A feature of the benefit is that a decision in principle can be obtained by a person while still in work. The decision is valid for a period of nine months, allowing the worker time to make related decisions about retirement. In line with the policy on reducing early retirement, the current intention is to restrict the number of claimants and recipients and to encourage greater commitment to the rehabilitation of older workers among employers, employees and health care professionals.

Disability allowance is the main benefit to compensate for and help meet the special costs of disability. It is aimed at people of working age who do not receive disability pension or insurance-based benefits and is not means-tested. Its expressed aim is to help persons with disabilities manage their lives, in work, education and day-to-day activities. Unofficial estimates suggest that as many as 80 per cent of disability allowance recipients are in work. There are three payment categories which are assessed according to the degree of disability, the need for continuous help or the extra expenses caused by the illness or injury. Disability allowance decisions are made by officials of the Social Insurance Institution. Costs are of concern to Government and the level of benefit is being held at 1995 levels until 1998.

Local authority disability benefits can be claimed from their local authority (Municipality) by people who are defined as severely disabled to contribute to some of the costs associated with their particular disability, such as transport, interpretation services, or a personal assistant. Municipalities also have discretion to award additional amounts for the costs of special foods or clothing. The benefits are not intended primarily to support disabled people in work but they may be combined with work and with other benefits such as partial employment disability benefit.

Benefits for vocational rehabilitation

Encouraging earlier return-to-work and facilitating work retention are current policy priorities in Finland. The aims of major reforms of rehabilitation legislation in 1991 included reducing the need for workers to transfer to disability pensions or other long-term benefits, increasing co-operation between agencies and encouraging rehabilitation in the workplace. Responsibility for undertaking measures to maintain working capacity lies with employers. People whose work and earnings capacity is significantly impaired by illness or injury are entitled to vocational training to maintain their working capacity.

Rehabilitation allowance is paid for a range of rehabilitation services arranged by the Social Insurance Institution (SII). The allowance is paid only if the objective is for the client to remain in, enter or re-enter employment. Incentives to encourage people to undertake rehabilitation programmes are built into the social security system: disability pensions can be retained and the amount of the award enhanced during rehabilitation; and after completing 30 days of rehabilitation arranged by the SSI benefit is increased by ten per cent. Employment pension institutes pay a rehabilitation allowance to employees in the labour market at a level set at 33 per cent above that of the disability pension they would otherwise receive. An equivalent *rehabilitation increase* is paid to existing disability pension recipients.

Subsidies and grants

The government employment services provide temporary subsidised employment for unemployed people if they cannot be matched in the open labour market or given training. Employers taking on an unemployed person can claim a subsidy for between six and ten months for non-disabled workers and for a maximum of two years for disabled people. For work in central government, the subsidy covers the entire wage; otherwise it varies from person to person. The duration of the contract now must exceed the subsidy period. Including trainees, who do not have contracts, in January 1996 there were in total 57,000 people in wage-subsidised jobs. Subsidised employment is increasingly the destination for unemployed disabled people helped into work by employment services, both as a route to competitive employment and as an end in itself. In 1994, out of 58,000 disabled jobseekers 13,000 were channelled to subsidised employment. The subsidy is intended to compensate the employer for reduced productivity and for extra costs of modifications and training. Most subsidised employment is in the public sector and policy debate has focused on ways of increasing participation of private sector employers, through possible modifications to the design of the scheme which discourages or prevents employers from substituting subsidised labour for a permanent workforce.

Other financial support available to employers includes grants from the Ministry of Labour and from the Social Insurance Institute for technical aids, adaptions to the workplace, adapting working conditions, assistance on the job and for training.

In the first half of the 1990s there has been a significant fall in the demand for labour in France. The unemployment rate fell in 1996 for the first time in the 1990s but the share of long-term unemployment rose to 40 per cent. Young people, women and disabled people have been particularly hit by long-term unemployment. Labour market strategies are directed at reducing unemployment. Key elements are training initiatives to bridge the skill-gap, measures to increase flexible working, notably part-time employment, and reduction of the indirect costs of labour. Financial incentives directed at employers, such as wage subsidies and relief of national insurance contributions, to recruit and retain disadvantaged groups, are central to active labour market policies in France. The idea that financial incentives might encourage disabled people to seek work is novel.

Since new legislation in 1987, the economic integration of disabled people has been viewed as the responsibility of the economic actors rather than, as previously, a social obligation founded on principles of compensation. There is a legal obligation on establishments with over 20 staff to contribute to raising the representation of disabled people in the workforce by meeting a quota of six per cent; an alternative means of meeting the obligation is to contribute to a quota-levy fund which is redistributed among enterprises of all sizes to promote recruitment and retention of disabled workers. There is an extensive programme of financial aid to employers, and latterly to disabled workers. At département level there are specialised agencies who assess the social and employment needs of disabled people and arrange placements. In addition, there is an expanding sheltered work sector. The employment needs of people with partial capacity for work are beginning to be recognised with some growth in part-time appointments and increasingly available practical help in the workplace.

Disabled people in the labour market

Disabled people have been hit by the falling demand for labour and high unemployment. Over 100,000 are in sheltered employment and between 500,000 and 700,000 in open employment. Of the 200,000 to 400,000 disabled people who are fit for work but unemployed 70,000 are registered with the French employment service. The increase in the number of disabled people among the unemployed has been greater than that for jobseekers as a whole. The average period of unemployment is very long (587 days) and is closely related to severity of disability. Half of the disabled but only one-third of all jobseekers have a low level of qualification. Unemployed disabled people are older than average.

Social security policy for disabled people

In France, income maintenance schemes for people whose capacity for work is limited through disability are based on compensatory principles and, although some benefits are assessed according to residual working capacity, they are not designed to promote return to work. Expenditure on disability benefits is not a policy concern. Nor is benefit dependency an issue.

Earnings-related *invalidity pensions,* introduced in 1945, are provided for persons insured under the social insurance system who have been unfit for work for more than three years. Invalidity pensions are part of the health care system and pensioners are transferred from sickness benefit. In the general scheme, *'first category' pensions* compensate for loss of earnings of people presumed able to work but unable to earn more than a third of their previous wage. The decision is made by a medical practitioner working for the pension fund, based on the insured person's residual working capacity, general state, age, physical and mental faculties, and level of vocational training. *'Second and third category' pensions* provide income replacement for disabled people deemed totally unable to work. The total number of recipients of invalidity pensions has remained stable since 1980 at around 430,000. The number of pensioners of the first category has also remained static, standing at 124,000 in 1993. There are no official statistics on the proportion of the latter in employment. Since 1987, invalidity pensioners have been covered by legislation to promote the employment of disabled people and the number of first category pensioners employed in establishments of over 20 staff has grown from 15,000 in 1988 to 25,000 in 1994, representing ten per cent of total beneficiaries under the law of 1987. The level of the first category pension is set low and the average pension is less than 30 per cent of the minimum wage. Accordingly, first category pensioners need income from work to sustain an adequate standard of living.

In France the concept of supplementing low incomes through the benefit system is unusual as normally workers are hired at a wage level which is equal to the 'convention' level; a nationally negotiated level for every employee in a given economic sector and fixed in a collective agreement. Disabled workers are a special case, as employers may reduce their wages in line with their productivity. Accordingly, the State provides a supplement to the employer to bring the wage packet up to the minimum wage level. This income guarantee for disabled workers *(garantie de ressources)* was introduced in 1975 for those accorded the status of 'disabled worker'. The provision is used extensively in sheltered work. In private sector open employment it is typically used where the disabled person needs support in the workplace; in 1995 there were only 7,000 beneficiaries.

Lump-sum integration grants

A lump-sum integration grant can be paid to disabled people on starting a job. It is supposed to encourage a positive attitude to looking for work. The measure was introduced as part of an extensive programme of aid to employers and disabled workers, managed by the quasi-governmental body (AGEFIPH) which disperses the quota-levy fund. All categories of disabled people covered by the law of 1987 in favour of disabled workers may benefit. A lump-sum integration grant is given also to the employer. The grants are generous and have proved exceptionally popular. Most are given for full-time permanent jobs. In 1995, they supported the recruitment of over 33,000 disabled workers and over the first six years 156,000 in all were supported by the grant. However, their popularity has diminished following a reduction in 1995 in the value of the grants, from 30,000 to 10,000 FF to the employee and from 40,000 to 15,000 FF to the employer. The grant has especially supported recruitment in smaller establishments of under 20 employees. The employment support services are instrumental in encouraging interest in the grant among potential employers. It is not easy to tell how far the lump-sum grant works as an incentive to disabled people. However, the level of take-up suggests that the scheme has been effective in promoting both access to work and job retention.

Grants for extra costs of work

Disabled people may benefit from a social assistance *compensatory allowance for work-related costs* which arise from their specific disability, introduced in 1975. It is presumed to act as an incentive to take up work, but appears to be little used because of very restrictive conditions. Claimants must be recognised as severely disabled (with 80 per cent incapacity), the benefit is means-tested and claimants must present invoices. Complementary grants for specific costs of aids and access to work are also available through AGEFIPH under much less restrictive conditions, mainly for disabled jobseekers, students, trainees and apprentices.

Subsidies

Since 1982 there has been an extensive system of state subsidies to employers to promote recruitment of disadvantaged groups. A large number of 'work contracts' have been created, including recognised disabled people among the target groups of unemployed people. The *CIE (contrats initiative-emploi)* exempt private sector employers from national insurance contributions and award a monthly lump-sum grant for 12 to 24 months. The job must be at least 16 hours per week. Under the CRE system which CIE replaced in 1995, ten per cent of contracts were awarded to disabled people in 1994 (19,500 contracts). In 1995 a total of 25,000 disabled people benefited from the two types of contract. Most recipients earn the equivalent of the minimum wage. The *CES (community work contract)* promotes part-time temporary community work in the public and voluntary sectors. Contracts normally last for three to 12 months but extension to 24 months is generally accepted for disabled people. The subsidy is between 65 and 100 per cent of wage costs and employers are relieved of employers' national insurance contributions. The employee receives the minimum wage. In 1995, six per cent of recipients were disabled people, out of a total 43,700. The programme has expanded from a total of 9,400 contracts in 1992.

GERMANY

In addition to the recession of the early 1990s, Germany has experienced unique labour market problems as a result of reunification. The most important objectives of federal employment and labour market policy are the maintenance of a high level of employment and the reduction of unemployment. These are viewed as primarily dependent on sustained economic growth and investment in improvement to production capacity.

The legal obligation to meet an employment 'quota' is a long-standing feature of policy for the employment of disabled people. Employers unable to meet their quota contribute to a compensatory levy. Other policy instruments are more concerned with improving the chances of the individual worker, for instance by vocational qualifications. For disabled people, the underlying principle is that of 'rehabilitation before pensions', leading to an emphasis on programmes of vocational rehabilitation. In general, research findings indicate that German employment policies are particularly effective in ensuring that severely disabled people and people who become disabled while in work retain their employment. The system appears to be less successful in fostering the recruitment of disabled people.

Disabled people in the labour market

There are 1.14 million registered 'severely disabled' people who are active in the labour market, of whom 1 million have jobs. About 150,000 are in sheltered employment. By 1996, there were 190,000 severely disabled people unemployed; about 60 per cent are aged 50 or over. The labour market participation rate of disabled people is currently half that of non-disabled people. In Germany, the policy approach to this situation is not to attempt to increase individual incentives to work but to address the problem of the demand for labour and to create more job opportunities.

Older disabled people usually retire early, taking advantages of a regulation allowing disabled people over 60 who have 35 years of contributions to retire on a full pension. This has caused substantial increases in the numbers of disabled people taking early retirement since the 1980s, and has been widely used by private sector firms wishing to restructure.

Social security policy for disabled people

The German social insurance system is a complex, comprehensive system involving all levels of government as well as worker and employer federations. There are many separate insurance schemes covering different risks such as unemployment, retirement and disability. Several funding agencies are responsible for the provision of both vocational rehabilitation measures and disability pensions. Early identification of an emerging disabling condition by social insurance office doctors should lead the local sickness insurance agency to call for a rehabilitation investigation. The agency in turn advises the rehabilitation agency of the measures to be undertaken. The aim is to avoid long-term receipt of benefit wherever possible.

Statutory pension insurance, covering about 85 per cent of employees, provides two types of disability insurance benefits; *partial (occupational) disability pension (BU) and full (general) disability pension (EU)*. For *EU*, the claimant must be deemed incapable of a regular income from *any* employment in the foreseeable future; this includes those capable only of working irregularly, or those whose earnings capacity is less than one eighth of a comparable person's. EU can be granted for an unlimited period. To be eligible for the *partial (occupational) pension BU*, the insured person's earnings must be assessed as less than 50 per cent of a comparable person's, for reasons of ill health or disability. In calculating earnings capacity, reference is made only to employment which is *commensurate* with the claimant's capacities, abilities and previous work experience. BU is, by definition, available only to skilled and semi-skilled workers. There are large numbers of older unskilled workers who do not qualify who must rely on unemployment benefits and/or social assistance payments. BU is granted usually for one year only, as recipients move automatically to EU.

Numbers of recipients of both benefits have dropped substantially since 1984 when restrictions on the qualifying period for the benefits were introduced. Since 1985, less than one in twenty new recipients has received a partial benefit, compared with one in three in 1965, mainly owing to the increased weight given to labour market considerations when deciding eligibility. This meant that almost all recipients of BU who could not be placed in employment within a year received EU. In 1995, 1.45 million and 112,400 people were in receipt of EU and BU respectively. Although it is possible to combine BU with employment, there is very little incentive to do so. In January 1996, an earnings limits for receipt of BU was introduced. Moreover, EU, which is payable after 12 months of unemployment, is paid at 33 per cent higher level. The lack of opportunities in the labour market also mean that very few BU recipients engage in paid employment, and for the vast majority BU functions as an interim pension before receipt of EU after a year. There are no official data on BU recipients in work but the number is thought to be negligible.

'Step-wise rehabilitation' allows claimants of EU and BU to combine earnings and benefit as they return to work by working a gradually increased number of hours over a specified period of time. A formal contract is drawn up between the employer and employee specifying the hours to be worked, start and end dates, and the level of salary to be paid. Earnings are deducted from benefits. Because benefit entitlement continues throughout the period of rehabilitation, there is no break in claiming, and benefit can be restored to the previous level if the attempt at rehabilitation does not succeed. This form of rehabilitation is regarded as being particularly successful. Employees report greatly increased levels of confidence when they return to the workplace.

Allowances for extra costs

There are a number of tax allowances and grants to disabled people for additional living and working costs. They are in the main intended as compensation for disadvantages faced rather than as incentives to work. A registered severely disabled person is entitled to an extra five days paid leave and registration gives access to several concessions to compensate for disadvantages faced. Severely disabled people (and some others) are entitled to a tax allowance, intended to provide compensation for additional living costs. This was introduced in 1974, and has not been uprated; its financial value is now regarded as negligible. Disabled people are also entitled to tax refunds in respect of travel to work; however, eligibility criteria are so tightly defined that very few qualify. Subsidies are available towards the costs of purchase or modification of a car for travel to work, and other supplementary assistance is provided from the levy redistribution fund towards costs of technical aids and modifications to the workplace, access to work, personal assistance and so on.

Benefits for vocational rehabilitation

From the beginning of 1997, disabled workers no longer have a legal entitlement to vocational rehabilitation benefits, as formerly. They are now discretionary, except for registered severely disabled people, who represent about ten per cent of participants. This change, which was made to accommodate serious budget deficits in the federal employment office and will reduce the numbers taking part, seriously effects the principle of 'rehabilitation before pension'.

Responsibility for rehabilitation is divided between the Federal Institute of Employment and the Pension Insurance Agency. There are four different types of benefit which can be obtained during vocational rehabilitation and training. Two available to both disabled and non-disabled people are *Substitutionary benefits for living (Unterhaltsgeld)* for participants in full-time vocational training, and *Assistance or subsidies for professional training* for those who are living independently of their parents, or who are unemployed, having worked for at least a year, or who are socially handicapped or educationally subnormal. Two benefits, which are the largest in terms of expenditure and numbers of participants, are solely for disabled people: *Interim benefits* can be paid instead of '*Unterhaltsgeld*' to disabled people taking part in vocational rehabilitation; and *Professional training benefits* are payable to those undertaking professional training, or vocational training if the claimant is under 22 years of age. In 1995, job centres were asked to reduce the number of awards of the two benefits specifically for disabled people with the aim of reducing costs. One result of this was an increase in the number of disabled people claiming the general rehabilitation benefits. Altogether both absolute and proportionate numbers of disabled people awarded vocational benefits declined in 1995 compared with the previous year. In 1995 93,000 people received the four benefits, 80 per cent of whom were disabled.

Subsidies

The main wage subsidy for disabled people in Germany, the *Integration Subsidy*, is intended to compensate the employer for the additional costs involved in hiring a disabled person. It is paid from the compensatory levy fund to an employer who takes on a registered severely disabled person who causes extra costs, has reduced working capacity, has a severe mental disability, is aged 50 or over or who has been unemployed for more than a year (as well as those leaving education, training or sheltered work). The subsidy lasts three years, tapering from 80 per cent in the first year to 60 per cent in the third (subsidies are extended for two years for people aged over 55). In 1996, 9,100 disabled people were subject to wage subsidies; of those, 1,700 had a reduced rate of output. These wage subsidies are generally regarded as ineffective; firms tend to view the subsidies as windfall profits, and the vast majority of grants are made to a small number of large companies. It is estimated that between 75 and 85 per cent of all placements would have occurred without subsidy.

There is also an extensive *general wage subsidy* scheme for priority groups of unemployed people, including severely disabled people. The subsidy is set at 50 per cent for the first six months and 40 per cent for the next 18 months. In the first half of the 1990s use of this job creation measure expanded considerably in the former East Germany; in 1995 the average number in subsidised jobs was 312,000, with a further 70,100 in the former West Germany.

NETHERLANDS

In the Netherlands, the level of labour market participation is comparatively low, part-time working high and a large percentage of the population withdraws from work at a relatively early age. The government expects to solve employment problems and reduce the public expenditure burden by re-shaping a highly institutionalised system into a more market-like arrangement through privatisation, deregulation and shifting of responsibility to individual economic actors. The role of the state versus the free market is intensely debated in the Netherlands. Considerable discussion, and proposals for legislative reform, have focused on the future of collective agreements over labour conditions, regulation of dismissal and hours of work, the role of public employment services, and income protection.

Disabled people in the labour market

There is no comprehensive information on numbers of disabled people unemployed or in work. There is a large sheltered employment sector and only a very small proportion of people with learning difficulties are in competitive employment, where people with mental health problems are also under-represented. Measures to promote open employment have focused on physically disabled people and on those with an employment history.

Social security and employment policies for disabled people

Policies to promote employment of partially disabled people have been driven by political and public concern over high sickness absence rates and increasing numbers receiving disability benefits. The financial consequences of the latter have led to a series of radical reforms to the social security system. These were accompanied in the 1990s by a series of new obligations on, and incentives to, the economic actors to assist the return to work of disability benefit recipients and to prevent workers who become disabled from entering the benefit system. Market principles are increasingly entering into service provision and into employer insurance against risks of sickness and disability.

All residents are insured under the national insurance scheme. This scheme provides a pension under the General Disablement Pensions Act (AAW) for non-employed people disabled from an early age and for self-employed people who become disabled. The social assistance scheme provides for a minimum income under the National Assistance Act. Separate employees' insurance schemes, run by the industrial insurance associations (until March 1997), provide benefits to full-time and part-time employees at times of unemployment, and long-term disability. Those who are sick and do not resume work after 52 weeks receive total or partial benefits under the Disability Benefits Act (WAO). (Employers are now responsible for coverage of sick pay for up to 52 weeks.)

The concept of partial capacity for work is fundamental to Dutch income and labour policy. As disability is a wage-related concept, degree of incapacity is expressed in terms of loss of

132

earnings capacity. Those who claim unfitness for work because of illness or infirmity have to undergo a medical and technical assessment. A computerised system matches restrictions and capabilities against the job demands of several thousand occupations. If a fit is found with at least three occupations, the person is deemed able to work. Whether any jobs are vacant at the time is not relevant. There are six partial disability categories, ranging from 15 to 25 per cent up to 80 per cent disabled; full incapacity is 80 per cent and over. About a quarter of the 860,000 WAO and AAW benefit awards are *partial capacity benefits*. Although partial capacity benefits were designed in 1967 to complement earnings from work, the way in which the system was implemented has meant that only about 13 per cent of beneficiaries are in open employment.

The TBA Act (Restriction of Claims on the Disability Benefits Regulations) 1993 limited eligibility for WAO and AAW to five years, changed the criteria by which lost earnings were assessed, introduced age-related rates, reduced the overall level of payment and introduced reassessment of existing claimants. After a drop in total recipients of more than 60,000 between the end of 1993 and the end of 1995, the last four months of 1996 showed an upward trend, with increasing intake and decreasing outflow. One year after reassessment fewer people than expected had resumed or increased work and a large number of those deemed fully or partially capable of work received unemployment and social assistance benefits or no benefit at all.

In 1996, a *WAO/AAW wage supplement* was introduced to bridge the shortfall in earnings resulting from the new system of assessing lost earnings capacity. This is designed as an incentive to the disabled worker. A person who is entitled to a WAO benefit may be granted a supplement to that benefit, for a maximum of four years' employment, if he or she accepts employment at a lower wage than his/her theoretical earning capacity. This statutory regulation came into force on 1 April 1996. There are also several small recently introduced work incentive measures for specified groups. For example, disabled people aged over 50 who have received benefits for over two years may receive an annual incentive benefit if they resume work. So far, take-up of that scheme is low.

Benefits for vocational rehabilitation

Benefits for rehabilitation are recent small-scale innovations. *Postponement of estimation of degree of disability after training* allows a WAO/AAW beneficiary to retain the original disability benefit for a full year after completion of training while searching for suitable employment. It is intended as an incentive to pursue training. *Re-integration benefit for trial employment* aims to give an employee with a partial disability, who receives both a AAW/WAO benefit and an unemployment benefit the chance to do unpaid work for a trial period of three months at the most, for a new employer in the private or public sector. For this trial employment the employee can apply for a re-integration benefit equal in value to the unemployment benefit. *Assistance with costs of work adaptations*, including transport, clothing and educational aids, is available to disabled employees. Provisions under the scheme are not bound to a specific place of work and can be retained by the employee.

Subsidies and grants

Several incentives to employers have recently been introduced. All are rarely used. Research has found that these measures have had very little effect. Awareness is low and procedures are over-bureaucratic. Subsidies are thought insufficient to counter employers' hiring preference for workers with no perceptible health problems. The incentives divide between relief of part of wage and sickness costs and compensation for the extra costs incurred in employing a worker who is disabled.

A disabled employee is normally entitled to the same wages as a non-disabled worker with a comparable job and the same working hours. Under the *wage dispensation* arrangements an employer may pay lower wages if the disabled employee's productivity is much less than usual. A *Wage cost subsidy* of 20 per cent of salary costs for four years can be claimed by an employer taking on a partially disabled person.

Relief of obligation to supplement sickness benefit applies in the private sector and only for new employees. If a person who has been declared partially unfit for work does return to work, but falls ill, the sickness benefit is increased to 100 per cent of the salary which they would otherwise receive. This means that the employer no longer has to supplement the sickness benefit previously set at 70 per cent.

Supervision subsidy can be awarded if it is evident that extra time and effort is necessary to integrate a potential disabled employee into the workplace. *Allowance for personal assistance* on the job applies to those who can work in mainstream employment only if some personal assistance is provided. There are also subsidies to adapt the workplace to the needs of employees.

SWEDEN

Labour market policy in Sweden is geared to the maintenance of full employment. This has been impossible to sustain during the recession of the early 1990s, with rising levels of unemployment, but remains a long-term goal. To this end active labour market policies are pursued. The principle of encouraging work activity, including training, vocational rehabilitation and work experience, rather than allowing individuals to receive benefit in a passive way, is an important aspect of Swedish labour market policy. The idea of providing individual financial incentives to work is not typical. Work is viewed as a normative aspiration for disabled and non-disabled people alike, and benefit claimants can be required to participate in labour market programmes. Creation of job opportunities is also emphasised.

Labour force participation remains high, with similar rates for men and women. Levels of part-time employment are significantly higher than the EU average and women are much more likely than men to be working part-time. All income-support and labour market programmes have a part-time option and partial benefits can be combined with part-time participation in a labour market programme or employment. Combining part retirement pension with part-time work is very common.

Disability policy has been integral to labour market policy since the 1940s. With policy based on a concept of 'work for all', a model of compulsory employment, such as a quota system, is unacceptable to all parties. However, a Disability Ombudsman was established in 1994, and non-discrimination legislation is under consideration.

Disabled people in the labour market

The Swedish definition of disability regards disability as a relationship between a person and the environment. Under the Work Environment Act, employers must adapt working conditions to individuals' physical and mental requirements and establish schemes for job modifications. A person is regarded as 'occupationally handicapped' if he or she has, or is expected to have, difficulties in obtaining or retaining gainful employment as a result of an impairment, medical condition or illness of a physical, mental, intellectual or social nature.

Participation rates amongst disabled and older workers are generally high in Sweden. The number of occupationally handicapped people who are unemployed has increased rapidly in recent years, however, from a monthly average of 20,200 in 1991/2 to 54,200 in 1995. Current projections suggest that disabled people will continue to experience great difficulty in the labour market over the next five years. In line with the policy requirement of greater representation of occupationally handicapped people in labour market measures, at the end of 1995, 11.2 per cent of those enrolled were occupationally handicapped, as against 10.3 of all unemployed jobseekers.

Social security policy for disabled people

In the 1980s absence from work due to sickness, and the number of long-term recipients of sickness and disability benefits, increased considerably. The policy response in the 1990s was to reduce compensation levels for sickness benefit, devolve to employers and social insurance offices the legal responsibility for rehabilitation of workers who become disabled and to practically abolish the right to work injury benefit. In 1996, the total number of disability pensioners declined for the first time in many years. Furthermore, from 1997 the labour market consideration in the eligibility criteria for disability pensions was abolished.

Partial disability pension is the single benefit-work combination specifically for disabled people. Disability pension, which may be full or partial, consists of two parts. The first tier is universal; eligibility is based on citizenship and long-term residency and is not conditional on past employment. This basic pension is the same for all claimants. The second part is an earnings-related supplement. Because of high labour market participation rates, few are ineligible for the supplement.

Social security policy, as well as labour market policy, assumes that disability or diminished work capacity is partial in most cases. Partial disability pension was introduced in 1960, both to recognise varying degrees of disability and to facilitate a combination of pension receipt with other paid or unpaid activities. It may be awarded at four rates; 100 per cent, 75 per cent, 50 per cent and 25 per cent. (Until 1993 the partial rates were a half and two-thirds.) Assessment of residual capacity for work is the responsibility of an insurance officer who consults a range of independent experts.

About a quarter of the 420,000 disability pensioners in 1995 received a partial pension; the proportion of new partial pensions awarded has increased in recent years. Partial pensions are uncommon in younger age groups and most common between the ages of 45 and 54. In all categories of pension there are more female recipients. The proportion of recipients of partial disability pension in work is not available but it is supposed that almost all male recipients also have part-time work, while some women may combine partial pension with unpaid domestic work. Combining work with pension does not lead to any additional entitlements, nor are any lost, although increased income will have an effect on means-tested benefits for housing and social assistance where these have been received. It is possible to return to the previous benefit at any time without penalty. Partial disability pensioners who do not work are not generally entitled to other benefits such as unemployment or social assistance.

Benefits for vocational rehabilitation

Rehabilitation has been given high priority since the early 1990s. Benefits are paid while undergoing an agreed programme of rehabilitation. The same social insurance office assesses an employee's entitlement to sickness benefit and rehabilitation benefit and is also responsible for planning rehabilitation of disability benefit recipients who are not employed. Benefits are paid at the same rate as the benefit payable before the period of vocational rehabilitation, whether sickness, unemployment or disability benefit. A special rehabilitation benefit, payable at a higher rate than sickness benefit, was introduced in 1992. This was intended to provide incentives to participate in rehabilitation and promote an early return to work. However, its value has now been reduced to the level of sickness benefit. Partial rates can be paid for part-time participation. Benefit can also be paid for planned training on the job, starting with a few hours a day and increasing gradually.

Extra costs of work

Grants may be made to disabled people and to their employers to cover the costs of technical aids, and to disabled people to cover purchase and modification of a car for work purposes. There is provision for employment of a personal assistant at work. Grants can be made available to disabled people wishing to set up a business.

Subsidies

Provision of wage subsidies is in line with the general principle of favouring employment rather than cash support to individuals. The policy intention is to compensate employers for the additional costs of recruiting a disabled employee, by subsidising reduced productivity. There are three main wage subsidy schemes. Open employment with wage subsidy is organised in all sectors of the economy. The Government-owned Samhall group of companies provides employment in sheltered workshops. In addition, sheltered work is available in the public sector for those with mental and psychological disabilities. Together with temporary work, these three programmes accounted for around two in five people disabled jobseekers obtaining work in 1995.

The level of the subsidy paid is negotiated, depending on the severity of disability. It can be paid to a maximum of 80 per cent of wages, plus corresponding insurance contributions; for severely disabled people a 100 per cent wage subsidy can be paid. Subsidy is available for part-time work as well as for full-time work. Many of those working part-time with wage subsidy are employed by Samhall. In theory, wage subsidies are intended to be temporary, for a maximum of four years. However, they can be renewed. There is therefore no incentive for either employee or employer to end the arrangement. Of those leaving work with wage subsidy, around 20 per cent go on to obtain work without subsidy on the open market. There have been few formal evaluations of wage subsidy and related programmes, but those carried out have generally been positive. The high labour force participation rate of disabled workers in Sweden is generally taken as evidence that they act as effective incentives to work. However, some disabled people view the subsidies as demeaning if the employee can perform as well as a non-disabled person.

UNITED KINGDOM

Policies in place before 1 May 1997 demonstrated a continued commitment to a 'flexible' labour market free from restrictive working practices, regulation and wage determination. Removing burdens on businesses was a prime concern. A series of reforms led to almost total deregulation of minimum wages. Promotion of individual responsibility and incentive to work were central themes of successive Conservative governments from 1979, alongside reducing the costs of the welfare state. Programmes for the unemployed, including long-term disabled people, focused on reducing the value of benefits, restricting eligibility, tightening their administration and introducing new programmes to assist access to work. Links between benefit payment and active job search were strengthened.

Past governments' commitment to non-interference in the labour market and promotion of individual enterprise have favoured policies which persuade rather than compel employers to recruit disabled people, encouraging them to adopt good employment practices and persuading them of 'the business case' for employing disabled people. There are almost no financial incentives to employers. The Disability Discrimination Act of 1995, which replaced the ineffective quota legislation, allows disabled people to take civil action against an employer who unjustifiably treats them less favourably because of disability, and there are no other regulations to investigate and scrutinise employers' practices.

Disabled people receive mainstream training for work and use employment support services open to all unemployed people. Programmes specifically for disabled people who need extra help include local Placement, Assessment and Counselling Teams; Supported Placements with host employers for severely disabled people, with wage supplements for reduced productivity; Access to Work, a co-ordinated programme of practical help; and Disability Working Allowance.

Disabled people in the labour market

According to the Autumn 1996 Labour Force Survey (LFS), 15 per cent of people in Great Britain of working age report work-limiting conditions. Nearly half are economically active, representing 8.8 per cent of the labour force. Their activity rate is half that of the rest of the population. People with mental health problems are much less likely to be economically active than those with physical or sensory impairments. Nearly one-fifth of economically active disabled people were unemployed in Autumn 1996, compared with under a tenth of non-disabled people. Unemployed disabled people are more likely to be unemployed for more than a year; half were long-term unemployed. People with learning difficulties and people with depression are most likely to be unemployed.

According to the LFS, two-fifths of disabled men and one-third of disabled women are in employment. Disabled men are significantly more likely to work part time than non-disabled men. Disabled people tend to be over-represented in partly skilled and unskilled manual jobs and under-represented in professional and intermediate occupations. In 1995 there were around 12,000 severely disabled people in sheltered workshops and 10,000 in supported placements.

Social security policy for disabled people

A large number of social security benefits are available to disabled people of working age. Benefits were introduced at different times, for different purposes and for different groups. There is no out-of-work benefit for disabled people partially capable of work.

Benefits relevant to disabled people include:

- *Incapacity Benefit (IB)* - a contributory benefit for the long-term sick

- *Severe Disablement Allowance (SDA)* - a non-contributory benefit for severely disabled people who have never worked or have insufficient national insurance contributions to qualify for IB
- *Income Support* - disabled people who are ineligible for IB or SDA, and recipients of IB and SDA, may apply for Income Support. A 'disability premium' (ISdp) is awarded if certain other qualifying disability benefits are being received
- *Jobseeker's Allowance* - available to disabled people not receiving Incapacity Benefit, SDA or Income Support who are unemployed for more than six months
- *Industrial Injuries Disablement Benefit* - a pension for people who become disabled as a result of an accident at work or due to industrial disease
- *Disability Living Allowance (DLA)* - a non means-tested, non-contributory benefit to help meet some of the extra care and mobility costs of long-term disability
- *Disability Working Allowance (DWA)* - an in-work, means-tested benefit to top up low wages of disabled people.

Public expenditure on benefits for sick and disabled people accounts for almost one-quarter of the total spent on social security benefits. The number of recipients of the main benefit increased by 250 per cent between 1977 and 1995. Growth was attributed to weak controls on access and continued receipt. Reforms which came into effect in 1995 sought to re-focus provision on those who were genuinely incapable of work; the new Incapacity Benefit (IB) was accompanied by a tighter test and reviews, through which large numbers were expected to lose or be refused eligibility. In the first year under half the estimated number was found incapable of work, less than a quarter of the estimated number claimed Jobseeker's Allowance, and very few used the augmented mainstream and specialist employment services and entered employment. A likely consequence of the new assessment arrangements is an increase in the number of jobseekers with partial capacity for work. DWA, introduced in 1992, is expected to act as a work incentive for ex-IB recipients although claims for DWA must be made in work within eight weeks of leaving the benefit.

'Exempt work' is available to recipients of IB and SDA under very limited conditions. It may be undertaken on the advice of a medical doctor if it 'helps to improve, or prevent deterioration in, the disease or bodily or mental impairment' which causes incapacity for work. Exempt work is limited to 16 hours per week and is subject to an earnings limit of £46.00 per week. Earning above that limit is taken as evidence of fitness for work and means complete loss of benefit. Similar, rather less restrictive arrangements which preceded exempt work were used by around two per cent of those eligible. Recipients of ISdp can work up to 16 hours a week if they declare their earnings and may earn up to £15 per week before their benefit is affected. There is a little used special exemption to work up to 24 hours if earnings are less than three-quarters of those of someone without a disability.

Disability Working Allowance was introduced in April 1992. This means-tested in-work benefit is intended primarily to encourage disabled people off benefits by making work more financially rewarding. It is paid on top of low wages or self-employed earnings, in work averaging at least 16 hours a week. DWA was designed for people who can do some work but are not fully able to support themselves. As partial capacity provision it has two main aims: short-term rehabilitation to enable disabled people returning to work to progress towards full-time work; and long-term financial support for disabled people who cannot work full-time because of a disability or who can only work full-time at reduced capacity. In addition, the benefit is designed to encourage disabled people to give work a try, without risk of loss of entitlement to IB if return to work is unsuccessful within two years.

To qualify, claimants must be in work receiving DLA (or analogous benefits) or have received IB, SDA or ISdp (or two other disability premiums) in the eight weeks before starting work. Initial claims are supported by a self-declaration that the claimant has a physical or mental disability which puts them at a 'disadvantage in getting a job'. For subsequent claims a self-assessment test may be required. The amount payable depends on the total income of the claimant's family and on family composition. There is a supplement for working more than 30 hours a week. Claimants have access to free NHS prescriptions, dental treatment and so on.

The results to date have been disappointing. It was estimated that about 50,000 people would be receiving DWA. By January 1997 (in GB) there were 12,000 recipients. In the four years from November 1992 altogether 17,500 new awards were made. Take-up was initially slow but numbers have risen steadily in the two years to January 1997. At first, very high proportions of claims were disallowed because the claimant was not in work at the time or did not receive a qualifying benefit; to a lesser degree, these difficulties remain. The effect of DWA in enabling people to leave IB and SDA has been small; by October 1996, IB or SDA was the main qualifying benefit in 5,000 out of the 17,500 new awards in the previous four years. It is difficult to say how far DWA is now meeting its short-term rehabilitative aims but a three-year evaluation commissioned by DSS found that most recipients were already in work when they first heard of the benefit. Its main impact has been as a long-term supplement to low earnings; 60 per cent of awards over four years were renewals.

Benefits for vocational rehabilitation

Unemployed disabled people can join mainstream *Training for Work* without the usual required period of six months' unemployment, proving that they are endorsed as disabled by Employment Services. They may receive the Training Allowance, which is equivalent to any benefit they are entitled to, with a £10.00 addition. Eligibility for IB is retained for two years. People can train part time if they have a disability. Under outcome-based funding arrangements, there are financial incentives to providers to take on disabled people.

Wage supplements, subsidies and grants

Wage supplements for reduced productivity in open employment apply on a modest scale, only within the Employment Service *Supported Placement Scheme* which has extended the notion of 'sheltered' work into open employment. Employers are not compensated directly for reduced productivity under the scheme; rather, the employer pays a portion of the wage and the State, through an agency, pays the remainder. The entry criteria are that a disabled person, who complies with the DDA definition, should be 30 to 80 per cent productive relative to a non-disabled person and cannot otherwise obtain or retain employment on account of the severity of their disability.

The few schemes giving direct subsidies to employers of disabled people have not been promoted as financial incentives. Rather, they are said to offer an opportunity to discover disabled people's skills and potential, and to deal with any practical concerns, so building on the argument that it makes economic sense to employ disabled people. Under the Employment Service *Job Introduction Scheme*, a private sector employer who takes on a disabled worker is paid a weekly grant towards wages during a 'trial period', usually of six weeks but exceptionally extendable to a maximum of 13 weeks. The job can be full-time or part-time but it must be expected to last for at least six months after the 'trial period' has ended. The employer is expected to pay the normal rate for the job. The value of the grant has not kept pace with inflation since it was introduced in 1977 and the scheme is under review.

Access to Work, administered by the Employment Service, can pay for physical alterations to the workplace, special equipment or adaptations to existing equipment, deaf awareness training for co-workers, job coaches to help familiarity with new tasks, adaptations of a vehicle or help with transport to work costs, a communicator at interview, and other practical needs. The programme is designed around the needs of individual disabled people and not available directly to employers. When it was introduced in 1994, half of entrants to the programme were meant to be unemployed; a year later 92 per cent of entrants were found to have been already in work.

CHAPTER 10
CONCLUSIONS

This concluding chapter draws together the evidence from the seven study countries on approaches to supplementing the income of disabled people with limited capacity to work and to earn. It looks first at regular supplements provided as direct benefits to disabled people through social security benefit systems and at the alternative approach of paying supplements through the wage packet. Secondly, it reviews the experience of countries other than the UK in supporting the transition to work through short-term benefits. The chapter then highlights examples of allowances for work-related costs and cash incentives in reducing the costs of working and in facilitating and encouraging employment. In conclusion, we discuss the role of income supplements in the overall context of national policies to promote employment of disabled people.

PARTIAL CAPACITY BENEFITS

The preceding chapters have described in detail the principles, structure and operation of partial capacity benefit provision in the seven study countries. Here we provide a synthesis of those accounts, concentrating on the relationship between partial and incapacity provision, origins and rationales for partial benefits, their coverage, and the significance of these benefits within national social security systems.

Partial capacity and incapacity benefit provision

Given the long history of compensation for disability in most western industrialised nations, it is not surprising to observe that in four of the seven study countries disability benefits were designed in the first instance solely to provide income in the case of total incapacity. Originally 'all or nothing' benefit systems prevailed. Subsequently, in two of those countries, Sweden and Finland, the system was reformed to allow awards of the benefit at a partial rate in recognition of partial capacity. In Sweden, partial capacity awards were added to the established disability insurance system in 1960; and Finland reformed the 'all or nothing' system, dating from 1956, by introducing a partial benefit in 1973.

In three study countries, partial and full benefits were introduced together. France introduced an invalidity pension which recognises partial earnings capacity in 1945, when the social security system was established. Germany's dual system of full and partial disability pension dates back to 1911. In 1967, the Netherlands introduced a disability insurance benefit which allows for six partial capacity benefits and one full disability benefit, integrating the occupational disablement benefit into the system at the same time.

In the UK and Australia, where 'all or nothing' benefits for people incapable of work (introduced in 1971 and 1908 respectively) remain in place, reforms in the 1990s to accommodate partial capacity departed with the model we see in the other study countries. In the UK, an additional benefit was introduced specifically for working disabled people with partial capacity, and the existing incapacity benefit system remained broadly unaltered. In Australia, on the other hand, the invalid pension was reformed to allow more disabled people to combine part-time paid work with receipt of what is still essentially a pension for those incapable of work. Here it has to be understood that Australian income support benefits are means-tested. The arrangement in Australia is similar to the 'earnings disregard' for recipients of a means-tested income support benefit in the UK, with the important differences in Australia of a liberal hours limit (30 hours) and an income taper which allows for earnings above a threshold. What seems anomalous about the Australian arrangement for combining disability pension with a substantial amount of work, from the UK perspective, is that the disabled worker is still regarded as incapable of work for the purpose of benefit receipt.

Advantages of a single system allowing for both full and partial awards, as in Australia, Finland, France, the Netherlands and Sweden, are that disabled people may move between full and partial benefits without the need to apply for a different benefit, and as, in principle, all partial benefits can be held in work they may also move in and out of work relatively easily. In the UK, on the other hand, the only partial capacity benefit is available in work only; previous recipients of the incapacity benefit must first leave that benefit and, when in work, apply for a new benefit. If work is unsuccessful, previous recipients of the incapacity benefit may return to it under certain conditions, however.

Rationales for partial capacity benefits

As we have indicated, in all countries apart from the UK and Australia, partial capacity benefits are very well established, dating back between 85 and 25 years. In some countries the original rationales remain. In others, incremental change has affected the original principles, sometimes fundamentally. There is seldom one discernable rationale and several principles may be at work in a single benefit. It is not straightforward to disentangle principles, which might be thought to guide provision, from ideological, political or economic objectives which prevail at the time of the study. Thus, our accounts of the rationales for partial capacity benefits reflect not only the principles articulated at the time of introduction, and since, but also intervening events and current political, social and economic priorities.

Provision in France remains embedded in traditions of compensation for the harm caused to disabled people by society. The insurance-based invalidity pension system has changed little in 50 years. Although the French system recognises a category of recipients with residual earnings capacity, the benefit is part of the health care system and is akin to extended sickness benefit. The number of 'first category' beneficiaries has remained static for over a decade, costs are relatively low and encouraging beneficiaries into work is not a key policy concern. Beneficiaries work, it seems, because they need the extra income to live.

In Germany, the principle of 'rehabilitation before pension' is intended to provide early intervention to return partially disabled people to employment and so avoid the need for benefit. A series of regulations has modified the purposes of the insurance-based partial benefit which in the past was intended to be combined with paid work; it now serves no real function in supporting partially disabled people in employment and is primarily a route out of the labour market.

In contrast to France and Germany, partial benefits in Sweden and Finland are explicitly intended to support people with partial capacity to work. Combining work with benefit is taken for granted within both systems. Swedish partial disability benefits were first designed to provide partially disabled people with some income which allowed them to pursue other activities (such as housework) but now the benefit is mainly intended to allow people with partial capacity to work part time. In Sweden, work is a normative aspiration and benefits are designed to support income from work. The 'work principle', which can be traced back to at least 1902, is based on the idea that work is superior to cash support. Traditional very high levels of labour market participation, along with a labour market policy designed to absorb increases in unemployment during recessions through public relief work, job training and job creation measures, mean that individual work incentives have not been a key issue in political debate.

142

In Finland, the employment needs of people with partial capacity for work are explicitly recognised in the social security system. The aim of the partial employment disability is to keep in some form of work for as long as possible those who are unable to carry out their usual work because of illness or disability. The narrower focus in Finland than in Sweden is explained by the fact that receipt of partial employment disability pension depends on an employment history and an adequate contributions record, while in Sweden partial disability pensions, are universal, based on citizenship or long-term residency. As in Sweden, the partial benefit is intended to enable disabled people to work part-time. However, in contrast to Sweden, there is no tradition of, or much desire for, part-time work, especially among women, and with the lack of job opportunities the partial benefit is little used. Finland has a tradition of active labour market policies, aimed at rehabilitation, access to work and job retention, as opposed to passive reliance on out-of-work social security benefits. The notion of individual incentives to work is gaining ground as the barriers in the present system come under review.

In both Sweden and Finland rising expenditure on disability benefits has been a factor in promotion of partial benefits. The partial pension was introduced in Finland with that in mind, and in Sweden recent reforms have led to an increased proportion of partial awards.

In Sweden and in Finland, separate partial benefits have been used to support in employment older workers who otherwise would have to retire on health grounds (although in Finland the original rationale was to support retirement). Policy moves to prevent early retirement have restricted use in both countries but the provision appears to have some value if used to plan partial retirement; in Finland, the benefit decision can be held in reserve so that an older disabled worker can weigh up the options for up to nine months.

The Dutch system of disability benefits was originally introduced in order to promote (re)integration into work. The Dutch approach, like the Swedish, assumes that disability is partial in most cases and is compatible with work. The starting point in the Netherlands is partial capacity to earn, however, rather than limited capacity to work normal hours. Thus, provision is designed to compensate for loss of earnings stemming from disability rather than to supplement earnings from part-time employment, as is the case in Sweden. In the Netherlands, then, there is no in-built assumption that employment should be part-time, although it often is so.

In contrast to the Nordic countries, the Dutch 'solidarity principle' historically has meant higher priority accorded to maintaining the incomes of those unable or partially able to work and less investment in rehabilitation. Recent changes to the system of assessing earnings capacity, alongside reviews of eligibility for benefits, seek to reduce disability benefit costs, in part through increasing the proportion of partial awards. The short-term result appears to be increased numbers of recipients combining partial benefits with unemployment benefit - a combination not possible in Sweden.

In the UK, incapacity and partial capacity benefits have a comparatively short history. An invalidity benefit was not introduced until 1971 (only two years before Finland decided to reform its 'all or nothing' system). By 1992, when Disability Working Allowance was implemented, reducing benefit costs and welfare dependency had emerged as key policy concerns and increasing individual incentives to work was an important policy objective, particularly relevant given the relatively low wages which benefit recipients were likely to command. The new partial capacity benefit (DWA) was designed as an incentive to people with a disability or long-term illness, primarily to encourage them to leave out-of-work disability benefits by making work more financially rewarding, but with a secondary objective of maintaining employment by supplementing low earnings. It allows people with partial working capacity to work less than full time, and specifically recognises that they may need assistance to progress to full-time employment.

In Australia, the new arrangements for combining work and disability pension, introduced in 1991, were also prompted by concern over growth in recipients of out-of-work benefits. The change was part of a wider reform movement, aiming to create an active society whereby people have more chance of achieving independence and self-determination through participation in the labour market, with a new emphasis on employment support services tailored to individual needs. The change was also underpinned by a social justice agenda aiming to realise the fundamental rights of disabled people.

In summary, then, evidence from the study countries indicates that there are three broad types of rationale for partial capacity benefits.

The first centres on meeting the employment and income needs of people with partial capacity for work. Three objectives can be identified:

- to facilitate entry to work and job retention for partially disabled people, where work is a normative aspiration
- to provide an incentive to enter or remain in work, particularly where low earnings are a disincentive
- to facilitate transition out of work and into retirement.

Here we can discern two distinct functions; to enable part-time working, and to compensate for lost or reduced earnings.

The second type of rationale relates more centrally to economic and ideological objectives; to reduce expenditure on incapacity benefits, to reduce benefit dependency and promote economic self-determination, and to realise disabled people's rights to employment.

Finally, partial capacity benefits, both in principle and in practice, aim to compensate those partially disabled people who are out of the labour market or who are unable to find employment. Exceptionally, they are intended to enable partially disabled people to undertake unpaid activities, such as domestic responsibilities.

It should be noted that in none of the study countries are partial benefits explicitly intended to cover the extra costs of working with a disability, although in some countries the level of the benefit may be higher than that of other benefits which can be combined with work.

Access to benefit/work combinations

As partial capacity benefits in most study countries are provided within the same benefit framework as total incapacity provision, criteria for access are similar. In the UK the criteria for Incapacity Benefit and Disability Working Allowance differ.

In the six countries with linked partial and full disability benefits (treating the Australian 'disregard' as equivalent to a partial pension) receipt for ex-employees typically follows an extended period of sickness benefit (or sickness pay in the Netherlands). In France the period is three years but the norm elsewhere is around one year. The period spent on sickness benefit, and the procedures for transfer from sickness to disability benefit, affect opportunities for combining benefit and employment. In France, for example, sickness benefit recipients need not apply for disability pension as the transfer is automatic, and in Sweden beneficiaries are prompted to transfer at the discretion of social insurance officers. In the Netherlands and in Germany, on the other hand, claimants must take the initiative and in Germany risk losing entitlement to disability pension if they fail to do so in good time. In the UK, there is no automatic transfer from Incapacity Benefit (IB) (which now includes the previous sickness benefit) to Disability Working Allowance; as we have already noted, DWA claimants must apply when in work. In any case, only a small proportion of DWA recipients previously received IB.

The assessment of employability at the point of transfer from sickness benefit/pay to the disability benefit system seems critical to return to work with a partial benefit There appear to be advantages in facilitating benefit/work combinations where assessment of eligibility for disability benefit and for services for return to work is co-ordinated, as in the Netherlands, Sweden and Australia. However, a year after onset of sickness or disability may be too late for successful re-integration. In the Northern European countries in the study, the current emphasis lies with early intervention for return to work, to prevent transfer to incapacity or partial capacity benefit. Doing so, challenges administrative resources. Germany is finding the principle of rehabilitation before pension hard to sustain in practice, and Sweden and Finland have recognised the need for more efficient administration.

As one might expect, there are different criteria for entitlement under insurance-based and means-tested schemes. Under the insurance systems in Finland, France and Germany, entitlement depends on employment history and social security and/or pension fund contributions. In the Netherlands and Sweden, all adults are covered by insurance. In the Netherlands, there are currently separate benefits for employees and for people with no employment history or an inadequate contribution record, while in Sweden there is basic rate for all and an earnings-related supplement for those with an employment history.

Claimants of partial benefits in countries with insurance based schemes must also have a reduced capacity, because of illness or disability,

- to work (Finland and, from 1997, Sweden)
- to earn the previous wage (France)
- to earn from commensurate work (Germany), or
- to earn from acceptable alternative employment (the Netherlands).

There is some variation in the types of condition which count as illness or disability for the purposes of partial capacity benefits. In Sweden, for example, alcoholism is included (for both full and partial benefits). In France, progressive illnesses are covered by the sickness insurance scheme, not the disability pension. Work-related injuries and diseases are generally not covered, except if, as in the Netherlands, there is no separate industrial disablement scheme.

In Australia, disability support pension is means-tested according to income and assets (as are all benefits in Australia) and employment history is not relevant. To qualify, the claimant must have an impairment of at least 20 per cent and a continuing inability to work more than 30 hours a week. Thus, in Australia access to benefit/work combinations is restricted primarily by income.

The in-work benefit in the UK is means-tested but eligibility also depends on existing or past receipt of one of a number of qualifying contributory and non-contributory, mostly non-means-tested, disability benefits. The claimant must complete a self-declaration that he or she is at a disadvantage in getting a job, guided by a list of functional disabilities. Here, type of impairment is not directly relevant to access. In theory, the scope of the benefit is wide but the disabled person must be in work in order to claim and also understand the system of qualifying benefits.

Characteristics of recipients

The rationales for partial capacity benefits and the criteria for access naturally determine the characteristics of recipients. For example, it is not surprising to find in Sweden a preponderance of female recipients, as the universal benefit was designed partly with the needs of women with domestic responsibilities in mind and as female labour force participation and part-time employment rates are high. To take a different example, the German decision to restrict eligibility to those who have worked for at least 36 months in the last five years helps explain why around five-sixths of recipients of the partial pension are men. The gender distribution, as well as the age distribution, is, of course, also affected by the availability of other pensions and benefits within national systems.

There is limited information available to us about the age profile and disabilities of partial capacity benefit recipients. Where partial and full benefits are provided within a single administrative system, statistics do not necessarily distinguish recipients of the two benefits. Comparisons of note are the relative youth of recipients (of full and partial pensions) in the Netherlands, where a third of beneficiaries are under age 45, compared with only 11 per cent in Germany. However, this is not surprising given that Dutch benefits cover young people disabled from an early age with no employment history. The differences in frequency of diagnoses between the two countries, with comparatively a high proportion of newly awarded beneficiaries with circulatory conditions in Germany (25 per cent compared with nine per cent in the Netherlands), may well relate to age. In both countries, the proportions of new beneficiaries with mental disorders were high (29 and 37 per cent).

There is very limited information about the characteristics of partial benefit recipients in employment, as few countries provide separate data on this group. People with learning disabilities appear to be under-represented in all countries, in part because they are not directed to open employment and in part because they are less likely to be covered by schemes which depend on an employment history. The comprehensive data on UK Disability Working Allowance recipients suggests that a high proportion are affected by exhaustion and pain. This type of categorisation of disability is not used elsewhere, however. Overall, there is very little information to show whether partial capacity benefits meet specific needs of people whose impairments affect their capacity to work.

Partial capacity benefits in context

Looking across those study countries where the benefit award can be either full or partial, we find that the proportion of partial benefits to full benefits is highest in Sweden, the Netherlands and France, where around one-quarter of awards are for a partial benefit. An analysis of trends shows that the proportion of partial benefits is generally static in France and Finland, has risen recently in Sweden and is set to do so in the Netherlands. In Germany, numbers receiving the partial occupational pension have been less than eight per cent of numbers receiving full general pension in recent years. In Germany and in France there is little policy imperative to increase the proportion of partial benefits. The system is under review in Finland. Only in Sweden and in the Netherlands are partial benefits being promoted, partly as a side effect of restrictions on full benefits.

The proportions of partial to full incapacity benefits do not necessarily reflect the significance of partial benefits in employment, however. Official data on partial benefit/employment combinations are available from Australia, the UK, and the Netherlands (possibly reflecting the policy importance attached to their promotion). In Australia, around six per cent of all disability support pensioners are in employment and in the Netherlands 13 per cent. Unofficial estimates suggest high proportions of recipients of partial benefits in employment in Sweden, very few in Finland and almost none in Germany. In France at least one-fifth are recorded to be in employment. In the UK, by the end of 1996 there were 12,000 recipients of DWA.

In all countries, apart from Germany, there is some policy interest in increasing the number of partial benefit recipients in employment. As already noted, reducing the costs of full incapacity pensions has been a driving force in several countries. In France, the policy imperative appears to be equitable treatment of pensioners who were previously denied coverage under employment promotion legislation; a similar concern for equity seems to have influenced Australian developments.

Summary

We have shown that in all countries there is opportunity to combine partial capacity benefits with income from employment but both the salience of the provision and its use are variable. A number of explanations for such variation have emerged and some of the more significant are outlined here.

- *Institutional context* - for example, location in a health care system appears to discourage active consideration of employment possibilities, while joint administration of labour and income policies locates income replacement firmly with the realm of employment policy.

- *Early intervention* - policies which aim to prevent progression to disability benefits, through rehabilitation as soon as possible after the disabling event, increasing employer responsibilities to pre-empt sickness absence, and action to support job-retention, may have the effect of reducing the significance of benefits which can be combined with work.

- *Labour market situation* - for people with limited capacity for work, the supply of suitable job opportunities is critical. Where there is a tradition of part-time working and/or a supply of part-time work, partial benefits appear to be popular. Conversely, a lack of opportunities in the labour market, and for part-time work in particular, does appear to limit the applicability of partial benefit schemes.

- *Tendency to award full benefits* - eligibility rules, such as the commensurate work requirement, and a history of semi-automatic awarding of full benefit have eroded the relevance of partial benefit/work combinations. Such trends can prove difficult to stem.

- *Conditions attached to claiming and receiving benefit* - the conditions attached to claiming partial benefit may be restrictive. For example, in the UK the claimant must be in work and must be receiving, or have recently received, a qualifying disability benefit.

Overall, the importance attached to partial capacity benefits as a means of supporting employment appears to be increasing in most study countries, although apart from in Sweden, they do not play a major role. The desire to reduce public expenditure and the general trend to emphasise individual responsibility seem to support adoption of incentive-based policies but there is at the same time clear recognition that employment is a right for disabled people and that one role of benefits is to support that right. The place of partial benefits in supporting disabled people who are unable to work falls outside the scope of this study but the casualisation of work suggests that benefits which allow disabled people to move in and out of employment will be increasingly necessary.

Partial capacity benefits combined with paid work have two functions. One is to enable people with limited capacity for work to engage in less than full-time employment with the security of additional income from benefit. The other function is to supplement their income if they are unable, because of disability, to produce as much as a non-disabled person when working similar hours. This distinction is not always clearly articulated and some partial capacity schemes, such as the UK Disability Working Allowance, combine the two purposes. In the UK, it is not necessary to make the distinction as there is no minimum wage regulation and thus no obligation on the employer to pay a standard wage to someone whose productivity might be diminished through disability. In other words, in the UK, the employer is able to pay low wages and, in the absence of a benefit or other arrangement for supplementing the wage directly, the individual worker bears the cost of his or her reduced capacity. If, however, a minimum wage obtains, the employer is liable to bear the cost. In such circumstances, wage cost subsidies come into play.

Wage supplements and subsidies

As we noted in the Introduction, wage supplements have for many years formed part of income security policies for disabled workers in sheltered employment. Particularly with the advent of supported employment - where disabled people with reduced productivity work in non-sheltered employment - income supplements in open employment are increasingly required. Typically, such supplements are paid to the employer who then adds them to the wage packet, as in the UK supported placement scheme and in a growing number of agency schemes elsewhere. They are also a necessary arrangement in France and in the Netherlands, where there is special dispensation for the employer to pay less than the usual wage to a disabled person with reduced productivity. Otherwise, outside the special context of sheltered and supported employment there is little evidence of use of wage supplements.

Social security benefits and wage supplements both serve the purpose of lifting the wage of a disabled worker, who might not otherwise be able to maintain employment. Wage supplements have additional advantages, however. Notably, they encourage the employer to hire someone who potentially might impose extra costs. In influencing hiring decisions they have an advantage over benefit provision as the employer is less likely to be aware of the latter. The wage supplement approach means that employers can acknowledge and act upon their social responsibility, while supplementing wages through the benefit system removes that responsibility from them.

Perhaps the most important consideration is that wage supplements are job-related; they recognise that occupational disability is a relationship between impairment and the demands of the job. Wage supplements may be used for rehabilitation to work, through a tapering arrangement, as in Germany, whereby the subsidy is phased out as the employee becomes adjusted to work. There is no evidence, however, of wage supplements being used to support someone with declining ability to work and in this respect a social security benefit may have the edge.

A disadvantage of wage supplements from the point of view of maintaining income in a flexible labour market, is that they are tied to a particular job and may be short term, whereas benefits are portable and normally longer term. Supplements (or more often, subsidies) have been criticised because they sometimes unfairly label a worker as unproductive and are thought to be demeaning. To obtain a wage supplement or a subsidised wage, the worker needs to be 'placed' with an employer, possibly with a restricted choice of job. In comparison, benefits have the advantage of privacy and dignity at work. On the other hand, placement under a subsidy scheme presents opportunities to tailor the work and working environment to the employee's needs.

Within the study countries there is more evidence of subsidies paid to employers as a job creation measure, within a wider labour market strategy to encourage recruitment of disadvantaged groups. They are heavily used in several study countries and may be accompanied by other incentives, such as recruitment bonuses or relief of national insurance contributions. In such programmes, the intention is that the employer should gain financially, over and above reimbursement of any extra costs involved. These subsidy programmes do not directly supplement low wages but they do provide disabled people with job opportunities which otherwise may not have been available. There is limited information on how far they meet the needs of people with partial capacity for work. Although subsidies are available for part-time as well as full-time work, schemes which specialise in part-time work are unusual. All subsidy schemes are time-limited, although in generalist programmes participation is often extended for disabled people.

TRANSITION TO WORK

Evidence from the study countries demonstrates a particular role for the benefit system in supporting the period of transition to work, either for a previously employed person during a period of recuperation after on-set of disability or illness, or to support training and job-search when seeking to enter or return to work from long-term benefit. There are also some interesting examples of work/benefit combinations for trial periods in work.

Rehabilitation benefits

Facilitating job retention and early return to work are notable policy priorities in Germany, Sweden and Finland, and benefits for rehabilitation feature more prominently there than in the other study countries. We have noted the well-known German system of 'rehabilitation before pension' which particularly supports the return to work of people who become disabled while in employment. Rehabilitation benefits in Germany are administered under a different system from disability benefits, which in principle should not be awarded unless rehabilitation has been fully explored.

We can distinguish between special rehabilitation benefits and arrangements which allow disability or sickness benefit recipients to retain their benefit during a period of vocational rehabilitation. In Australia, the separate rehabilitation benefit was abolished in the reforms of 1991 and now disability support pensioners retain their benefit during rehabilitation. In Sweden, on the other hand, a special rehabilitation benefit was introduced in 1992; there, rehabilitation benefit is paid at the same rate as the benefit received previously, whether sickness, unemployment or disability benefit. When first introduced, it was paid at a higher rate than sickness benefit, to provide an incentive to participate and to promote early return to work. Finland has a well-developed system of incentives built into the social security system to encourage participation in rehabilitation programmes; typically, the benefit is enhanced to stand 33 per cent above the level of disability pension and there are also incentives to continue with a programme.

In the UK, there is no similar special provision within the benefit system for disabled people. Reviews of eligibility for Incapacity Benefit have highlighted the needs of ex-recipients with partial capacity for work who typically move to a lower rate of benefit for the period of job-search.

Combining benefits with trial work

The international trend is towards facilitating rehabilitation on the job. As already noted, this may be achieved through wage subsidy schemes but the latter tend to lack the flexibility that many individuals require on entering or re-entering work. Here we give three different examples from the study countries of the use of benefits for trial work.

In Sweden, rehabilitation benefit can be paid for planned training on the job, with the existing employer or another employer. It may start with a few hours a day and increase gradually, so that the individual can test working capacity and relieve the stress of piece-rates and of normal working hours.

'Step-wise' rehabilitation in Germany involves recipients of disability pensions, both partial and full, in working gradually increased hours over a specified period, according to a formal contract. Earnings are deducted from the benefit. There is no break in claiming and if the rehabilitation does not succeed the benefit can be restored at its previous level. In one sense, this arrangement is similar to the 'linking rule' which enables recipients of Disability Working Allowance in the UK who previously received Incapacity Benefit to return to that benefit if the job does not work out. In the German example, however, the programme is individually tailored and the participant supported through the transitions.

Until recently, an obstacle to unpaid trial work opportunities in the Netherlands has been the lack of a supplement to a partial benefit which can be retained in work. Under a new arrangement, a re-integration benefit for trial employment replaces the unemployment benefit which the partially disabled person had previously combined with a partial benefit, so that the person does not lose out financially. If permanent employment does not result after a three month trial period, the person may return to the previous benefit combination without penalty.

Extra Costs of Working

We have reviewed so far arrangements for enhancing the income of disabled people in work, in transition to work and in trial employment. As far as we can tell, none of these arrangements was specifically designed to take account of the extra costs of working with a disability. In designing the study we had expected to find evidence of allowances in cash and in kind which would reduce demands on benefit/work income, and so enhance the disposable income of disabled people in work. The evidence from outside the UK was more limited than expected, however.

Two regular allowances are of some interest because of their emphasis on supporting employment. The Finnish disability allowance is not dissimilar to the UK Disability Living Allowance (although more limited in that it cannot be combined with disability pension) but is noteworthy because of its stated objective to help disabled people to manage their lives in work and in education, as well as in day-to-day activities. Unofficial estimates suggest that as many as 80 per cent could be in some form of paid work. Mobility allowance in Australia is meant solely for people in at least eight hours a week employment, vocational training or voluntary work who are unable to use public transport without help.

Most study countries have programmes to subsidise the costs of access to work, extra help or personal assistance in the workplace, aids and adaptations and so on but, given that payments are often made to the employer rather than to the disabled worker, it is difficult to determine their value in reducing the out-of-pocket costs of people with partial capacity for work. Moreover, it is not clear that such grants are used by many people working less than full-time.

150

INCENTIVES FOR RETURN TO WORK

Lump-sum incentives to take-up work are a feature of labour market policies, notably targeted at 'discouraged workers', just as recruitment subsidies are aimed at changing the attitude of employers towards marginalised groups. Incentives directed at disabled people are not usual, however, although incentives to their employers are widespread. An exception is France, where an extensive programme of lump-sum integration grants, set at a generous level, has proved very popular among disabled people taking up work and their employers (who also receive a lump-sum grant). This programme is financed from the levy-redistribution fund and not from the benefit system. The Australian employment entry scheme, which gave smaller lump-sum payments to disability support pensioners returning to work under certain conditions, is now discontinued. There are also small-scale examples from the Netherlands, such as an incentive benefit, paid to older disabled people returning to work after two years on benefit, which amounts to 60 per cent of the benefit that was saved.

PARTIAL CAPACITY PROVISIONS AND THE POLICY MIX

So far, we have reported on one type of policy response to the disadvantaged employment situation of disabled people with partial capacity for work - financial provision to supplement income from work. As the country reports demonstrate, however, social security benefits and other arrangements for supplementing wages comprise only one element in the range of national policies and services devised to improve disabled people's participation in employment. Policies with special relevance to promoting the employment of people with partial capacity for work can be grouped into four main types.

The first type of approach aims to adapt the social and working environment to accommodate disabled people whose capacity to work is otherwise restricted. Measures include over-arching legal requirements to adapt work conditions, remove architectural barriers and ensure that working environments do not cause disability, and requirements under anti-discrimination legislation to make reasonable adjustments so that individuals are not treated less favourably on grounds of disability.

The second two policy approaches aim to influence the demand for labour. Labour market policies try to increase participation through creating job opportunities and by encouraging demand through financial incentives to employers to recruit marginalised groups. The third approach imposes obligations on employers to ensure that disabled people are fairly represented in employment, through quota schemes and legislation to prevent discrimination in employment.

The fourth policy approach concentrates on services and benefits targeted at individual disabled people which provide practical help, rehabilitation and employment services, and on financial benefits to improve individual competitiveness. These can be described as supply-side measures.

The study countries accord different weight in their policy mix to environmental, demand-side and supply-side policies. Sweden, for example, has been strongly committed to minimising the disabling effects of the environment and, like Finland, pursues active labour market policies to create job opportunities in times of economic downturn. In both Germany and France, there are legal obligations on employers to increase the representation of disabled people in the workforce, as well as economic incentives, in France in particular. Dutch policy is now moving beyond legal obligations on employers to employ disabled people to include financial incentives directed at both employers and employees. In Australia, individually-based services predominate, backed by subsidy programmes to influence demand.

FOCUS ON THE UK

The UK stands out for its historic lack of emphasis on demand-side policies. Approaches to influencing employment have concentrated on persuasion, rather than on obligation and job creation. The main policy investment has been in incentives and practical help to disabled people and the UK is unique among study countries in the over-riding emphasis on supply-side measures. The pattern of policies has been shaped by a belief that the benefit system should provide incentives to work, and by a commitment to non-interference in the labour market and reduction of burdens on employers.

The evidence from the study suggests that potentially effective policies to promote disabled people's employment not only encompass both the demand side and the supply side but also address the interface between them. Here we need to take account of the role of mediating services in creating the link between employment needs and job opportunities. While some disabled people take advantage of available incentives and find jobs independently, others, particularly if they have spent time out of the labour market because of disability, may need the support of a mediating organisation to find suitable work. Policies to affect the demand side will be ineffective if suitable job applicants do not come forward. There is an observable trend in several study countries towards strengthening the links between local providers of employment support services, employers and disabled people seeking employment.

Further investment in placement services may represent part of the solution for the UK.[1] However, further links may need to be encouraged between service providers and those who might benefit. Particular difficulties have stemmed from divided responsibilities for assessment of benefit eligibility and for guidance on vocational opportunities. This problem is salient in the UK following the tightening of eligibility for Incapacity Benefit and the consequent outflow from the benefit into unemployment. The two stage approach, where disabled people found ineligible for Incapacity Benefit must then apply for another mainstream benefit can mean that some may disappear from the benefits system altogether without finding employment. Examples of co-ordinated and case-managed income maintenance and vocational services in the Netherlands, Sweden and Australia have been cited.

Use of services for return to work by people with partial capacity may be encouraged by rehabilitation incentives. The UK situation is unusual in that unemployed disabled people who are not sufficiently incapacitated to be eligible for Incapacity Benefit do not have recourse to a form of income support which recognises their partial capacity and, moreover, normally experience a drop of income during the work preparation and job search period. We have noted examples from study countries where enhanced levels of benefit are payable in the short-term as an incentive to undergo rehabilitation. Lump-sum entry payments, payable through the benefit system or in conjunction with employer incentives, may act as an additional incentive.

UK partial capacity provision differs significantly from that of the other study countries; Disability Working Allowance must be applied for and is available only in work, and there is no partial capacity benefit for disabled people not in employment. In a number of the study countries the *same* benefit, payable at different levels, may be held while the recipient is

---

[1] In the Budget speech on 2 July the Chancellor of the Exchequer announced an extra £200 million to be directed towards training and placement services for disabled people.

incapable of work, during the period of employment rehabilitation and in work itself. The combination of continuity and flexibility in a single benefit which can be held both in and out of work appears to play some part in facilitating work and sustaining income.

The study reported here has been led by the UK interest in the role of social security benefits as an incentive to partially disabled people to return to and retain employment. An alternative policy approach to reducing benefit dependency and increasing disabled people's representation in the workforce is to act to prevent loss of employment and entry into the benefit system in the first place. One option is to encourage employers to retain employees whose employment is at risk because of disability, though supporting adaptations to the organisation of work and to the working environment, and through arrangements to enable employees to return to their jobs after extended absences. Ideas such as these, while promising for those who already have the advantage of an employment history, do not address the employment needs of the growing number of people with limited capacity for work who have never had a chance to give work a try.